The Seeker on the Quest

Each of us begins our spiritual journey as a pilgrim—the Fool—standing at the edge of a cliff, unsure of what lies ahead. At times the path will be unsteady, full of hidden dangers and unexpected turns. But those who persevere in this sacred quest for enlightenment will eventually find balance and heightened awareness. Keep walking past the upheaval of the crumbling, lightning-struck Tower and you will encounter the peace and hope of the Star.

Tarot Awareness is an essential guide for the serious student of Tarot as he or she travels the road toward Truth. The seventy-eight images of the Tarot represent much more than answers to questions like "Will I get a raise at my job?" While the cards can offer valuable advice on affairs in the external world, thoughtful study offers rewards far beyond simple divination. For the dedicated seeker, entry through the portals of Tarot actually becomes a glimpse into the mysteries of the psyche.

For centuries, practitioners of the Ageless Wisdom have used the Tarot for divination, in ritual, and as a spiritual tool. As a result, we have inherited a body of Western metaphysical thought, including astrological, Qabalistic, and numerical correspondences that add depth and a richness of meaning to a Tarot reading. *Tarot Awareness* presents this esoteric wisdom in an engaging and accessible format designed to promote contemplation and a deeper understanding of this complex system.

For those who embark upon this strange and wonderful path toward higher consciousness, the inspiration and knowledge gained from the seventy-eight cards of the Tarot will be a guiding light along the Fool's continuing journey.

About the Author

Stephen W. Sterling received a Bachelor's degree in Psychology from San Francisco State University. He has applied this academic training in his work as a Certified Hypnotherapist. Teaching and providing spiritual counseling form the core of his professional activities, he has also had over twenty years of practice in reading the Tarot for clients. Currently, Stephen teaches Metaphysics and Tarot at the Mandala Labyrinth Center in Carmichael, California, as well as regularly giving workshops on Tarot and its use in psychological well-being.

To Write to the Author

If you wish to contact the author or would like more information about this book, please write to the author in care of Llewellyn Worldwide and we will forward your request. Both the author and the publisher appreciate hearing from you and learning of your enjoyment of this book and how it has helped you. Llewellyn Worldwide cannot guarantee that every letter written to the author can be answered, but all will be forwarded. Please write to:

Stephen W. Sterling
℅ Llewellyn Worldwide
P.O. Box 64383, Dept. 1-56718-676-9
St. Paul, MN 55164-0383, U.S.A.

Please enclose a self-addressed stamped envelope for reply,
or $1.00 to cover costs. If outside U.S.A., enclose
international postal reply coupon.

Many of Llewellyn's authors have websites with additional information and resources. For more information, please visit our website at http://www.llewellyn.com

TAROT AWARENESS

Exploring the Spiritual Path

Stephen Walter Sterling

2000

Llewellyn Publications

St. Paul, Minnesota, 55164-0383, U.S.A.

First Edition
First Printing, 2000

Cover Illustration © Robert Place
Interior Illustrations © Merle Insinga
Cover Illustration coloring: Anne Marie Garrison
Cover Design: William Merlin Cannon
Editing and book design: Tom Lewis

Library of Congress Cataloging-in-Publication Data
Sterling, Stephen Walter, 1949–
    Tarot awareness : exploring the spiritual path / Stephen Walter Sterling.
       p. cm.
    Includes bibliographical references and index.
    ISBN 1-56718-676-9
    1. Tarot. I. Title.

    BF1879.T2 S746 2000
    133.3'2424—dc21

                00-060661

Grateful acknowledgment is made to Builders of the Adytum, Incorporated, 5105 North Figueroa Street, Los Angeles, CA, 90042, for permission to use their Tarot Keys. The permission granted for the use of materials by Builders of the Adytum, Incorporated, in no way endorses the suggested exercises, meditations, prayers, or other material presented in this book.

Illustrations from Universal-Waite Tarot Deck reproduced by permission of U.S. Games Systems, Inc., Stamford, CT 06902 U.S.A., Copyright ©1990 by U.S. Games Systems, Inc. Further reproduction prohibited.

Llewellyn Worldwide does not participate in, endorse, or have any authority or responsibility concerning private business transactions between our authors and the public.
    All mail addressed to the author is forwarded but the publisher cannot, unless specifically instructed by the author, give out an address or phone number.

Llewellyn Publications
A Division of Llewellyn Worldwide, Ltd.
P.O. Box 64383, Dept. 1-56718-676-9
St. Paul, MN 55164-0383, U.S.A.
www.llewellyn.com

 Printed in the United States of America on recycled paper

To my father
who passed on not really understanding me,
but always loving me;

to my mother,
who loves me,
but still rolls her eyes at my Sagittarian ways;

and to Gram,
in whose eyes I could do no wrong.

And to my students,
for their unfailing encouragement.

Contents

The Seven Universal Laws—
VIII. Strength to XIV. Temperance

The Seven Levels of Spiritual Unfoldment—
XV. The Devil to XXI. The World

Part Three
The Minor Arcana—
Consciousness from the Garden to the Battleground

Part Four
Tarot in Practice—
Reading the Cards

Preface

ONE OF THE GREAT TRAGEDIES OF HUMAN EXISTENCE IS FORGETTING THE SECRET WE knew so long ago—that Consciousness looks at the Universe through our human eyes. Unfortunately, we easily neglect to keep the "lenses" polished and sparkling, as our perceptions are so often refracted through the clouded eyes of an unfocused ego. This unclear vision then results in the human self getting caught up in what the Buddhists call "the thousand things."

When we are distracted by the thousands of complex activities that the world offers, we often allow our awareness to shift focus and concentrate on unwise and detrimental thoughts. Thoughts which eventually lead to unwise and detrimental *deeds*.

It is here, in the distracted moment, that we are most vulnerable. When we let our awareness cloud over, we waste precious energy on nonessentials and leave our consciousness open to contamination with selfish and unworthy pursuits.

In this state of unawareness we absorb into our consciousness, our personal energy field, innumerable fog-shrouded illusions. Like hungry ghosts, these distorted fantasies devour our natural innocence, sucking the life-affirming juices from our will. They are the phantoms that haunt our consciousness—phantoms like fear, arrogance, and greed.

The intent of *Tarot Awareness* is to help the seeker remember that Consciousness, the Energy that knows Itself, permeates the subtleties and activities of *all* our life. When the seeker knows that we "live and move and have our being" within Spirit, Consciousness—God, the view of the Landscape becomes luminously clear, and then we apprehend the world from a non-egoistic perspective. For not only does Spirit see the panorama of the outside world, but It observes the Inner Landscape as well, a realm of insights, feelings, concepts, perceptions, and so much more.

Tarot Awareness will stress the value of the virtues to help keep the ego steady on the path. The seeker will better understand the nature of his or her individuality by consciously practicing such virtues as reasonableness, discipline, and compassion. Through practical application of the ancient symbolism and meanings portrayed in the seventy-eight cards of the Tarot deck, the text will illustrate thought processes that encourage the seeker to see the virtue in adopting a distinct, more conscious recognition of the workings of Spirit in his or her life.

The text will also illustrate how Spirit actually experiences Life *through* us: through consciousness, through personality, through the senses. The study of Tarot will show the seeker that focusing our consciousness on this Reality, this so-called "Presence of God" in and around us, will also help us to remember our purpose—and our nature.

In addition, it is the objective of this text to awaken the seeker, to lead him or her to participate fully in the Examined Life, to evoke thoughts like: Am I aware that Spirit is looking at the world through my eyes right now? When Spirit peers into the reflective pools of my subconscious, are the waters clear and calm? Does Spirit experience a symmetry to my thinking, or does Spirit experience a chaos of tangled gears and pulleys?

In *Tarot Awareness*, we will explore these and other spiritually-minded inquiries through study of the meanings behind the Tarot symbolism. Practical use of Tarot will help the seeker to draw attention away from the thousand distractions along the path, thereby opening the way to a more aware and vibrant communication with the Inner Self, the Divine Spark within.

Across the centuries, the Ageless Wisdom inherent in Tarot is always *contemporary* as it takes into account the fact that Life offers us the daily gauntlet, no matter what age: Alarm clock, cold dawn rain, crowded bus, parking lot full, fender bender, timecards, assembly line, bureaucrats, friends, enemies, children, pastors, husbands, wives. Whatever the situation—anxiety, sorrow, distress, and adversity, to name a few—wait at every turn. The numbed ego soon panics and then, in the unguarded moment, succumbs: Laxity, excessiveness, worry, rigidity, anger . . . Ageless Wisdom teaches that chaos comes in many forms.

Confused egos stumbling and brutally beaten in the gauntlet are eventually traumatized into anxiety-ridden sleepless nights, psychosomatic illnesses, problematic relationships, overextended credit cards, or heart attacks. When an individual exists unaware of the Real, then he or she will eventually lose perspective and control of what happens in the outer and inner life.

How can the study and practical application of Tarot help the seeker find his or her way back from the mad carnival of the outer world—to the natural inner world of Awareness? The text will provide guidelines that encourage a spirit of dedicated introspection and practical application that can help bring the seeker back to the very Source of our strength and well-being. And when that happens, problems are solved and goals are reached.

We will also study the Tarot reading, an interpretation of the meanings and patterns of a group of cards in a particular moment in time. And the reading is, above all, a challenging, daring, and intriguing entryway into the subtle realms.

Some teachers feel memorization of ancient meanings help block the creative, intuitive process. Others feel that memorizing phrases for each card is an essential foundation for a meaningful Tarot reading. The approach of this text falls somewhere in between.

We will avoid cookbook-like phrases, but we will learn astrological, alchemical, and psychological relationships for each card. We will also learn how to read the cards for self-healing as well as—if the seeker has the dedication and sincerity—healing for others.

Tarot Awareness will show the seeker how to illuminate the Golden Path that our soul takes on its journey up the mountain, the mountain we call Life. Our consciousness can be reawakened—but only through introspection, the Baptism of Fire along the way. Then, at the pinnacle, our purified human selves enter the Temple, the Holy of Holies, the Kingdom of Heaven Within. It is there that we face our true Inner Self, regaining perspectives lost long ago . . . perhaps even perspectives from *before* this earthly sojourn.

With its powerful imagery, hidden meanings, and sometimes earth-shattering revelations, Tarot can surprise you like a sudden lightning flash across the evening sky. It must be stressed, however, that the foundation of these insights is gathered from various traditions and religions dating back to ancient times. And, hopefully, the information provided within this text finds agreement with Ageless Wisdom in general.

Take, for example, the idea of God's omnipresence. The Christian might say, "God is the Creator of the Heavens and the Earth, and He is everywhere." The Jewish pilgrim might repeat a mantra such as "Master of the Universe." In China they might say, "There is only the Tao (meaning 'the Way'), and no other." Each approach to Spirit should feel comfortable with the eclectic meanings behind the Tarot cards.

Prayer, meditation, and good works, along with insights gained from the study and the common sense utilization of material from the text, can help the pilgrim to achieve a blissful clarity. For it is here in this state of vivid awareness that we can work miracles for ourselves and others as we touch the sacred healing energies of the Life-power.

Part One

An Introduction
to the Lay of the Land

Chapter 1

Tarot and Consciousness

ALTHOUGH SPIRIT IS ONE AND OMNIPRESENT, THE GREAT "ALL IN ALL," IN another sense we can think of It as the personal unfoldment of Consciousness through the four Planes of Existence: from the Spiritual, to the Emotional, to the Mental, and to the Physical. Down through the ages, through both oral tradition and the written word, certain ancient sages explored these four Planes and portrayed their understanding of mystical wisdom into a master plan, a conception of the universe which has come to be known as Tarot. Their metaphysics examined the meaning and application of the Universal Principles and the nature of Reality, of Consciousness Itself.

From Biblical Israel to the early Christians and beyond, to spiritual knowledge from India, Egypt, Persia, China, Tibet, and Japan—to all the other continents of the Earth, Tarot draws from a wealth of inspired thoughts from many sources.

In addition, certain disciplines and philosophies contribute to the treasures found in Tarot's Temple of Ageless Wisdom: The study of the movement of the seasons, the planets, the Sun and the Moon, for example, prompted astrologers from all ages to apprehend the mysteries of Nature; then the alchemists (mystics from medieval times) performed their magic to transmute the dross of ignorance into the gold of enlightenment.

But who invented Tarot, and why? There is much controversy surrounding the origin of Tarot, and opinions range from the mystery schools in ancient Egypt or Greece to the temples of Atlantis. Somehow, somewhere, we know that ancient adepts created a pictorial diagram that reaches beyond language and cultural barriers; Tarot is nothing less than a symbology devised to convey Truth to the subconscious of all humans for ages to come.

According to one tradition, in order to save the Ageless Wisdom from total obliteration by the intolerant Church of the Dark Ages, about eight hundred years ago adepts from all over the known world came together for a three-year conference in

3

Fez, Morocco. It was during this time that the city of Alexandria in Egypt, the center of human thought at the time, was destroyed. Since the Church burned both books and those they considered heretics, these sages of many lands and cultures disguised the Ageless Wisdom in a series of pictures that eventually took on the outer form of a deck of playing cards,[1] thereby throwing the suspicious, book-burning inquisitors off the track. In reality, however, the Tarot deck is a powerful, personal 78-page guidebook to the Holy of Holies, the Divine presence within and without.

Many forms of enlightened writings have come down to us in order to contribute to our spiritual advancement. Pythagoras, Plato, the Bible, the Upanishads of ancient India, the Tao, St. John of the Cross, Emerson . . . but in Tarot, the Ageless Wisdom is profoundly portrayed in pictures—all without comment. The seeker's own subconscious must shade in the meanings.

Mystical scriptures from the Hebrew Zohar of the Qabalists to the inspired writings of the Sufis, Spirit imparts Wisdom through the prism of the human mind.

To begin our study of *Tarot Awareness*, we will look at the Four Planes of Existence that make up Tarot's dimensions:

In the first Plane, the realm of Spirit, we are in the rarified atmosphere of Idea and pure Awareness. Some of the ancient sages identified the Spiritual Plane with the Element *Fire*. In Tarot, the Spiritual Plane is illustrated by the Suit of *Wands*.

Then in the second Plane, Awareness "moves" into the realm of the heart and pure feeling and the Element *Water*. In Tarot, this Emotional Plane is called *Cups*.

In the third Plane, Awareness operates as pure intellect and enters the thinking mode and the Element *Air*. Tarot calls this Mental Plane *Swords*.

Finally, in the fourth Plane, we reach the realm of manifestation, the planet we live on, and pure matter. This is the Element *Earth*, and in Tarot the Physical Plane is called the Suit of *Pentacles*.

To illustrate Awareness moving through the four Planes of Existence from Idea to manifestation, think of the process an artist might go through. First, he or she becomes inspired and is filled with the burning desire to paint something worthwhile (Fire—Spiritual Plane—Tarot Suit of Wands); secondly, the artist experiences flights of imagination, and the pictures and the patterns begin to unfold (Water—Emotional Plane—Cups); thirdly, the artist begins to hone in on a visualized picture. Materials, colors, approach, subject and other nuances round out the thinking (Air—Mental Plane—Swords); and, lastly, as the artist enters the world of manifestation, the charcoal and brush touch the canvas. A period of time passes where the artist sketches, paints ,and shades until the canvas is finally filled with a completed picture (Earth—the Physical Plane—the Suit of Pentacles). Filled with inspiration

(Fire) and imagination (Water), Consciousness thinks (Air) and toils until reaching the result: the finished product (Earth).

The study of Tarot along with meditation and good works can help the seeker stay aware in the Spiritual Plane, calm in the Emotional Plane, wise in the Mental Plane, and productive in the Physical Plane. Examining our experiences and looking at ourselves within leads to a free flow of energies through these Planes. And the seeker can rediscover the lost treasures from Ageless Wisdom, the Holy Laws behind all existence (in chapters 11–17 we will study them in depth). Adherence to the Law will allow the energies operating in the seeker's life to flow unimpeded: Talents, aspirations, desires, and problem-solving abilities will stand out in bold relief.

In the world of manifestation, we generally allow blockages and obstacles to interfere with the natural flow of Consciousness through the Planes. Then as we continue our lives, the obstructions influence our thinking in a variety of ways: The personality may become bloated with arrogance in the Spiritual Plane, live in illusion in the Emotional Plane, obsess in the Mental Plane, or self-indulge in the Physical Plane.

In this brief life we are eventually supposed to get a sense of what Spirit wants us to accomplish. "To do God's will," in other words, and we're supposed to be humble about it ("Whosoever therefore shall humble himself as this little child, the same is greatest in the kingdom of heaven." Matt. 18:4). In order for us to be in alignment with Spirit, we need to guard against wasting precious energy on nonessentials, because without balanced discipline, the personality becomes willful. And willfulness within the Landscape leads the seeker to wander off into evil gardens. Lust, envy, avarice, anger, sloth, gluttony, and arrogance. As we will see, sometimes within its imagery Tarot holds a mirror up to the vices.

Unconscious traumatic contents negatively influence the waking consciousness; informed contemplation of the principles of Ageless Wisdom found in Tarot will help the seeker to observe the impediments to clarity, and eventually correct them. The seeker can use Ageless Wisdom to examine the contents of consciousness as well as to look at the nature of an inquiry.

A woman may ask, "Why is there so much conflict in my office?" Genuinely wanting to know the answer, she takes that thought with her into a Tarot meditation on XVI. The Tower, an indication of upheaval. Contemplating the image on the card, the seeker might get any number of messages or impressions. She might get a flashback seeing herself complaining unfairly and secretly to her boss about an employee she considers a rival. The employee, very popular with the staff, is eventually fired. People in the office are edgy and don't know why. But after meditation on the nature of the conflict, the seeker suddenly realizes that *she* is the one at fault for the anxiety in the office. Examining the contents of consciousness through a Tarot meditation can shine a light on the core of the situation.

Sometimes it takes a bit of stamina to enter Tarot's atmosphere; facing one's own injurious attitudes and behaviors can be overwhelming, but as long as the seeker approaches with sincerity, the experience will be enlightening, at least to some degree. The Examined Life, although painfully frank in spotlighting unhealthy thoughts, words, and deeds, can assist the seeker in consciously dissolving the various impediments to clear seeing. It takes work and dedication, however.

In *Tarot Awareness* the seeker can learn the basic principles and meanings behind the Tarot cards discussed in the text; then in meditation on particular cards, new insights will come into the seeker's life.

Another aspect of Ageless Wisdom involves the illustration of virtues and talents as well as the obstacles. For example, the seeker can meditate on a certain card when he or she is discouraged by the progress of the current project. (In this case, the *Three of Pentacles*[2] would be appropriate, and will be discussed in greater detail when we get to the Minor Arcana in Part Three). Here the Inner Self can use the medium of Tarot to convey a message to the waking conscious, triggered by the imagery of the Three of Pentacles (A young artisan is working on a cathedral, watched approvingly by two patrons).

The messages could go something like this: "Bring a sense of sanctity to your performance." Or, "Enjoy the mastering of the craft. Diligent work on the project brings its own rewards." Or the Three of Pentacles might evoke thoughts like, "Don't worry. Your work is more appreciated than you think."

The ancients who conceived Tarot handed down to humankind a hidden treasure, a jewel intricately designed to highlight the benefits of practicing the virtues. Virtues like self-discipline, poise, and goodwill.

You see, *Tarot likes to teach lessons.* The seeker might ask something like, "How can I help myself not to take in so much anxiety?" Tranquillity and compassion are two of many characteristics of Spirit, and since we are "Children of God," it is our natural birthright as the outer manifestation of the Inner Self to already have these traits in potential. The lesson is that to reduce anxiety we need to remember who we are: Human beings with the peace of God within our hearts. Meditation on the Ace of Cups, for example, will remind the seeker of this.

One of the most important tools the seeker can use along the journey is the *Tarot Journal.* Writing thoughts and impressions in a blank book chosen specially for the Tarot Journey will give the seeker an opportunity to reflect on the myriad of experiences that occur as we study and contemplate the Tarot imagery. One could treat the Journal as a spiritual diary with daily entries, or the entries could be made under certain sections.

Relaxation Exercises

It is a good idea to prepare for meditation. Choose a quiet place where you are not likely to be disturbed, preferably at the same time every day. You might try some soft music, incense, and candles to help you get in a relaxed mood. Reading spiritual literature beforehand is also helpful.

For a general meditation that will work with each of the cards, you can follow these guidelines or write your own in the Journal: Sit with your spine straight, take a nice deep breath, close your eyes, and begin to feel the calmness . . .

> Notice your breathing as you slowly inhale and exhale.
> With each breath, let yourself feel more comfortable
> and more relaxed.
> Let the tensions of the day begin to fade . . .
> and feel all the tightness in your muscles wind down . . . melt away.
> Notice the rhythm of your breathing.
> Exhale slowly . . . and release more of the tension . . .
> the stress . . . the tightness.
> When you inhale quietly,
> notice a cleansing purity entering your personal atmosphere . . .
> Exhale, and feel more relaxed . . .
> Repeat this conscious breathing a few more times.
> You will notice that . . . your body . . . is beginning to feel . . . lighter.
> Your neck has lost all stiffness . . . your shoulders relax . . .
> Your arms . . . your back . . . your legs . . .
> let your whole being relax.
> Allow the last remaining tensions to drain out through your feet.
> Just drift . . . and let your mind float into a total state of peacefulness.
> Count backwards from 10, and when you are ready,
> open your eyes. . . .

Impressions and Messages
Received from Meditation

In Tarot, the seeker's attitude, frame of mind, and grounding are very important as he or she approaches the time for meditation. First, it is beneficial to sincerely study the meaning of the card or cards in question. Involving the intellect in the preparation, along with a heartfelt desire to learn, gives the individual walking the path a sure footing as the personal consciousness enters the special atmosphere of Tarot.

After a general understanding of the card's meaning, you can contemplate the imagery of the card for a few minutes. Follow this with a time for quiet reflection. Later, enter some thoughts about the experience in the Journal. If we are prepared on the Mental Plane when we look at the imagery of Tarot, then our consciousness is enriched from our understanding of the meanings. In addition, when we *think* about the imagery pictured, the personal subconscious is impressed.

Answers to Various Questions Posed from the Text

From time to time questions may arise. With II. the High Priestess, for example, we could ask something like, "How clear am I about my motivations in this situation?" Or, with the Hermit, we might wonder, "How can I apply what I have just learned to be more helpful to my coworkers here in the Physical Plane?" The Rider in VII. The Chariot might ask, "How can I better prepare myself for the difficulties I must face?" When we look at the figure of Justice we could ask ourselves, "How must I adjust my thinking to perceive what is Real?"

Many teachers believe that it is important to clearly formulate a question first before entering the atmosphere of Tarot. A question acts like a beacon light leading along an unsure path ahead. When reading cards for another person it is especially beneficial because without a specific question, we could wander off into nebulous territory.

Formulating questions using words like how, what, why, what if, help expand the consciousness: "Why don't I feel my job is in conformity with the ultimate plan for my life? Where is my conduct best reflecting God's Law? What is God's Law?" These questions are better than, say, "Since I feel lucky this week, should I buy lottery tickets?"

Write the answers to the questions in the Journal and refer back to them from time to time.

Notes from the Text and Other Spiritual Readings

Keep your notes from reading in the Journal. This will provide a handy summary of what you have been learning so far. (Selections from the *Bibliography* are highly recommended.)

Poetry

Each of the twenty-two cards of the Major Arcana has a poem inspired by the imagery and meaning of the particular card. In the Journal you could write your own original poetry for any and all cards in the deck.

Dreams

Freud said that dreams were like letters sent to us from our subconscious; the only problem is, we usually leave these letters unopened. If you should do a Tarot meditation before sleep, it is possible you could get messages about it in your dream that night—especially if before going to sleep you intend to get a revelation about an issue. Some seekers actually sleep on the card.

When you wake in the morning, lie still, gather your thoughts, and then grab a pen and the Journal and start writing your impressions. The resulting information could be invaluable.

The Personal Mission Statement

In this original manifesto we strive to design a foundation for the cathedral we intend to build to the heavens. We will attempt to recognize our persona and who we really are. We will try to discover (or at least get some hints about) what the blueprint for our soul is supposed to be. Therefore, in our Personal Mission Statement, we want to answer questions like:

- What are my objectives, the True North of my journey?
- How do I intend to keep my "house" in order?
- Am I busy with activities that I find valuable and/or amusing?
- Am I able to objectively observe my thought processes, and what do I see?
- How clear am I about the project(s) I wish to complete?
- Where am I missing the mark?
- What do I value?

As we proceed on the Tarot Journey we will be able to observe how our life unfolds within the Great Mystery. The Personal Mission Statement will help you plot your strategy so that you can better sense the Light of the Holy Presence shining through your personality.

After a Tarot meditation, certain insights might encourage you to add to the manifesto. Over time you can write in new amendments as you adapt your Statement to your life and vice versa. For example, after meditating on say, IX. the Hermit, some questions may arise: What do I consider to be worthwhile sacrifices? How can I best share my knowledge (even with a disagreeable person)? Is my sense of purpose gaining steam?

The Tarot Journal will stand as a living chronicle of your many insights along the way.

Tarot meditation and study illuminates certain tendencies and potentials inherent in the seeker's character. If the seeker applies the power of concentration to the imagery in the card or cards at issue, hidden influences will reveal themselves, allowing the Inner Self to communicate more clearly to the seeker's consciousness.

From birth our consciousness, our personality, our *entire energy field* is affected by various karmic, celestial, and sensual influences. Fortunately, human consciousness was given the basic free will to focus or not to focus and, as a result, we remain free at our core. That's why *Tarot likes to offer choices.*

"Do I heed or reject the warning? Is all the effort really worth it? Has the time come for me to change this obnoxious behavior?"

We can keep the glass polished and sparkling, or we can splatter it with mud. Spirit provides us with the choice. As we experience Life, if we are in alignment with Spirit, our choices will reflect the harmony of that relationship. If not, we approach the question with typical human near-sightedness. And that's where our study and meditation can be of great benefit because Tarot raises a lantern aloft and casts a light on the various angles of the question.

One angle might involve *anxiety.* Look at the *Nine of Swords* (in the Suit of Air, the Mental Plane, chapter 27), a pictorial representation of apprehension and worry. In this case, the figure has opened the floodgates to the influence of what Jung might call "the shadow self." To emphasize the vibration involved, nine Swords rise eerily in the dark night Air.

Another angle might portray consciousness *victorious* over uneasiness and distress (as in the *Six of Wands,* chapter 25, where a young man wearing a wreath on his head receives accolades for his triumph as he rides before the throng). Or Tarot can illustrate an angle that shows Spirit bestowing *blessings* on human consciousness. In the Ace of Pentacles (chapter 28), for example, we see the Hand of the Divine extending forth in a gesture of great givingness. The card can inspire us to give thanks for our many blessings in the Physical Plane, and can also heighten our awareness of grace, Spirit's eternal stream of love and protection. *Tarot likes to portray the gifts of Spirit.*

The cards encourage us to be more cognizant of another of Spirit's precious gifts: *Intuitive potential.* Study and meditation on the *Ace of Wands* in particular could help with better psychic attunement.

Other gifts portrayed in Tarot include the drive to achieve, expansion of the capacity to know, and the deeper appreciation of the harmony underlying all of creation. As a result, Tarot is complex, expansive, and always benevolent, even if at times confrontational, with shocking imagery and uncomfortable, unexpected revelations.

In the Major Arcana (0. The Fool plus 21 other cards) the emphasis is on the *Inner* Landscape: The Seven Modes of Consciousness (Cards 1 to 7), the Seven Universal Laws (Cards 8 to 14), and the Seven Levels of Spiritual Unfoldment (Cards 15 to 21). In the Minor Arcana, on the other hand, the seeker finds imagery illustrating more of the *Outer* Landscape, that is, circumstances and situations in the seeker's life. Job, family, projects, relationships, duties, behaviors, failures, successes . . . In the Court of the Minor Arcana we encounter the character traits, Spirit expressing through the pattern of the human personality. Pages (Earth and sensation), Knights (Air and thinking), Queen (Water and feeling), and Kings (Fire and inspiration) symbolize the individualization of consciousness and the psychological functions; how much Light is reflected through this prism depends upon the degree of clarity or pollution in the personality. Sympathy or indifference, compassion or cruelty—the possibilities are vast.

Examining consciousness with Tarot as our guide, along with faith and good works, we continue along the Golden Path—which is another way of saying that only through awareness and application do we advance toward the goal. Tarot, a profound tool for observing ourselves, helps clear the way for ultimate realization of the compassionate power of the Inner Self, Spirit's love unfolding.

Notes

1. Paul Foster Case, *The Tarot: A Key to the Wisdom of the Ages* (Richmond, Va.: Macoy, 1947), p. 2.

2. There are many decks of Tarot cards to choose from, but particularly recommended are: 1) The Major Arcana is illustrated by the self-coloring Tarot deck, Builders of the Adytum (B.O.T.A.), 5101-05 North Figueroa St., Los Angeles, Calif. 90042; 2) The Minor Arcana is illustrated by the Universal Waite Deck, re-colored by Mary Hanson-Roberts, drawings by Pamela Coleman Smith (U.S. Games Systems, Inc., Publishers, Stamford, Conn. 06902, 1990).

Chapter 2

Tarot along the Ecliptic
The Ancient Wisdom of Astrology

THE SAGES OF OLD—THE ASTROLOGERS, THE ALCHEMISTS, THE QABALISTS, the adepts of all ages—used similar symbology and correspondences to illustrate their respective approaches to Spirit. The astrologers painted the planets and stars into the Landscape, analyzing the cosmic energies that stimulate certain inclinations, tendencies, and potentials hidden deep in the subconscious. The alchemists in turn worked their magic with the elements.

From the point of view of the human on earth, the sun follows a path, the *ecliptic,* around a belt of fixed stars called the zodiac (meaning "circle of carved figures, or animals"). At the Spring Equinox, the power of light rushes forth (the Fire of Self-expression). During the Summer Solstice light is warm and nurturing (the feeling nature of Water). At the Autumnal Equinox light fades and the intellect comes into prominence (the thinking processes symbolized by Air). And during the Winter Solstice darkness overcomes, and the personality develops practical endurance (matter and sensation, Earth).

Tarot blends the symbols, patterns, and correlation of astrology and alchemy with aspects of Hebrew, Christian, and Eastern mysticism.

Significantly, both astrology and Tarot share the same alchemical correspondences. Aries, Leo, and Sagittarius—the three Fire signs of the zodiac—are the same Element of Fire that blazes in *Wands.* Like the Wands of Tarot, Fire in astrology is purposeful, vital, and enthusiastic.

As consciousness becomes more aware, the door opens so that inspiration may visit the personality. However, the Element of Fire also challenges the temperament: The Aries personality can be impulsive, Leo obnoxious, and Sagittarius scatter-brained.

Astrologers use the Element of Water—the signs of Cancer, Scorpio, and Pisces—in the same way Tarot uses *Cups.* We are in the Emotional Plane. Astrology says Cancer is reflective, Scorpio intense, and that Pisces, the last of the twelve signs, is the most sensitive in the zodiac. In the Water signs, the consciousness is often highly sympathetic to the feelings of others, and when aware, freely allows spirit to move through the emotions. But Water must also challenge the consciousness. As we will learn from Cups, emotions can explode in the personality. Cancer gets hysterical, Scorpio raises its stinger, and after the attack, Pisces drifts off into space.

The three Air signs, Libra, Aquarius, and Gemini, correspond to *Swords*. The Element of Air in astrology is the same Mental Plane of Tarot. The Air sign Libra seeks balance, Aquarius exhibits originality of thought, and Gemini dazzles with superb powers of communication. In the Air signs, as in Tarot, the major expression of the consciousness is through the intellect. However, it must be remembered that Air is also *unpredictable*. Libra, void of his natural elegance, demands peace no matter what the consequences, Aquarius violently espouses extreme opinions, and Gemini blathers.

In the physical realm, Capricorn, Taurus, and Virgo correspond to *Pentacles* in Tarot. Here we are walking the Earth: Forging ahead in Capricorn, steadfast in Taurus, and conscientious in Virgo. We get in trouble, though, when we forget that we are in the realm of the senses. Capricorn in detriment is distant, almost detached; in sexual and other relationships, should Taurus be "afflicted," then human consciousness is often preoccupied with carnal interests; and Virgo in the extreme is absurdly fastidious.

Tarot incorporates astrological symbolism into its atmosphere because the signs and planets of the zodiac enhance the hidden meanings of the cards. Consciousness exists within waves of Energy—pulsating, subtle vibrations. Symbols in astrology point to the power of Spirit influencing these vibrations. The signs (twelve in all) describe the personal environment, while the ten planets (which include the two illuminaries, the Sun and Moon, plus Mercury, Venus, Mars, Saturn, Jupiter, Neptune, Uranus, and Pluto) have come to symbolize what astrologers believe to be a particular set of vibrations influencing the personal environment. Twelve signs + ten planets = twenty-two, each one representing a Tarot card of the first twenty-two (called Trumps or Keys) in the Major Arcana (or "Greater Secret").

Many astrologers assert that at the moment of our birth, as we left the womb and took in our first breath, our personal atmosphere was struck by the solar energies at unique angles, depending on the time of the year and the place of nativity. As a result, our subconscious in that moment was imprinted with those tendencies, inclinations, and potentials corresponding to the consequences of our previous actions, our *karma*. Skills, faults, attractions, repulsions, strengths, virtues, and vices, all reside in the vast reservoir of our Inner Self. The timing and composition of that first breath was influenced by the content of our prior existences. However, it must be remembered that in the current moment we always can draw on the power of our free will to consciously work with the beneficial tendencies, inclinations, and potentials—and reject the harmful ones.

The natal chart is like a photograph of the heavens at the moment of birth, and properly interpreted, can reveal the blueprint the Inner Self has chosen to fulfill its mission in this particular lifetime—along with the strengths and weaknesses, the potentially easy roads as well as the treacherous roads, that will be taken by the soul on its journey.

In astrology, the sign represents a unique environment reflecting twelve types of temperaments, influenced by a dominant element as well as the planetary positions.

The Fire Signs (*Masculine, Active*)

From the time of birth, humans reflect the qualities of Nature during that season. Those born at the time of Aries absorb the primal thrusting energy that affects matter at the beginning of springtime. Astrology compares this energy to a Ram forging up the mountainside. Briefly, the typical Aries personality is dynamic, pioneering, and bold. He proclaims to the world, "I am." If unevolved, however, Aries is reckless and quarrelsome.

The sign of Leo, the self-assured and authoritative lion, makes potent use of the dramatic energy of Fire. He says, "I will." Charismatic and tireless at his best, vain and domineering at his worst, the Lion's roar commands attention.

Sagittarius the Archer is aspiring, idealistic, and filled with fiery enthusiasm in his search for truth, asserting, "I perceive." Unevolved, the Archer wanders the earth aimlessly, a dabbler.

The Water Signs (*Feminine, Receptive*)

In Cancer, the summer begins and the solar energies affect the emotions. Symbolized by the tenacious Crab, the Cancer personality is dominated by emotion and protectiveness. She says, "I feel." However, the Crab can be timid, sentimental, and cloying.

In Scorpio, the emotions are intense. The evolved Scorpio (the soaring eagle) is highly principled and profoundly sympathetic to the feelings of others. Scorpio says, "I desire." When this consciousness is in the Scorpion mode, however, the personality can be bitter, sarcastic, and suspicious.

In Pisces it is the imagination that is intensely active. A dreamer, creative, spiritual, and kind: "I believe," she says. Pisces is symbolized by two fishes—one travels confidently upstream, the other is pulled downstream in a torrent of irresponsibility, bad habits, and self-deception.

The Air Signs (*Masculine, Active*)

In Libra the solar energies flow in the autumn equinox, a time of year when growth is subsiding and internalizing. This personality seeks harmony through use of the intellect, symbolized in the zodiac by the scales. Libra says, "I balance." However, when out of balance, Libra is gullible, tactless, and uncouth.

When evolved, Aquarius the Water Bearer is a visionary, open-minded, humanitarian, revolutionary. He says, "I know." However, when Aquarius is unfocused, the personality becomes eccentric, a victim of muddled thinking and erratic iconoclastic behavior.

Gemini the Twins (a blending of the masculine and feminine energies) is mentally agile, logical, and very active. Gemini states, "I think." The Gemini are the debaters of the zodiac. Sometimes too clever for their own good, Gemini can be intolerant of others, restless, and in constant need of stimulation.

The Earth Signs (*Feminine, Receptive*)

In Capricorn, the energy is more focused in the material. The Capricorn personality is ambitious and persevering like its symbol, the Goat. She says, "I use." Unevolved, Capricorn is haughty, narrow-minded, and unsettled.

Taurus the Bull is kind-hearted and loves beauty, structure, and things. Taurus says, "I have." But when Taurus gets too comfortable, the personality can become slow, obstinate, and lazy.

Virgo the Virgin is dignified and hard-working, detail-oriented. She says, "I analyze." If afflicted, Virgo is overly critical and prejudiced.

The Three Qualities

Astrologers describe the celestial energies affecting our personal atmosphere, that is, our subconscious and personality, and overall approach to life, as having three different rates of vibration, or qualities: Cardinal (dynamic energy unfolding, the beginning of a cycle), Fixed (the energy stabilizes), and Mutable (the energy harmonizes with the surrounding environment; change, ending of a cycle).

The four Cardinal signs of Aries, Cancer, Libra, and Capricorn remind us of the energies manifesting at the beginning of the season: Aries in spring, Cancer in summer, Libra in fall, and Capricorn in winter; Fixed signs maintain the energy of their respective Element: Fire (Leo), Water (Scorpio), Air (Aquarius), Earth (Taurus); and, finally, the Mutable signs (Sagittarius, Pisces, Gemini, and Virgo) adapt to the energies and harmonize them with the beginning vibrations of the next emerging Cardinal sign.

Tarot uses Cardinal, Fixed, and Mutable categories to correspond to the Numbers of the Minor Arcana. The Aces incorporate the meanings of all three signs of the Suit (i.e., The Ace of Wands reflects the meanings of Aries (Cardinal Fire), Leo (Fixed Fire), and Sagittarius (Mutable Fire); the Twos, Threes, and Fours are Cardinal; the Fives, Sixes, and Sevens are Fixed; and the Eights, Nines, and Tens are Mutable. The Two of Wands, for example, would be Cardinal Fire (Aries), the Five of Wands would be Fixed Fire (Leo), and the Eight of Wands, Mutable Fire (Sagittarius). This attribution will be discussed further in Part Three, The Minor Arcana.

The Planets

The light-force emanating from the Sun interpenetrates every physical manifestation of our solar system—from tiniest cell to the largest planet. Therefore, the influence on human nature is not necessarily a ray from the planet itself, but energies flowing through it from the Sun. The planets are focal points of solar radiation, and like celestial prisms, color the character of the radiation streaming down upon the Earth. And depending on their angle from Earth (and each other) at the time of birth, certain kinds of unconscious activity can be influenced if there is no interference by the human will.

When the planet enters a specific sign, the energy is affected by the atmosphere of that sign. The planet is said to "rule" the most like its own vibration. When a planet enters a sign that enhances the power of its vibration, it is said to be "exalted" there. If, however, the planet enters a sign that is opposite to its nature, then the energy is weakened and is said to be in "detriment." The general meanings of the planets are as follows:

1. **The Sun** is the principal Illuminary, the source of life in the solar system. The Sun symbolizes the Essence of the Inner Self, the center of beingness, the will. The characteristics endowed by the Sun in the natal chart are the most dominant, signifying the person's individuality. The Sun is said to rule the sign of Leo because during the season of the Lion, the angle of the Sun's rays compliment the creative energy, stateliness, and leadership qualities of Leo. In the self-confident atmosphere of Aries, the Sun is exalted. (Tarot Trump XIX. The Sun will be discussed in detail later in chapter 22.)

2. **The Moon** is the second Illuminary. Portrayed by Isis in ancient Egypt, this body reflects the light of the Sun, and therefore represents the personality, the reflection of the Inner Self. The Moon influences the tides and the rhythms of the body and as such is the principal symbol for the nature of Water. Since the sign of Cancer is the most emotional of the zodiac, the Moon rules there and is in detriment in the emotionally detached atmosphere of Capricorn; she is exalted in peaceful Taurus (associated with II. The High Priestess).

3. **Mercury**, in Roman mythology, was the winged god (corresponding with Hermes in Greece, Thoth in Egypt) and was known as "the Messenger of the Gods." In Tarot and astrology, Mercury is the mind as the "messenger" between the personality (Moon) and the Inner Self (Sun). Mercury, the quickest of the planets (it completes its orbit of the Sun in only eighty-eight days) rules our powers of communication and mental agility, and therefore is most like volatile Gemini and analytical Virgo—but loses concentration in ethereal, Mutable Sagittarius. However, the thinking processes of Mercury are exalted in the stable, Fixed Air of Aquarius (associated with I. The Magician).

4. **Venus** is the Roman goddess of beauty and love (Aphrodite in Greece). Harmony. Refinement. Aesthetics. The solar energies operating through the Venus vibration stimulate the consciousness to respond to others in friendship, cooperation, romance, sympathy. Venus rules Taurus and Libra, is exalted in Pisces and is in its detriment in Scorpio and Aries (associated with III. The Empress).

5. **Mars** is the Roman god of war. This planet is a fiery, aggressive energy and stimulates the passions. Mars is the first planet to orbit outside of the Earth, and this outward push gives it a sense of initiative, corresponding to the signs it rules, Aries. Mars is exalted in the ambitious sign of Capricorn, while an angry Mars is in its detriment in the diplomatic sign of Libra (associated with XVI. The Tower).

6. **Jupiter** symbolizes the philosophical mind and is considered, as the largest planet in our solar system, to bring expansiveness to thinking. Growth, wisdom, benevolence, fortune, good humor. Jupiter rules the free-spirited atmosphere of Sagittarius and is exalted in Cancer, as it expands the nurturing quality of the Crab. However, Jupiter hinders the ability of the volatile Gemini to concentrate (Associated with X. The Wheel of Fortune).

7. **Saturn** is known as the Challenger or the Lord of Karma. Saturn is restrictive and provides the seeker with obstructions along the path. Saturn teaches patience and persistence and therefore governs Capricorn and is exalted in Libra's pursuit of justice. Saturn's detriment comes in Leo where he constricts the lion's heart (associated with XXI. The World).

8. **Uranus** represents freedom and independence. Individualism is heightened. Uranus can bring about sudden change in the course of events and awaken the consciousness to new realities. Uranus rules the inventive atmosphere of Aquarius and is exalted in the probity of Scorpio. However, Uranus in detriment can exacerbate the prideful tendencies of Leo (associated with 0. The Fool).

9. **Neptune** constitutes vision and mysticism. Here the solar energies bestow intuition and idealism. Neptune is the higher octave of Venus, and the love vibration expands outward to all beings. Neptune, the god of the sea, rules the watery, sensitive sign of Pisces and is exalted in the compassion of Cancer. Neptune is restricted in the critical atmosphere of earthy Virgo (associated with XII. The Hanged Man).

10. **Pluto** is known as the god of Hell. However, Pluto actually signals rebirth and illumination. Here the soul becomes regenerated. The planet Pluto's discovery is relatively new (1930), and it completes its orbit around the Sun every 247 years. Modern astrology assigns its rulership to Scorpio (associated with XIII. Death).

Decanates

The ancients asserted that when God first spoke to consciousness, He spoke in numbers and letters. Besides astrology, alchemy, and many spiritual traditions, Tarot also blends the meanings of numbers and letters into its system. Pythagoras, a Greek philosopher living during the fifth century B.C., asserted that numbers were veils for the secret workings of Spirit. The Qabalists, Jewish mystics of the Middle Ages, agreed with this description and contributed to Tarot the attributions of numbers 0 through 9, their combinations, as well as the sacred meanings behind the 22 letters of the Hebrew alphabet, Aleph (א) through Tav (ת).

In the Minor Arcana (the so-called "Lesser Secret"), the four alchemical elements combine with the planets ruling the signs in the realm of Numbers. Tarot incorporates the meanings of seven planetary influences (Sun, Moon, Mercury, Venus, Mars, Jupiter, and Saturn) in the Two through the Tens in the Minor Arcana.

For example, the meaning of Two in the Suit of the Element Fire (the Two of Wands) is influenced by the meaning of what happens when the fiery radiation of Mars enters the fiery atmosphere of Aries (where he rules). In the chapters on the Minor Arcana, the meaning of the Two of Wands will be explained in greater detail.

One school of thought[1] divides the 360° eliptic (the path followed by the Sun through the signs of the zodiac) by the twelve signs, equaling 30° each. These 30° divisions of the signs are called "decanates." The first 30° decanate is Cardinal and divided by 3 into 10° for each card (Tarot numbers 2, 3, 4), the second 30° decanate is Fixed (5, 6, 7) and the third 30° decanate, Mutable (Numbers 8, 9, 10). A different planet "rules" each 10° of the series (Tarot cards 2 through 10). The Aces, as was stated before, contain attributes of all three Qualities (Cardinal, Fixed, and Mutable). Israel Regardie in *The Golden Dawn*,[2] Aleister Crowley in *The Book of Thoth*,[3] and Muriel Bruce Hasbrouck in her book *Tarot and Astrology, the Pursuit of Destiny*[4] all use the so-called Chaldean system of attributions for elements and planets in Tarot.

The Court of the Minor Arcana

As consciousness awakens in the physical plane, from birth until passing, the individuality, the core of the personality, learns things. Negative/positive, passive/active, feminine/masculine: The Chinese call it *yin/yang*.

The One Energy has two poles at either end of the continuum. Astrologers use terms for aspects of the Energy like feminine Moon (*yin*) and masculine Sun (*yang*). Tarot illustrates these female/male aspects in the Minor Arcana, most prominently in the human personalities of the Court; in the realm of consciousness, Tarot in the Major Arcana displays the One Energy as twenty-two Personages or Trumps.

The Court of the Minor Arcana is personality divided into the four Planes, Suits, and Elements and the twelve signs and ten planets. In this most human atmosphere, the Tarot Court is the personification of the traits. For example, an adaptable, idealistic woman decides to travel to Yucatan in Mexico in order to see the Mayan Pyramids. "What areas should I explore?" she asks herself before looking through the cards. Suddenly her gaze focuses on the Queen of Wands, emotional Fire. (In Tarot the Kings = will, Fixed; Queens = emotion, Cardinal; Knights = mind, Mutable; Pages = body and a combination of the three signs of the suit.)

The Queen of Wands would climb the gigantic pyramid at Uxmal and feel a heightened spiritual sense as she gazed down at the jungle below—initiated by a strong determination to reach the top.

The Queen of Cups (emotional Water) personality, on the other hand, might travel to the Yucatan in order to experience the heightening of her sense of beauty.

While walking in the Yucatan jungle, the Queen of Cups would revel in being greeted by the myriad of butterflies along the paths.

The Queen of Swords, being of airy intellect, would find the history of the Mayan peoples fascinating. Instead of the jungle, though, this Queen might visit the huge cistern where the Mayan priests tossed their human sacrifices.

The Queen of Pentacles, the earthiest of the Queens, would savor the spices and flavors of the Mayan cuisine.

In the Suit of Wands, the personalities are more concerned with ideas, and they often express themselves through what they have learned. When Spirit flows freely, the Wands personality gets inspiring ideas (the King of Wands). If the Wands personality is ego-driven, however, then the ideas become more self-serving, more crass (the Knight of Wands Reversed personifies these negative traits). In Cups, the personalities are more emotional, in Swords more intellectual, and in Pentacles more worldly oriented. (The Court will be discussed in detail in Part Three: The Minor Arcana.)

Entering the Landscape

Tarot activates the seeker to ask questions like, "What is my attitude toward what's happened to me along the way? How conscious of my responsibilities am I? What are the results of my self-indulgence?"

Now look at the Devil (Capricorn). Here is an example of the evil we have invited into the Garden. Although the imagery in this card was intended by the ancients to poke a little fun at the menacing Beelzebub of the Medieval Church, the undercurrent of their message was serious: The consciousness needs to be vigilant about the demanding, harmful urges of the will corrupted by instinct, or what Freud called the "id." In Church dogma, this instinct is called "Satan." In Tarot he is selfishness in disguise, wryly illustrated in the Devil. Much more will be said of this trump later in chapter 18.

Tarot stimulates curiosity, thereby encouraging the seeker to discover truths about the Inner Landscape—as well as the outside world.

Meditation and study of Tarot can help the seeker to sharpen focus. Then the consciousness can get a better picture of the goals to be reached in this lifetime. Soon the forgotten details of the life plan, goals set aside long ago, begin to reveal themselves after a lengthy slumber. The seeker gradually feels purpose once again and wants to look deeper into things. More questions arise: "What am I supposed to accomplish? How do I best make use of my talents? What is my duty?"

In Sanskrit the word is *dharma*, and it translates not only as "duty," but also as "religion" in its original meaning: A binding principle between a spirit and what is divine.

By clearly defining the goal and reaching it with principles and idealism intact, we fulfill our duty, our *dharma*. The process of reaching the goal, living the ideal, becomes our true religion. It takes faith, a practical discipline, and a sense of joy. And it takes endurance. But as long as the seeker approaches the task with a sincere attitude of confident expectancy and a humble heart, at the very least, little flashes of awareness will come. Tarot is a spiritual set of diagrams and pointers designed to vivify the emotions, stimulate the intellect, and purify the senses. Working with Tarot can also enhance intuitive abilities. Through consistency of effort, combined with a simple faith in the power of spirit, we prepare for entry into what the adept from Nazareth often described: "But seek ye first the kingdom of God, and his righteousness; and all these things shall be added unto you." (Matthew 6:33) Tarot study and meditation provide the seeker with some rather vivid hints on how to get there.

Notes

1. This "school" is believed to have originated with the ancient Chaldean astrologers. Charles E. O. Carter, *The Principles of Astrology* (Wheaton, Ill.: Theosophical Publishing House, 1925), pp. 21–22.
2. Israel Regardie, *The Golden Dawn* (St. Paul, Minn.: Llewellyn Publications, 1990).
3. Aleister Crowley, *The Book of Thoth* (Berkeley, Calif.: Kashmarin Publications Ltd., 1969).
4. Muriel Bruce Hasbrouck, *Tarot and Astrology, the Pursuit of Destiny* (Rochester, Vt.: Destiny Books, 1989).

Chapter 3

0. The Fool
The Life-Power Manifesting

Alchemical Element: Air

Astrological Correspondence: The independence and originality associated with the planet Uranus.

Hebrew Letter: Aleph א (meaning "ox" or "bull" as a symbol of the movement of the creative energy. It is meant to evoke the image of oxen pulling a plow, the force of agriculture, and its symbolic effect on early civilization.)

The Inner Atmosphere: The fire of Spirit ignites; the element Air and the power of the Life-Breath in expression. It is Spirit innocent of experience. Guilelessness. Consciousness ready for increased awareness.

Statement: "I am the Fool, and the Life Force limits itself in me, descending; it is my business as a manifestation of this Power in the Physical Plane to ascend from one level to the next. I am a ray of light forever unfolding through the realms of existence. I am the seeker on the path, and I am you who read these words."

Quotation: "If any man among you seemeth to be wise in this world, let him become a fool, that he may be wise." (1 Corinthians 3:18)

The Challenge: The ego must avoid careless thinking and ill-considered behavior.

The General Atmosphere of The Fool

The Zero, as the ancient adepts asserted, was the great Nothingness before manifestation. The Qabalists, medieval Hebrew mystics, speak of the Limitless Light (*Ain Soph Aur*, in Hebrew). Zero is a glyph for Spirit, the source of "beingness," pure consciousness and the essence of will—the energy that is aware of itself. The Zero is idea before manifestation, "the circle without circumference," the infinite center without a point. It is the absolute expression of the power of love and wisdom moving through the four Planes of Existence.

Tarot calls this Zero the Fool. He[1] can be understood from many angles, one of which is consciousness before the moment of conception. The ancients chose to portray him as a carefree youth about to step off a precipice. In fact, one of the most important questions Tarot asks in the atmosphere of the Fool is, "After he falls off the cliff, where does he land?" The answer is, "Into waiting human hands—as he takes his first breath."

Another even more basic question is: "Why is he called the Fool?"

First, you must ask yourself what a fool really is. Your immediate reaction is probably something like, "Dupe! Idiot! Buffoon!" Although the surface meaning is one of inexperience and unbridled enthusiasm, the word "fool" actually comes from the Latin *follis*, meaning windbag, or bellows, giving you a suggestion of the alchemical element represented: Air.

From another vantage point you can see the Fool as the soul on the journey you call your life. He is the pilgrim who travels the path in order to gather experience and refine his awareness of the divine essence within. Look at the white Sun above him. The seeker as the Fool is a ray of light emanating from that white Sun, the divine Source of Life, the white fire of Spirit within and without.

The title of the trump refers to something else, however. It is believed that before birth we existed in the "other world" (which some call Heaven); the imagery of the

Fool asserts: "I would have to be a fool to choose to leave this blissful state, this Paradise—to be cast out into the world of the senses—especially with a body and mind created for the purpose of imprisoning me!"

Choosing birth in the Physical Plane, this place we call Earth, is the direct result of the soul desiring sense experience (the "Fall" of Adam and Eve). Or, as the Bible puts it, eating the forbidden "fruit" of Eden's tree. In a moment of instant decision—taking the fateful "bite"—the soul allows itself to be pulled into the sacred vortex generated by the sperm's entry into the egg. The point is, we've *all* done it.

The trump of the Fool challenges the seeker to stay awake to his or her Inner Self, the fiery essence of the Life-Breath. The ancients assigned the first letter of the Hebrew alphabet, Aleph (pronounced AW-leff), to the Fool and the element Air (the word "air" comes from the Greek αηρ, "breath").

The imagery of the Fool in Tarot gives many hints that point to that living, breathing Essence: Beyond definition, beyond boundaries, the Life-Breath expresses itself through the seeker's own life experience. *Tarot Awareness* teaches that to the degree that we consecrate our life to the expression of Spirit, in equal measure will we experience bliss along the journey. However, if our lives run contrary to the awareness of Spirit, that is, we become intoxicated with sense experience, then the ego—the soul's "point of contact" with physical reality—stands before the lens and blocks consciousness off from the flow of Spirit's inner light.

The little white dog in the picture symbolizes the desiring senses under control of the ego. If, however, the ego becomes forgetful of its true nature, then it becomes willful and selfish, and the playful little dog transforms into a snarling beast—a beast of obsession and indulgence, ready to devour the seeker.

The Fool—Aleph—is of the Spiritual Plane, carrying a Wand over his right shoulder, a Wand that reminds him that he brings into this life a divine heritage and innate appreciation, and longing for, the Sacred. Aleph says, "Here in the Spiritual Plane I am awakened, and I am inspired with a Vision. I shall lead a life of awareness, a life that embodies the highest ideals. My consciousness shall continue on the path of ascension to become a kind of living example."

However, the Fool also presents a challenge: After the fall from the cliff into the physical plane, it must be remembered that the seeker is free to choose any number of paths toward enlightenment. Often, however, the ego immediately asserts its power, and the seeker is vulnerable to choose a more difficult, disorienting path. He or she ignores the divine potential, and then, ego-bound, takes routes that, among other things, can reek of ennui, carelessness, despair, and lassitude. Or the distraction from Spirit can come from a more sensually desirable self-indulgent path.

The Fool holds a white rose in his left hand, the hand of the subconscious. This flower represents the purity of Spirit and the potential of the ego to reflect that purity in virtuous, ethical thoughts and behavior. Further, the white rose represents the divine tranquillity one can achieve when wisdom and love guide the seeker. If, however, the seeker chooses to live in a semiconscious state, then the flower can wither. The emotions begin to rule thought, and existence changes into a raging torrent of anxiety. *Tarot Awareness* encompasses the idea that you can be a slave to past abuses by dwelling on resentment, or as a personality receptive to influence, you are also free to imagine pathetic future anxieties for yourself and others. The ancients have always warned us that *the price of living unaware is high.*

Tarot Awareness tries to illuminate paths that work to eliminate ignorance. For example, the human mind can become a tower of worry—with imagined fears chaining the ego to its walls. Psychology calls this condition the *neurotic paradox.* Here the ego is too afraid to escape from its imagined fears, fears thriving in a torrent of uncontrolled thought (symbolized in this book by the Eight of Swords).

In the realm of feelings, the Emotional Plane (Cups) can indeed be treacherous, but by visualizing positive images, such as seeing yourself with purified motivation fulfilling the vision, the Emotional Plane can be a state of mind where you can have a direct experience of God's beauty. Aleph carries the white rose to remind himself (or herself) of this.

The youth walks beneath a yellow sky, the ancients' way of portraying the Life-Breath permeating the atmosphere of the universe. Aleph is Spirit manifesting as the soul's life in the Planes of Existence. After the "Fall," the Fool becomes the microcosm of the seeker's life in the macrocosm of the universe. In Tarot, the yellow sky is the airy manifestation of God in the planes—the Life Force as Consciousness. Universal mind, Air transcendent.

The Air of Wisdom (Swords exalted) combines with the Fire of Initiative (Wands), and Life breathes. The Life-Breath also expresses itself through lovingkindness, the highest octave of the heart-feelings (Cups). And in Pentacles, the ethereal aspect of the Life-Breath becomes tangible. *Tarot Awareness* emphasizes that if the seeker stays aware of spirit within and without, then in the Physical Plane consciousness experiences inner calmness, intelligence, and beauty.

The Fool in the physical plane, the path our soul now walks, is consciousness in the realm of sensation. It's also the realm where we experience achievement or failure, health or sickness, freedom or slavery. In the physical plane of Pentacles our will, our decision-making abilities, take form in word and deed. With aspiration and enthusiasm from the spiritual plane (Wands), tranquillity from the emotional plane

(Cups), and common sense from the mental plane (Swords), our consciousness will eventually exist in a physical plane that manifests as the Garden of Eden (Pentacles).

Unfortunately for most humans, we let our ego slip into a fog of blurry perceptions and relinquish our God-given power of choice to mindless indulgence. The result is a life filled with confusion and pain.

It also must be pointed out, however, that the atmosphere of the Fool is charged with unpredictability. Anything can happen. And awaiting the impressions of experience, the newly incarnating soul enters the physical plane innocent (the white rose). Then as the life unfolds, through trial and error, the individuality begins to form.

This process reflects the spiritual meaning of Uranus, the planet most associated with the Fool. As the soul forges ahead on the path, consciously trying to learn from experience, the ego can get sidetracked in energy-wasting emotional, mental, and physical activities. It is at this time that a certain force can be activated deep within the psyche, a force that disrupts the ego's pattern of negative thinking and resultant troublesome experiences. This is the "Uranus mode of thinking." It stimulates the ego to suddenly realize that through ignorance it has closed the spiritual eye. The planet Uranus is there to shock the ego into recognizing the pain of spiritual darkness, and then urges the seeker to choose an appropriate route back to salvation. That's why astrology calls the planet Uranus "the Awakener."

The urge toward freedom of expression brought the soul into incarnation, and in a sense, the soul is a pioneer in a new era—and a new paradigm: The emerging life of the individual. The influence of Uranus activates the atmosphere of the Fool and pushes the ego along the path in unconventional ways. The so-called "flower children" of the 60s, for example, were viewed by the older generation as rebels and misfits, embodying the unorthodox extreme of the planet Uranus.

Uranus was discovered relatively recently by Sir William Herschel on March 13, 1781. As a result, we don't have a record of what the ancients may have thought about the planet. Modern astrologers assign revolution to Uranus, as well as fate and opportunity. Aleph in the Uranian atmosphere will ask questions like: "What is my destiny this time around?" or "Will I take advantage of my inherently wonderful talents?" "Will I take the right opportunities?"

When the Fool is conscious as he continues along the path, he soon revels in what Robert Pirsig calls "the high country."[2] He starts to recognize the intricacies of the world around him and rejoices in the harmony of the patterns he sees. He is in a state of confident expectancy as he rounds the next curve. For the Fool is *optimistic*. He intends to fulfill his dream, his plan for success—in spite of obstacles.

The Fool afflicted, on the other hand, adopts a gloomy philosophy. He walks in lockstep with the disillusioned masses, forfeiting the drive of his individuality as he allows himself to be crushed by the socialist state. Or he becomes an iconoclast and debases a revered tradition with bile and invective. When in a reading the image portrayed on the card comes up reversed, the youth that first gazed expectantly into the unknown, now appears to be in a state of confusion. The Fool Reversed in Tarot indicates that in order for the seeker to neutralize serious negative outlook, or at least become distracted from the continuous pessimism, he or she may need to rediscover the natural fascination with the mysteries of existence and the meaning of the quest.

The Fool, when exalted, desires to experience the adventure of the real, unvarnished and vivid. And he wants to fulfill the admonition of the Oracle at Delphi: "Man, Know Thyself." The planet Uranus rules the astrological sign of Aquarius, the Water-Bearer. Consciousness, represented by the Fool, sees far across the landscape. Unbiased and pure, Uranus in Aquarius brings independence and originality of thought to the ego; if evolved, the ego chooses a scientific, as well as spiritually directed, path.

Since Uranus takes eighty-four years to orbit around the Sun, it stays in one sign for seven years, and astrologers say that he therefore affects large groups of people with the same angle of vibration. The planet Uranus is considered the first of the "nonpersonal" planets, with the orbit of Saturn being the last outpost of the "personal." Stephen Arroyo says in *Astrology, Karma and Transformation*, "In many cases, the influence of Uranus can be defined culturally, for Uranus starts where Saturn ends. Saturn marks the boundary of personal ego consciousness, symbolizing the collective cultural norms and standards (a kind of cultural "super-ego" in Freudian terms).[3] Uranus is related to nations and generations, while Saturn (and the other six "planets") emphasize the individual character. Uranus affects the masses and rules humanitarianism and global thinking."

But Uranus is variable in his orbit. In fact, some astrologers think his movement, compared to the other celestial bodies of our solar system, is "eccentric." Therefore, the planet Uranus also corresponds to the erratic tendencies operating in the Fool's environment. When the human ego foolishly becomes preoccupied with personality and tries to wrench control away from Spirit, they say your "Uranus is afflicted."

Other Symbols in The Fool

Aleph before manifestation has assimilated countless experiences that have prepared him (or her) for the current sojourn in the physical plane. He carries them in the bag tied to the end of his Wand. Typically, right after death in the last life, as reported by the ancients (and ordinary people returning from an after-death experience), the entire life passes before the inner eyes. Consciousness still retains the free will and is given the opportunity to review and learn from the events of his previous life. The process can take years, but in Earth-time it seems like only a moment.

If on Earth the ego has wallowed in selfishness and addictions, he will experience in minute detail the severity of the pain he has caused himself and others. (The Grim Reaper carries a scythe, symbolizing the Biblical axiom, "What ye sow, so shall ye reap.") The ego's own craven desires will remain raw and unquenchable. The object of his desire, be it money, drugs, sex, or whatever, cannot be touched in the other world, and the appetite screams unsatisfied. The ego soon realizes that the torment is more savage than in the Earth life because there is no dense body left to mitigate the rawness.

Some religions liken these painful experiences to fire and call this state of consciousness "hell." They consider hell to be a place of eternal punishment, a literal "lake of fire." However, since the universe, the body of God, is an infinitely evolutionary process, it can be assumed that painful realizations in the afterlife eventually do end (similar to the Catholic Purgatory), and the consciousness "sees the Light." This relief only happens when the consciousness finally acknowledges his/her ignorance of divine law and divine love—and depending on the level of awareness, the "purgatory" could last centuries. The time spent in pain just seems like it is eternal.

The red feather in his hair is his animal nature while the green wreath represents the plant kingdom (and his victory over the desire nature). The white undergarment symbolizes his spiritual nature, while the outer black coat signifies his ignorance of the mysteries of life. The circles and flames of his outer garment remind him that he is vibration, particles, and waves, whirling in the universe of his body and his aura.

The golden belt that encircles his waist is the ecliptic, reminding him that if he is to advance, to never be imprisoned in flesh and time again, he must learn all the character lessons that the twelve signs of the zodiac offer him. The number of lives needed to accomplish this incredible feat depends on the accumulation of expanded consciousness achieved in each life—because lessons left unlearned in the physical plane draw the soul back to Earth. In other words, ignorance is *not* bliss.

As we can think of Zero, the limitless light of pure Spirit, each of the other numbers has a spiritual meaning as well. The Qabalists illustrated their approach to these sacred numbers in a glyph they called the Tree of Life (see Figure One).

0. **Zero** is the Unlimited Absolute. The so-called "Tree of Life" "floats" in, and is penetrated by, Its Infinite Power. Out of this Nothingness of Zero, the flash of Creative Energy begins Its descent into form—the first moment of which is called *Kether*, the "Crown," number One at the tip of the Tree of Life:

The Tree of Life
Figure 1

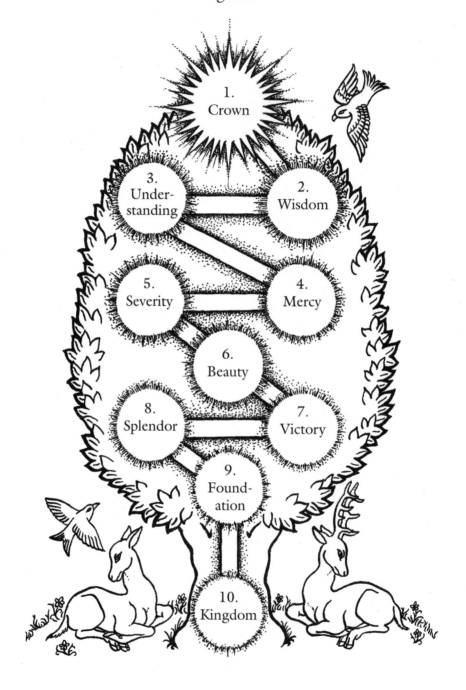

1. **Kether,** The beginning, the first movement of the primary Essence, the starting of something new. The Life-power begins to focus. The original initiative of God proclaiming "I am."

2. **Chokmah,** "Wisdom" on the Tree of Life. Correct judgment, duality, polarity, rhythm, cycle, reflection, choice, opposition, change.

3. **Binah,** "Understanding" on the Tree. Growth, multiplying. The opposing forces come together and a third force is created.

4. **Chesed,** "Mercy." Stabilization, solid foundation, tradition, methodical, materialization, security.

5. **Geburah,** "Severity." The impersonal exactness of universal law. Karma, the striving to break free, disruption, struggle, arguments.

6. **Tipareth,** "Beauty." Equilibrium returns. Opposites balance again. Adaptation. Love, compassion, sharing, contentment. The "Christ Consciousness."

7. **Netzach,** "Victory." Success, transcendence over the animal nature, mastery, control, insight.

8. **Hod,** "Splendor." The Power behind the magnificence of creation is perceived. Strength, will, healing, dominion.

9. **Yesod,** "Foundation." The vitality of the Life-power. Substance on the astral plane about to enter the physical plane. The involuntary system of the body. Achievement, goals, skill, the inherent need to know truth, the ideal.

10. **Malkuth,** "Kingdom." The Zero has manifested itself in the physical plane. Rebirth. The ending on one rung of the spiral and the beginning of another.

As Zero, the Fool (Aleph) begins his Journey through the Major Arcana. We will see that included on his travels will be encounters with the sacredness of numbers, as well as an experience of the planets, signs of the zodiac, the letters of the Hebrew alphabet, and the Elements of the four Planes of Existence.

Guided Visualization for The Fool

Each of the cards of the Major Arcana will have a guided visualization designed to help the seeker get a sense of the personage and mode of consciousness in question. Before each visualization enter a relaxed state (see chapter 1, "Relaxation Exercises in the Tarot Journal"). Then you can listen to a recording of the Visualization with your eyes closed or have someone read it to you.

See yourself surrounded by a . . . living yellow light.
You feel the subtle pulsation of this light
illuminate your being.
You become aware that you are a part of this soft yellow atmosphere,
and notice its light flowing in and through you.
Then . . . in the distance, you see purplish pink mountains,
and you realize that you are walking along a craggy path in these mountains.
Over your right shoulder in your right hand
you are carrying a Wand with a bag attached to the end;
in your left hand you are carrying a white rose.
Then you realize that you are looking through the eyes of the Fool,
the Journeyer,
the pilgrim
walking confidently on the path.
You are Aleph—the Life-Breath,
Spirit—
the Energy that knows Itself—
coalescing into a personality:
With feeling and humility
as Aleph the Fool
you say,
"I will add to my experience as I travel this path,
this journey to the Holy of Holies.
I will enter through the tabernacle of my heart,
filled with Love.
And my mind shall be directed by Wisdom.
I place my faith in the Divine beneficence of the Life Power
and my conviction in the exactness of the Law."
At your heels you hear barking,
and you look down
at a little white dog.

It is the ego,
Spirit's best friend and companion.
Then you smell the fragrance of the white rose
and become intoxicated with its purity.
You feel yourself within the Holy Presence
where there is innocence and youth,
faith and confidence
and an endless enthusiasm for Life.
This is the state of mind for Aleph, Zero the Fool . . .
After taking a few, slow deep breaths,
and feeling relaxed . . .
you can begin to count
slowly backwards from 10 to 1
becoming more and more consciously awake
10 . . . 9 . . . 8 . . .
As you begin to return fully conscious to the room
feeling more and more aware,
more and more refreshed,
filled with a sense of gratitude
for any of the knowledge gained,
you can begin to open your eyes,
still retaining a childlike enthusiasm
for the next adventure.

The Fool in a Reading

The ability to "read" the cards is an extension of *Tarot Awareness* enhanced by meditation and study. Much more will be said of what the ancients called "divination" in Part Four, but for now we will concentrate on some shor-hand phrases for particular cards that can trigger meanings—should you decide to read for yourself and/or others.

The more you become familiar with the intricacies of the cards, the more you will have a "feel" for the vibrations associated with the atmosphere of each card. And for a more rounded reading you also should be aware of proximity, that is, how the meanings of other cards appearing in the reading affect the card in question (see chapter 29).

- The beginning of a new adventure.
- Innocence.

- Wide-eyed, though not necessarily well thought-out, idealism.
- Taking the risk.
- A trusting nature.
- A consciousness often operating in the moment.
- Seeking answers to the hidden mysteries.
- Unconventional.
- A need to be more carefree.
- Spontaneous.

If the card is Reversed, the Fool can be looked at from another angle, even negatively:

- Foolish or erratic behavior.
- Haphazard thinking.
- Iconoclastic personality; anarchy.
- Immobile, fearful to take a risk.
- Blind trust.
- A jaded attitude toward life; a need to rediscover the long-forgotten enthusiasm of childhood.
- A foolhardy choice could be made if practicality is not considered.

Meditation on The Fool

In the midst of the chaos we experience in the world, taking time out to disengage our consciousness from the "thousand things" becomes crucial if we ever hope to reconnect with our natural state of spiritual inner bliss. In his aphorisms, Patanjali says, "Sickness, mental laziness, doubt, lack of enthusiasm, sloth, craving for sense pleasure, false perception, despair caused by failure to concentrate and unsteadiness in concentration: these distractions are the obstacles to knowledge."[4]

Before beginning the sojourn through the deck of Tarot cards, it is highly beneficial to first meditate on the meanings and imagery presented by the Fool. Certain spiritual, emotional, and intellectual responses will be evoked as the consciousness becomes acclimated to the terrain of the Inner Landscape illustrated in the Tarot cards.

It is important here to recognize the fact that there is nothing miraculous about the cards themselves; rather, it is the connection that our consciousness makes with the ancient meanings that brings on the "magic." As a result, meditation should be approached in an attitude of humility and a desire to know the truth about oneself in relation to the Holy Presence, within and without. Tarot meditation can dislodge long lost transgressions and weaknesses (other items also in that bag at the end of the Fool's Wand), and examining the contents of consciousness can at times be unsettling. It is highly beneficial for the seeker, however, to trust in the idea of personal redemption and the grace brought on by ultimate awareness. This is what Jesus of Nazareth spoke of in the Beatitudes when he said, "Blessed are the pure in heart, for they shall see God." (Matt. 5:8)

After reaching a state of relaxation as described earlier, read the poetry for the card under consideration slowly and think about the words in connection with the meanings and imagery. Then contemplate the card for a few minutes.

Any number of questions might arise: How can I apply what I have just learned to the circumstances of my own life? What are the challenges I must overcome? How should I adjust my thinking so that I can accurately perceive my weaknesses? Where am I at fault? Am I showing enough sensitivity to the feelings of others? Do I neglect my own needs in order to satisfy the demands of family, friends, lovers, or employers? In addition, meditation on the Fool could activate thoughts regarding the life mission, motivation, gaining efficiency. . . .

The ancient adepts understood human fear and vulnerabilities, delusions and arrogance long before Freud, and in an act of supreme compassion, devised the Tarot. To the average person, Tarot looks like a deck of cards. In actuality, however, Tarot is a book, a mystical treatise, almost miraculous in its execution and construction—containing meaning and imagery woven into sublime patterns.

Meditation in *Tarot Awareness* helps focus the mind and open the consciousness to a new sense of what's real. The Fool is a good card to meditate on when you want to add a new spontaneity into your life, when you want to let go of tired, useless behaviors, when you want to start that new project fresh and unprejudiced.

The Fool's Invocation

I am a ray of light
in search of myself . . .
My head aloft,
I wander the Earth,
a Fool.
I chose to come here—

in a timeless
moment of forgetfulness,
and I must refine my vision
as I walk this Path of Return.
But the precipice yawns before me.
I can fall into this gaping chasm . . .
but I know that Thy hand will steady me.
May I always remember my Divine Origin,
a pure Spirit
forged from Thy Holy Fire:
poised, vigilant, awake—
I am now ready to overcome the obstacles
that Thou must put before me.
Amen.

Notes

1. A note on gender: Although consciousness is neutral, neither male nor female, and yet both at the same time, the pronouns used in this book will usually correspond to the gender of the personage of the particular card. For example, the High Priestess is portrayed as female and will be referred to as "she." The Fool, although androgynous, will be referred to as "he," for convenience's sake.

2. Robert M. Pirsig, *Zen and the Art of Motorcycle Maintenance* (New York, N.Y.: Bantam, 1974).

3. Stephen Arroyo, *Astrology, Karma and Transformation* (Sebastopol, Calif.: CRCS Publications, 1978), p. 41.

4. Patanjali, *How to Know God, The Yoga Aphorisms of Patanjali* (New York, N.Y.: New American Library, 1953), p. 44.

Part Two

THE MAJOR ARCANA

Portals to the
Inner Landscape

The Seven Powers of Consciousness

I. The Magician to VII. The Chariot

Chapter 4

I. The Magician
Reflecting the Divine

Astrological Correspondence: The communicative powers associated with the planet Mercury.

Hebrew Letter: Beth ב (meaning "house" as a symbol for the personality perfected).

The Inner Atmosphere: As the outer persona becomes more aware of its subtle Essence, the more it reflects Spirit's special blend of Power and Love. In the atmosphere of the Magician, the ego acknowledges its powerlessness in the face of Spirit. The Magician's emotional and thinking processes "allow" the Lord to operate through him (or her). His ego is calm and observant, aware of Spirit flowing through him unhindered in the Physical.

Statement: "I am conscious of Myself. . . . Here in the Major Arcana I am that aspect of awareness the ancients called the Magician. I am Consciousness awake—and

Consciousness aware—of my true spiritual Nature. As I continue on in the current of my life, I will consciously explore my connection with the Creative."

Quotation: "The greatest magicians know themselves to be no more than channels for the Life-power, clear window-panes through which the light of wisdom within the house of personality streams forth into the objective world." (Paul Foster Case, *The Tarot*)

The Challenge: The ego must learn to overcome arrogance. Here the personality can self-righteously believe it is all powerful, with the self-destructive intention of dominating and manipulating others.

With the first breath, the Fool begins the journey. As he or she enters the Physical Plane, the human consciousness is a clean-slated mind—the mind before life imprints its effects. Ready to gather experience, the soul incarnates as a *tabula rasa* (the "erased tablet" in Latin), and encounters the world of the senses, a world that will soon etch its mark. And then in a short time the human personality begins to show itself.

The next card in the Tarot deck (actually the first card, as the Fool is the Traveler on the journey through all of Tarot) is the Magician, which portrays the personality at its zenith.

The ancients viewed the number One as the point in the center of the circle, self-consciousness, the "I am." Here the aware mind, a psyche filled with light, functions as the center point in thought, emotion, and deed. And symbolized within the number One, the Magician, is a frame of mind where the thoughts are focused on one's relationship with God. At this time in the journey, the Magician realizes that the more he functions in the world with an aware mind, the more he will think and feel the presence of Spirit. The ancients would say that he is "preparing the Holy Tabernacle Within." Why? The Magician is aware that Spirit is the initiator in and through all his life, and he wants his ego to remain in a non-interfering mode.

On Mount Horeb, when Moses stepped on holy ground before the burning bush, he asked God that all-important question. "'Behold, when I come unto the children of Israel, and shall say unto them, The God of your fathers hath sent me unto you; and they shall say to me, What is his name? what shall I say unto them?' And God said unto Moses, 'I am that I am.'" (Exodus 3:13–14)

Like Moses, that moment shall guide us throughout our own journey. In *Tarot Awareness* we like to think of the Magician as the human ego spiritualized. But what does that mean? Actually, the answer is very personal, and you, as a seeker, need to discover it for yourself. St. Francis of Assisi gives us a hint in his famous prayer, "Lord, make me an instrument of Thy peace."

As we begin our journey, we will visualize a portal or doorway, an entrance into a particular aspect of the Ageless Wisdom. There we will meet the various personages of the Major Arcana, and as spiritual travelers, like the Fool, we will enter each Portal in search of knowledge.

Visualization to the First Portal, The Magician

You are feeling calm and relaxed . . . *
Now see yourself as the Fool
—the Eternal Pilgrim—
walking down from a mountain path to a meadow . . .
Smell the fragrances . . .
see and hear the water
of the creeks around you.
Notice the colors of the wildflowers
blooming in the meadow—
the vibrant orange of poppies,
and the seemingly endless expanse
of yellow mustard flowers . . .
Then at the edge of the meadow
you begin to notice an entryway in front of you.
As you get closer you can see a huge archway
fashioned from garlands of hanging red roses.
And you realize that you are now standing
in front of the First Portal . . .
Take another deep breath,
and feel very calm as you exhale . . .
Then you decide to walk under the archway of roses.
Upon entering you notice that the roses continue,
forming a scarlet canopy over your head.
You also become aware of the yellow sky above you,
the Limitless Light,
and you can feel your consciousness infused
with the Life-power's loving pulsation.
Suddenly, a few feet in front of you,
you see him . . .
He is young and vital,
dressed in a cloak of fiery red
over a glowing white tunic . . .

* Refer to the General Relaxation section in chapter 1.

His right arm raised,
he holds a two-headed phallic symbol.
Then you notice something entirely startling.
Coiled around his waist,
you see a greenish-blue snake,
biting its tail . . .
Then in the yellow sky,
hovering above the Magician's head,
you observe the infinity symbol,
a white fire forming into a horizontal figure eight.
You pause at the sight,
and as though staring into a mirror,
you gaze into the Magician's beautiful, dark crystal eyes.
You then feel a tremendous surge of power
overwhelm your being.

With an echo-like voice,
the Magician smiles back into your eyes,
and says,
"So, young Pilgrim . . .
you have come wandering into my garden.
Tell me, what is it that you seek?"
You reply, with a little hesitation,
"Uh . . . To know you better . . .
To try to put you into words."
"I am the simple within the complex," he says.
"Maybe you would like me to show you glimpses into my nature,
is that it?"
"Oh, yes, very much."
"Raw spirit is always so eager," he laughs,
"that blind enthusiasm for unpredictable experience!
It could get you into a lot of trouble . . .
But, then, how can it be any other way?"

You think about his words . . .
relax with them
and take in the impressions
that are meaningful to you.
"I'll tell you something, Good Pilgrim,
to begin with, when I consciously think and act

from the knowledge of my true Being,
I am able to envision ecstatically.
And from that state of consciousness,
with wisdom and love,
I plan precisely what I must do for my own good
and the good of all sentient beings.
That is how I fill my existence with magic—
and why they have always called me
the Magician."

A little bewildered, you thank him for the insights.
Then you see his form begin to drift away
on the light-filled breezes,
and you ponder the experience
as you feel enveloped in the loving vibration
of the Limitless Light . . .

You can now begin to slowly count backwards
10 . . . 9 . . . 8 . . .
And finally, as you reach number 1,
you open your eyes,
feeling refreshed and relaxed.

The Atmosphere of the First Portal, The Magician

When we look at the card of the Magician, we see human personality as a *conduit* for the light of Spirit. In the Magician's state of mind, the atmosphere of the First Portal, we are able to express clarity and decisiveness, and yet show humility—for we know that we are not the power, but only its vehicle.

As ego with a free will we are, of course, at liberty to negate these virtues and turn toward laziness and vacillation, selfishness and arrogance. The eventual result is often confused thinking processes and emotional distress which eventually lead to a loss in direction. The personality then feels threatened; it is only a matter of time before some extremely faulty and/or dangerous decisions are made.

The Magician teaches us that it is critically important to stay awake to virtue, balance, and clear intent. In the chaos of this world, jostled by numerous interruptions, *Tarot Awareness* is a method that encourages the seeker to manifest a calm spirit—the crown jewel of a life well spent.

The ancient wise ones who devised Tarot, for example, chose the Magician to illustrate the highest level of awareness: Self-conscious attention to the real as well as the ideal.

From an astrological standpoint, the Magician represents the planet Mercury. The mind. The pursuit of knowledge. Eloquence and oratory. The intellect as the intermediary between the spiritual and the physical. Agility of thought, communication. Mercury's symbol is the *caduceus* (two snakes winding up and around a wand with wings at the top) intimating the power of the mind to heal. Active, alert, precise.

However, when the workings of the mind become too dominant, the Mercury atmosphere turns detrimental; the erratic and quickness of thought can then lead to irresponsible action. Restless, excitable, harshly critical. The mind adopts an illusion of power and the ego becomes conceited.

Likewise, the Magician in detriment, either reversed or surrounded by negative cards in a reading, suggests a tendency to muddled or selfish thinking. Dissatisfied. Overevaluation of the self. In a tragic misunderstanding, the ego does not see itself as a channel for the power and instead uses mental agility to manipulate others. Self-righteous.

Beth (meaning "house") is the second letter of the Hebrew alphabet and is given to remind us that our bodies are the "house" of our mind, and that our mind is the "house" of our divine Essence. Psalm 127:1 says, "except the Lord build the house, he labors in vain that builds it." Activated by the power of a focused will, self-consciousness, the thrusting male principle of the universe (the yang of yin/yang), initiates action.

Above the head of the Magician we see a horizontal figure eight, a symbol of infinity. Through concentration, our thinking processes will open to the infinitude of the Spirit within. The snake biting its tail has similar meaning: The infinite circle of life. The red roses symbolize the senses, while the lilies represent pure motivation in the pursuit of truth. His red outer garment is the desire nature, the desire to bring down the power of the Life-Breath into the personality. The white robe underneath is the spiritual self, the Initiator.

The position that the Magician takes with one hand pointing upwards and the other down suggests that what is seen in the microcosm is reflected in the macrocosm. His pose also suggests the power of concentration, an essential ingredient in Tarot meditation.

However, Tarot gives a warning here. Be careful what you concentrate on, because thoughts are things, and they eventually will manifest in your outer world if you put enough energy on them. Knowing that Beth represents the power of self-consciousness, awareness in the Now, the Observer, and that his highest power is the ability to concentrate (to focus or not to focus), *Tarot Awareness* holds that the Magician is the exact center-point of free will.

On the table in front of him, his "field of attention," we see a Wand, Cup, Sword, and Pentacle (a gold disk with a five-pointed star emblazoned on it). He must be able to harmonize the aspects of all four Planes represented by his implements on the table: Wands, Spirit and initiative; Cups, emotion, beauty, and love; Swords, intellect and the pursuit of Truth; and Pentacles, illumination on the Physical Plane.

The Magician in a Reading

Look at the card of the Magician. Notice the symbolism in the illustration and reflect on its overall meaning. Should the Magician turn up in a reading (in Part Four we will look at the dynamics of giving a reading to yourself and others), it could indicate that:

- A well-focused frame of mind is called for in this situation.
- Draw on your powers of communication to solve the problem.
- The Magician is measured and decisive.
- Be confident in the use of your Will, providing you are operating from the wise, constructive, well-focused frame of mind indicated earlier.
- The Magician does not scatter his energies or waste time on nonessentials.
- Understand that you are powerful, and you need only bring this Truth to the surface of your consciousness.
- When the Magician shows up in a reading you should feel sure-footed in your innate ability to handle a difficult situation.
- The Magician suggests that there is a need to bring the idea to fruition; he is a call to action.
- In a reading, should the Magician fall near another card that indicates uncertainty or confusion (i.e., the Two of Swords Reversed), the Magician card suggests that a renewed sense of reality, plus accurate observation, needs to be brought into the seeker's consciousness.
- Near a card that indicates difficulty, the Magician reminds us that no matter how bad things may get, we always have the power to become a channel for the Life-power and rise above any amount of despair the wounded ego may hold. This is what Jesus of Nazareth meant when he said, "Of myself I do nothing; the Father which dwelleth within me, he doeth the works." (John 14:10)
- The Magician brings a tremendous force of initiative to the reading.

The Magician Reversed in a reading could indicate the following:

- Arrogance.
- Self-righteousness.
- Manipulating others.
- Unfocused, scattered thinking.
- A need to be more decisive.
- Ruthlessly critical, condescending.
- Regarding the project, energy peters out (especially near the Eight of Pentacles Reversed and the Three of Pentacles Reversed).

Thoughts for Meditation on the Magician

If the seeker is feeling panicked or considers his reactions to life as too egocentric; if his or her thinking is unfocused or he is plagued by feelings of emptiness and a disjointed existence, meditation on the Magician repeatedly for five minutes a day over a period of one week—plus sincere study—can bring a new sense of initiative into the seeker's life. Heightened awareness will follow.

The Magician's Prayer

I am a focused beam, one-pointed,
And I dedicate my life, anointed,
to Thee.
My body, my intellect, my emotions, my soul—
When I am awake, I know them as one Essence, unfolding,
For in my heart I am holding
this sacred thought of Thee:
It is You who work through me, O Lord,
and I stand in awe and humility before Thy Divine Power.
Make me Thy vehicle in this difficult hour
So that I may bring Light into this poor world.
I direct my energy for my own good
and the good of others.
Help me to hold my Ideal before me always,
in the highest position—
For only then can I truly be called Magician.

Chapter 5

II. The High Priestess
The Eternal Reservoir

Astrological Correspondence: The reflective quality of the Moon.

Hebrew Letter: Gimel ג (meaning "camel" as the vehicle that links one area to another).

The Inner Atmosphere: As children of the Most High we are entities that share by nature—as we all exist within the same substance.

In the case of the Second Portal, this aspect of sharing within the mind of God is represented in Tarot as the High Priestess. And yet within this portal, we are reminded by the imagery that there is so much more yet to experience. For behind her veil the High Priestess hides the infinite Mystery.

Statement: "I am infinitely evolving within the vastness of my potential . . . and am the Substance that moves within all four Planes of Existence. I hide a breath away from consciousness, forever awaiting impregnation by the Magician, your self-consciousness. And what is it that I wait for? I await the Idea."

Quotation: "If your heart were sincere and upright, every creature would be unto you a looking-glass of life and a book of holy doctrine." (Thomas á Kempis, *Imitation of Christ*)

The Challenge: The ego is dominated by negative unconscious motivation and must guard against overly emotional reactions.

Visualization to the Second Portal, The High Priestess

The Traveler continues in a relaxed state of mind, leaving behind the first Portal of the Magician, the garden where we experienced the power of self-consciousness and the concept of "I am."

In order to get the most benefit from a visualization within the atmosphere of *Tarot Awareness*, it is a good idea to take some time to do the Relaxation Exercise from chapter 1 before beginning. The purpose of the Exercise is to get you feeling more calm, peaceful, and receptive to the ideas behind the imagery . . .

Now as you approach the Second Portal,
you are surrounded by a bluish nightfall.
In front of you a hill rises at the edge of a field . . .
Then the sudden glow of the Moon surprises you.
As you approach the hill, you see it:
Her temple—silver, shining and mysterious.
You first notice the columns . . . majestic,
fashioned from gleaming gray stone . . .
a huge door, silver-polished and imposing.
And that Moon . . .
The door to the Temple opens,
and you begin to float through the columns.

Although serene,
you notice that your physical senses
feel a slight chill
in the Temple's silver-blue atmosphere.
Then, in front of you,
the Moon Goddess is sitting calmly

on a gray stone cube.
A veil decorated with palm fronds and pomegranates
hangs behind her throne.
Although you are immediately struck by her cool beauty,
you are absolutely transfixed by her blue robes,
which flow with living waters . . .
Within your reverie you are suddenly aware
that in this Second Portal
you are in the realm
of the eternally reflective subconscious.
Then you notice her silver crown,
in the form of a waxing and waning moon
which further hypnotizes you with its fluctuations . . .

"Come forth, Pilgrim,"
she intones in a voice deep and remote.
"What is it that you seek in my temple?"
"I . . . I would like to see what's behind your veil."
She almost laughs,
but maintains her dignified composure.
"That is an interesting request . . .
Well, then, let me ask you something:
Are you bold?
Are you open?
Are you poised?
For only the most worthy may glimpse there."
You reply confidently,
"Let's say that I always try to forge ahead."
"Yes, that is commendable, brave traveler,
but the question is—
are you awake?"
"I am coming to learn my responsibility in that matter,
and, therefore, I often think of myself
as the eternal seeker,
coming to you to learn
what it is that you would impart to me."

Slowly her blues begin shimmering in the moonlight.
"Know me as I am," she says.

"I am feeling, the eternal flow of emotion . . .
I am Universal Subconsciousness,
and I am forever receptive to impression.
I am virgin potential,
unlimited.
Do with me as you will,
but do not defile me with your petty, selfish desires—
or I will make you insatiable."

You are speechless,
and your thoughts drift with her blue wavy vibrations.
The scene dissolves into a blue haze . . .
and you suddenly find yourself lying in the meadow
looking up into the Moon.
You feel the peacefulness of the landscape
and let your thoughts wander outwards
into the starry night.
Then, floating on the cool evening breezes,
you hear her silvery voice.
"The Life-power is your Essence," she says.
"Past. Present. And forever . . .
As with me,
unlimited potential is your destiny—
and your birthright."
Her voice begins to fade . . .
"For you are born of Divine Fire:
The Life-Breath itself beats within your heart."
Faintly, the last words you hear are,
"Attune your memory to this,
and you penetrate the Veil."

You contemplate her words
as you slowly begin to come back into the room.
Begin to count backwards,
10 . . . 9 . . . 8 . . .
Then when you are comfortable,
you can open your eyes.
You awake feeling refreshed and alert.

The Atmosphere of the Second Portal, The High Priestess

The High Priestess is the unlimited invisible Essence behind all creation. We live and move and have our being within this substance, which can also be thought of as an aspect of Universal Mind. As the Magician—self-consciousness—we are able to consciously *think* into this mind, which interpenetrates all space. In so doing, we activate a certain Universal Law: Self-consciousness is given the ability to imprint on this unlimited potential, this Universal Substance, his *desire*.

The High Priestess is presented as a virgin to suggest the infinite possibility of the fulfillment of desire, as well as her infinite receptivity to impression by the self-consciousness of the Magician. The Universal Substance will always respond to the force of the Magician's focus.

And what is the main thrust of his energy? Self-conscious Will.

We, as human beings, have not yet evolved to a complete realization of our potential. In Joel Goldsmith's words, we are "consciousness unfolding," bringing into experience all that we can conceive. There is simply no limit. The problem comes in our understanding of the Law. The more we know about how the universe works, the more our potential for successful living will increase. That which manifests in our outer environment will be similar to the thoughts we have deliberately dwelled on. This is the Law written on the parchment on the lap of the High Priestess.

The Law is impersonal and it cares not whether the thinker is genius or buffoon; it will return to the self-consciousness whatever it is that the Magician thinks into it.

The movement of the High Priestess is the movement of *deductive reasoning*. Plant a tulip bulb and you will get a tulip, never a cactus. There is an inevitable result from the first action. The "ripple effect." If this happens, then this will happen and this will happen . . . until the final result is reached. The High Priestess responds to the will of the Magician and carries out the desire—no matter what. He instructs and she continues through without comment.

However, for health, progress, and ingenuity there needs to be an equilibrium between the self-conscious and the principle symbolized by the High Priestess. What is it? It is the second mode of the Life-power called subconsciousness.

The palm fronds and pomegranates on the veil symbolize the male initiative energies and female resistant energies, respectively. Similarly, on the right of her cube (representing the Physical Plane) is a white pillar—the positive, conscious, solar, masculine polarity; on the left, the black pillar stands for the negative, subconscious, magnetic feminine polarity of the life force. The High Priestess is the balance in between, symbolized by the equal-sided cross on her breast.

Study and meditation while journeying through the Inner Landscape can bring the masculine and feminine polarities into creative harmony. In fact, equilibrium between the Magician and the High Priestess is crucial to well-being. Strife between the two fills the individual with confusion and pain.

The addict (hooked on drugs, sex, food, etc.), for example, is enslaved because the personal subconscious is in chaos. And from the cauldron of this chaos, the craving demands of the wild animal body emerge. Exquisitely formed images of the craved object come into full focus—never a problem visualizing those.

When the raw sensations of the body make their demands, and you let the Magician's ideal aspect withdraw, then the Priestess turns into a banshee with a whip. "I want it!" is the resultant cry. It doesn't seem to matter that satisfying harmful physical, mental, emotional demands eventually paralyze the free will of the Magician; he becomes an ego in a whirlwind of confusion, blinded and stumbling off the path. Eventually, his willpower dissipates into despair, weakness, and death.

We were not made for this.

The destructive urges of the body, mind, and emotions *can be controlled*. We, as evolving beings are, however, required to expend time, effort, and most importantly, desire, to facilitate the altering of the original destructive commands to the High Priestess. Commands like, "Give me this—Give me that! And I don't care how you get it. I want it NOW!"

The rolled parchment on the lap of the High Priestess is written with the Hebrew word, "TORA," which means "law." This is where the subconscious records the varying shades and impressions of our experience. In Sanskrit the word is *Akasha*, the infinite impressionable substance; some call it the ether, others "the Book of Life." Every thought, word, and deed is recorded on her parchment.

The two pillars, one black and one white, signify duality, from one end of the continuum to the other: light-dark, male-female, positive-negative. The veil is symbolic of the hymen, virginal unlimited potential, decorated with pomegranates (yin-female-receptive desire) and palm fronds (yang-male-projective will). Her crown in its fluctuations of the Moon signify the cycles of life. The flowing blue robes intimate the invisible waves, while the yellow floor of the temple are the visible particles of God's Limitless Light. The yellow floor is also a reminder that the Life-Breath permeates everything.

The High Priestess says, "It will do you well to have clear, precise, correct desires. The problem is that unless you feel, think, and act within the clear, loving intent of the Magician's Ideal, you are very likely to give me the entirely wrong impression, to put it mildly."

The impressions of destructive, demeaning thoughts forced into the subconscious all lead to their inevitable conclusion: Harmful actions to the seeker and to others. The idea is to examine the contents of our lives so that we can bring the light of Spirit to bear on our ignorance. Hidden truths will be revealed and the veil will be lifted. Although it takes some effort to unlock the door and find the healing within, the key is never far from our grasp. Jesus of Nazareth says it well in Matthew 7:7, "Ask, and it shall be given you; seek, and ye shall find; knock, and it shall be opened unto you."

Through the Second Portal of the High Priestess we learn that we need to examine our *motive*. The Magician's Ideal is to do the job well, remain in concert with our conception of the Most High and abide in God's peace.

We also learn that self-serving interest, especially at the expense of others, corrupts motivation. Thoughts that we dwell on infuse our atmosphere and affect our emotions and our behavior.

Marcus Aurelius said that "our life is what our thoughts make it."

From an astrological standpoint, the High Priestess represents the Moon ("the Queen of Borrowed Light")—personality as the reflection of our true Self (the Sun). Energy is produced by the electricity of the Sun with the magnetism of the Moon.

The Moon is the personal subconscious, emotion, receptivity, femininity, the involuntary functions and rhythms of the body, instinct.

The Moon rules patterns and habits, as well as moods. And like the parchment of the High Priestess, the Moon rules memory—remembering everything precisely. The self-conscious, in turn, must cultivate memory as well so that the ego can properly evaluate what we have discovered about our experience and our Nature. Within the atmosphere of *Tarot Awareness* the High Priestess reminds us that the most important thing is to remember who we are.

Our subconscious, our High Priestess, does not choose; that is the responsibility of the Magician, the self-conscious. Rather, the subconscious "waters" accept the premise and the impressions made by the self-conscious, without interference of any kind. However, if these impressions are confused, then the waters get polluted, and we suffer. So a question to consider here is: "What is the nature of my intent?"

In addition, cultivating the ability to make the correct choice enhances our balance and clarifies our perspective. This is one of the most important of the Magician's many skills. But how does he employ it? His observations must be clear, poised, and precise. He must form reality-based perceptions from what he sees and send exact instructions to his subconscious High Priestess regarding the fulfillment of his goal—fully aware that she will carry out these directions exactly as presented to her.

For example, if your blind date sends out signals of rejection that last the entire evening, and you cannot get any romantic response from him or her, it would not be wise to present the High Priestess with an image of this person as the ultimate desire of your life!

If the Magician is aware, he or she will form a logical, concise premise from clear and real impressions of the situation (i.e., the disappointing blind date). The Magician plants the seed (the premise) in the garden (the subconscious, the virginal substance of the High Priestess): You observe your blind date's snide and insinuating remarks, arrogant attitude . . . the cold kiss. You then don your Magician's robes, so to speak, and send an unmistakable message to your High Priestess. "I don't think I want this guy to be the father of my children." Think how many divorces could have been avoided if the communications between the observant Magician (Mercury) and the compliant High Priestess (Moon) were accurate?

The Moon aspect of the High Priestess is feeling and mood rather than intellect (Mercury). It is the realm of subconscious motivation, inward reflection, and dreams. For in the Temple of the High Priestess we learn to appreciate the Mystery of Life. Essential to fulfillment in the Physical Plane is the self-conscious effort to visualize positive outcome. The Magician must impregnate the High Priestess with logical, reality-based images, and then picture the result: A manifestation of the idea—beneficial to others as well as to oneself.

The function of the self-conscious (Magician) to the subconscious can be compared to sculptor creating a statue. The artist is the Magician (Beth), self-conscious mind. Awake, he chisels into the medium represented by the subconscious High Priestess (Gimel): the marble, in this case. Both artist and marble are needed to make the statue (in the Third Portal of the Empress we will learn about the nature of this statue).

It is up to the subconscious to bring the images impressed upon her by the self-conscious into concrete form in the Physical Plane.

The High Priestess in a Reading

- Subconscious influences, hidden beneath the surface.
- Equilibrium returns when the mystery is solved, which may be concealed in memory.
- Remembering past accomplishments helps soften the blow of current setback.
- Pay attention to the subtleties.
- Making use of one's potential.
- A time to reflect on Divine Law and see how transgressions are affecting the problem at hand.
- Make sure the wish is clear, concise, and resolute—for the greatest good for yourself and others.

REVERSED

- Emotionally on the defensive, or emotionally distant.
- Criticism and judgment are inappropriate in the atmosphere of the High Priestess; a need to be more accepting of the fluctuations, the natural ebb and flow of life.
- A need for reality-based perceptions; overly impressionable (especially near the Seven of Cups).
- A time to deal with bad habits.
- Fresh emotional responses to the difficulty are called for.
- A more flexible, receptive frame of mind may be needed.
- Secretive, vengeful thoughts (powerfully negative near reversed Court cards of the Suit of Swords).
- Keep watch over emotional reverie (especially near the Six of Cups Reversed).

Meditation on the High Priestess

If the seeker feels plagued with overly emotional reactions to events, or feels trapped in a problem that seems insurmountable, meditation on the High Priestess can bring hidden motivations to the surface. Once the seeker can understand what fuels the underlying painful patterns, he or she can begin to take steps to clear the way for insights.

Questions to consider for meditation might center around thoughts like: What are some of the underlying patterns operating just beneath my personality? Am I making use of my unlimited potential?

Do I have any secret, vengeful thoughts I need to neutralize? Am I clear about what I want to accomplish?

Write your impressions in the Tarot Journal.

Prayer

I open my eyes to the vision of Thy vastness.
With knowledge of Thee,
I see the workings of Thy Law.
I cleanse my temple in thy honor
so that Thine eyes will see no blemish.

But, oh, how I am distracted!
I stumble into agonies,
blaming the outside for my pain.

I forget that my selfish thoughts,
my conniving words, my foolish actions,
were born from inner fogs
deep within my brain.

Lift the veil so that I may gaze upon Thy splendor.
Help me to remain receptive to Thy wisdom,
to focus my senses on Truth,
and to speak clearly into Thy tilting ear.

Chapter 6

III. The Empress
Beauty Unfolding

Astrological Correspondence: The creative, harmonious aspect of personality, Venus.

Hebrew Letter: Daleth ד (meaning "door," as the passageway through which all creation emerges—within and without, incarnating and evolving).

The Inner Atmosphere: Awareness of the eternal creative flow of the Life-power. Our level of consciousness rises to a finer vibration when there is a combination of the accurate observations of the self-conscious with the action triggered by the deductions of the subconscious. As the Magician focuses, the Energy becomes more personalized, and he partakes in the Creative.

Statement: "I am that aspect of your subconsciousness which helps bring the Magician's image to fruition—through his union with the High Priestess. When you enter the realm of Gimel, the High Priestess, and remember who you are, God's Holy Light shines through your eyes. And with that Light, God encourages you to make use of It in your life for the highest good."

Quotation: "And for all this, nature is never spent;
          There lives the dearest freshness deep down things . . ."
          (Gerard Manley Hopkins, *God's Grandeur*)

The Challenge: To bring the ego out of its stagnation, its lost interest in new ideas, and its concentration on the superficial.

Visualization to the Third Portal, The Empress

Sunrise.
The sky is a softly vibrating yellow,
and you are tranquil within its warm light.
Ahead, you see massive, but graceful trees
responding to the golden currents of air.
They are cypress, trees sacred to Venus,
and their presence tells you
that you are approaching the Third Portal,
the garden of the Empress.

As you walk through the grove of trees,
you see the Empress sitting on a gray stone bench.
She is in a wheat field at the edge of a river,
a river rushing with the waters from the blue robes of the High Priestess—
the "Stream of Consciousness."

In her left hand she holds a scepter
with a globe and a cross at the tip.
In her right she holds a copper shield with a dove.
Five red roses are at her left arm.
She is crowned with twelve golden stars and a wreath of myrtle.

Although the High Priestess appeared cool, distant, and virginal,
you see something completely different
in the young blonde woman before you.

She is rosy-cheeked and brimming with the vitality of the Life-power.
You notice that the most striking feature about her, however,
is the fact that she is pregnant.

"That is a result," she beams,
"of the last intimacy of your Magician
with your High Priestess."
"Yes, Majesty, I was wondering about that,
but it seems as though you read minds . . ."
". . . I only reflect your own thoughts."
"Then you know why I'm here?"
She answers: "Apart from being the third stop on your travels,
you want to see my crops before the harvest, is that it?"
"In a manner of speaking."
"I suppose you could say that as I progress from the High Priestess,
I help birth the Magician's idea from the Cosmic Womb.
If you notice that waterfall over there
with the stream plunging into the pool,
you'll get the idea."
For a few moments the spray from the pool distracts you,
and your thoughts become misty.
She speaks to you without moving her lips
and instructs you on the nature of the Third Portal . . .
You hear her emphasizing the need to observe the events
of the external world . . .
to sense the inner world of other individuals
as well as your own moods and feelings.
"You must present me with deliberate positive imagery,"
she seemed to be saying.
"Only then can I deliver enlightened progeny to you."
You now begin to refocus
and agree that you have received enough information for now
but feel compelled to inquire a little further . . .
Then you notice her standing in front of you.

"Before I go, can I ask you something?"
"Yes, please," she says, gracious as ever.
"Could you tell me exactly what it is that's forming in your womb?"
She pauses a moment and then stares deeply into your eyes.

"I hold all that you've learned so far
on your journey through the Portals."
"Then tell me something:
When is the delivery?"
She smiles. "When you complete your travels on this rung of the spiral."
"Thank you for your great wisdom . . ."

As the scene fades before you,
you hear her intone one last phrase.
"You must pay attention to what you think," she says.
You take a few deep breaths,
noticing that you are relaxed and at peace . . .
Count backwards 10 . . . 9 . . . 8 . . .
After a few moments you open your eyes,
feeling refreshed and awake.

The General Atmosphere of the Third Portal, The Empress

When the Magician, a highly focused consciousness, is alert to his motivations, as well as possessing an aware determination to explore the contents of that consciousness, he can then form the most positive image of success possible. It is vital that we objectively observe the outer events of our environment as well as our own inner psychological world. We also need to have at least some awareness of the thoughts and feelings of others around us. It is important to always remember that thoughts are things, and like a train, once they leave the station, they head directly to their destination: Manifestation in the Physical Plane.

Depending on the nature of the image, focused thought can lead to the building of a cathedral or the hanging of a murderer. We are always given the ability to choose the degree of movement on the polarity (i.e., from happiness to misery, say). The Eternal Moment exists in the exact center, and the more you observe from that point, the clearer your perception and the more control you will have over your thoughts and emotions.

The Magician, through conscious thought processes, etches the canals so that the "water" can flow properly to nurture the desired areas of the Empress' garden. Through *inductive reasoning* the self-conscious observes an object or event and forms a conclusion. Whether his conclusion (which reasoned from the particular to the general) is true or false, is deeply connected to the accuracy of his observations. If the conclusions are in line with what is true, then the garden is appropriately watered; if the observations are tainted and the subsequent conclusions foolish, then the water is wasted, and eventually the Garden of Venus turns into a desert.

The Empress symbolizes Nature, fertility, abundance, the manifestation of the Idea. As the Fool represents the Inner Self, or Superconsciousness, the Magician is self-consciousness, and the High Priestess, subconsciousness in general, the Empress is the individual's subconscious in particular. She is the feminine aspect of the Life-power giving us the capacity for unconditional love, and she is that aspect that imagines worlds into eventually becoming the Physical Plane.

Her crown of twelve stars indicates the signs of the zodiac and that the soul must experience the characteristics of all twelve before moving on. Astrologically, the Empress is Venus, the Goddess of Love and Beauty. Feminine, a gentle and refined nature; love of harmony. Aesthetic appreciation—poetry, music, art, literature. The vibration of Venus expresses itself in simple affection all the way to compassion. Venus is nurturing, gracious, sociable, charming, sensitive, diplomatic. If afflicted, Venus is vanity, possessiveness, indulgence, social dysfunction, isolation, jealousy; the emotional nature causes destructive tremors in the Landscape.

The Empress can represent the project as it approaches completion, the potential (High Priestess) fulfilled by initiative and determination (the Magician). She brings consideration, empathy, and nurturing to the enterprise, a "mothering" touch. When we see the card of the Empress we are reminded that we have access to the limitless creative urge of the Life-power, subconscious knowledge always available—rolled up in the parchment of the High Priestess. Her affiliation with the loving vibration of Venus also reminds us that if the personality is egocentric, then the thinking processes of the Magician become disjointed or bland, and the power of awareness clouds over. One of the worst tragedies in this life occurs when the personal self, through ignorance, never realizes the need for union (yoga) with the Inner Self.

From the inner realm, the Empress shows us the path. She stimulates our reaction to beauty and encourages us to elaborate on the workings of Nature (art). When we see the Empress we are reminded of the need to harmonize the discrepancies and correct the imbalances in our life. The Empress, in combination with Venus, is the realization of virtue and a high sense of ethics. The Empress is the fruition of our hopes and desires, the embodiment of our sense of value.

Graceful and peace-loving, the Venus aspect within promotes harmony and encourages us to imitate her in a myriad of ways. The shades of soft color in a painting by Renoir, the powerful lines in a Rodin sculpture, the stirring crescendo of Gershwin's music in *Rhapsody in Blue*—beauty in art expresses itself in many forms. The soul's particular reaction to this beauty in the language of Tarot is called the Empress.

The Empress also reminds us of the benefit of living the ethical life. If we can dissolve the blockages and impediments to clear thinking, then the Empress aspect of our being helps us bring forth new life. In effect, we are encouraged to envision the absolute best for ourselves and others, all symbolized in the fertility of her garden.

But who exactly is the Empress? She is our creative imagination, one of the greatest gifts bestowed upon us by the Life-power.

The Empress in a Reading

- The project approaches fruition; growth in the Physical Plane.
- Love, balance, harmony, well-being; affectionate relationships.
- A nurturing attitude helps the problem; supportive.
- Artistic talent and appreciation; refined tastes.
- The ability to relate to another's difficulty.
- Productivity.
- A cooperative frame of mind is indicated.
- Peacefulness attained in communing with Nature.
- Elegant demeanor.
- Imagination put to good use.
- The Empress encourages trust in the personal vision.

REVERSED

- A tendency toward laziness.
- A fear of intimacy needs to be balanced with a more open heart.
- Sterile ideas, sterile environment, and a lack of imagination; seek more stimulating thoughts and activities.
- Contrary, inconsiderate attitude; unappreciative.
- Difficulty in expressing love.
- Inordinately extravagant; employs trickery, especially with sexual allure.
- Overly sentimental (intensifies near the Queen of Cups Reversed).
- Often responds to the superficial (especially with the Page or Knight of Cups Reversed).

Thoughts for Meditation on The Empress

A good time to meditate on the Empress is when you need to stimulate your natural creativity. Performing the meditation in Nature is particularly beneficial (as with any

Tarot card). Think of the water in the card (which actually is the subconscious water flowing from the blue robe of the High Priestess) fertilizing the garden of the Empress.

Notice the symbol of femininity on her shield, the cypress trees and the wheat field, all evoking the meanings of the Venus aspect of the card. The idea is to bring the creative imagination into focus.

Prayer

In thy fertile garden,
I see the waterfall, the stream—
and I see union:
yin-yang, female-male, negative-positive.

My eyes gaze upwards—
the first glistening point in the evening sky.
Venus.
And my imagination livens.
Your light illumines my vision . . .
and forms appear everywhere.
I have fertilized you with my seed,
my idea, a zygote now,
and I struggle for patience
as I anticipate a new birth of Awareness.

In thy fertile garden,
my soul flows forth
moving amongst the petals and the dewdrops.
I hear the song of the green finch
and the stream that rushes from the wellspring of my subconscious.

May the waters there run clear and free,
as I pray for the dissolution of any selfish debris.

Chapter 7

IV. The Emperor
The Fire of Mind

Astrological Correspondence: The force and power of fiery Aries.

Hebrew Letter: Heh ה (meaning "window," as in "the eyes are the window to the soul.")

The Inner Atmosphere: The flame of thought in the realm of intellect, measuring, planning, organizing, and regulating.

Statement: "I am visionary Mind employing the human brain as my instrument."

Quotation: "He who is satisfied with wisdom and direct vision of Truth, who has conquered the senses and is ever undisturbed, to whom a lump of earth, a stone and gold are the same, that one is said to be a saint of established wisdom." (*Bhagavad Gita*)

The Challenge: The ego must avoid emotional coldness and aggressive behavior.

Visualization to the Fourth Portal, The Emperor

We leave behind the soft refreshing mists of the Venusian Portal to undertake a more strenuous, a more dehydrating route upward to the abode of the Empress' consort, the Emperor.

It is as though you are looking over the shoulder of the Fool,
and in doing so,
you see the fiery expanse of orange stone above you.

You feel its dryness.
The watery world of the High Priestess
and fertile imaginative world of the Empress
turn arid in the realm of intellect.
However, far below the ridge
at the bottom of the orange canyon,
you see the stream still flowing from the blue robes of the High Priestess.

This river reminds the Emperor of the need
for exploring his emotions
and opening his mind
in the midst of his prized thought processes.

He is Aries, the Ram, the pioneering Spirit,
the supreme leader of the personality,
energized by the power of the Mars vibration, the ruler of Aries . . .

You climb steadily upwards
where at last you reach the top ledge of the mountain.
Here you see a powerful being with a white beard
sitting on a gray stone throne carved with rams' heads.
He turns to you and says sternly,
"Why do you climb to me, brave traveler?"
"I . . . I . . . want to sit on your throne,"
you reply a little nervously.
"What?!" he thunders.
"I want to experience your powers of dominion."
"So—you think you can withstand my Fire of Mind?"

Then, with a charming confidence, you point your chin to his chest.
"I come to you with the accurate attention of the Magician,
attuned to the perfect memory of the High Priestess
and active with the creativity of your wife, the Empress."

With a scowl, he turns his white head to you:
"But here in the fiery range of my red stone mountains,
let me ask you this:
Can you dedicate your consciousness to logic,
to preciseness—to order?"

You are silent and ponder his question . . .
Then he breaks the silence.
"I like to think of myself as a benevolent despot," he says.
"Emotion tends to blunt the preciseness of my objectivity,
but I am perfectly aware of the ego's need
to develop the feminine side of its nature
as well as the masculine."
"But do we need to—"
"Drawing conclusions is my mettle,
and I am most active in the mind of the mathematician
and the inventor," he says.
"Purify your High Priestess with the Magician's clear vision,
and reap the fruit of the Empress' womb—
Creative Imagination.
Then you may sit in dominion on my throne."
You listen attentively to his words.
"And something else, bold Pilgrim.
If you don't want to be burned to a cinder in my fiery atmosphere,
you must adopt my modus operandi."
"What is that, Sir?"
He turns his flashing red eye toward you and says,
"Discipline!"

You are stung by the word,
and recovering from the shock,
you manage to say,
"But regulation stifles my creativity."

His laughter, which rumbles like thunder down through the red canyon,
startles you awake.

General Atmosphere of the Fourth Portal, The Emperor

The Emperor is the composer among the personae of the Major Arcana and, at this point in the journey, the ego-aspect of the Fool has assimilated the finest qualities of an attentive Magician, a yielding High Priestess, and a bountifully creative imagination (the Empress).

The Portals of the Major Arcana exhibit a magnificent diversity, giving the Landscape an infinite gradation of awareness. In the realm of the Emperor, we experience a consciousness dedicated to *order*.

Precise. Logical. Here Tarot teaches control of the mental processes as we meditate and study the meanings behind the Emperor's Fourth Portal. In fact, to continue on the path, the seeker must adopt the Emperor's discipline to study and meditate, the discipline to "keep on" message and find enthusiastic joy along a sometimes difficult road toward achievement. Also, along this road, the seeker must face the challenging discipline of controlling the instincts.

Spirit (the Fool) coalesces into the self-consciousness of the Magician, interpenetrated by the subconscious of the High Priestess and enhanced by the creative imagination of the Empress. The ego then scales the heights of the Fourth Portal in order to grasp the Emperor's most sublime characteristic: Reason.

From the Emperor we learn that we can gain an amazing control over the ordering of our world, that the intellect can have incredible power over what is to happen. In fact, the meaning of the word emperor comes from the Latin root "to command."

The movement of mind must work in harmony with the logic of things, with Reality. This achievement gives us dominion (symbolized by the globe in the Emperor's left hand) over our environment; it is also the ability to follow our individual destiny. In the Fourth Portal we are filled with an energy that flows toward activation, to achievement of the Ideal, the Ideal of Awareness.

The Emperor's scepter is the Egyptian *ankh*, a symbol of Life, and his Arian throne is made of stone and is supposed to represent the material world.

The ancients link the Emperor with the sense of sight. Tarot therefore encourages us to direct our "seeing" inward through the window (the Hebrew letter Heh) of the house of our personality (Beth the Magician) so that we can examine our consciousness and clearly view the Landscape.

We take this process of seeing, along with our self-consciousness (Magician), our memory (High Priestess), our imagination (Empress), and press onward on the path to do battle. Armed with the potential to organize our world for our greatest good and the good of others, we must eventually face one of the most hideous of beasts: Chaos.

Conflict and chaos often antagonize our thoughts until our willpower degenerates into a total lack of order. An atmosphere of helplessness makes us feel degraded because on some level of awareness we have a vague memory that somewhere, somehow, our nature is one of Light, and that we are living far below our greatest potential. If we can bring our powers of Reason to bear upon the chaos operating in our life, we will eventually "see" a comforting symmetry underlying the seeming surface disorder and randomness. Meditation on the Emperor can help activate these powers of "seeing."

One of the goals of our existence is to eliminate or neutralize harmful vibrations from our personal atmosphere. In the realm of Intellect we are susceptible to one of the worst, the paralyzing thoughts of fear (see Eight of Swords). Fear of loving. Fear of being. Fear of the unknown. That's why it is imperative that we try to understand our personality, our nature—and that Spirit is at the center of our awareness. The Bible tells us emphatically that we "live, and move, and have our being" (Acts 17:28) within the Mind of God. The Emperor is there to remind us that we have a very beneficial tool indeed when we bring the light of Reason to bear on our thought processes. Vera Stanley Alder puts it this way: "The mind has power over everything that it can understand and visualize."[1]

Aries, the astrological attribution of the Emperor and the first sign of the zodiac, rules the head. Aggressive, strong-willed, enthusiastic, Aries is Cardinal, masculine Fire—the butting Ram forging up the mountainside. Awakened from the slumber of winter, Aries is the new surge of solar energy infusing the Earth. Alive, animated, Aries unfolds as the budding power of springtime.

The Aries character is forceful and self-directed ("I am"), although he or she can be passionately stubborn, impatient, and close-minded to constructive criticism. And he can be rash and intolerant of restriction. Aries excels in roles of leadership, but can be inflexible in his decrees. He needs to be aware of the river below him flowing from the High Priestess' robe. Compassion and understanding for the needs of others must never be forgotten in the Arian atmosphere. Forgetting can result in scorn and alienation. Aries needs to direct his forcefulness to fulfill his Ideal rather than lording his exploding self-expression over anyone else. Besides, in the atmosphere of the Emperor, crude egotism is ultimately *unreasonable*.

Aries brings lofty achievement to the human endeavor. When he takes his responsibilities seriously and transmutes his Martian aggressiveness into initiative, the world is enriched. However, Aries is afflicted with a tendency to lose interest in a project after the initial burst of energy. The Ram is challenged to reactivate the boldness and dedication he exhibited in the beginning so that he can eventually complete his task.

The Emperor consciousness is a state of awareness where the ego puts a premium on mastering his own fate (the globe). He logically sets up situations and applies his expertise so that he can make a success of his endeavor. He is the executive power of the Major Arcana, and his mind is drawing conclusions from accurate observations (Reason).

The Emperor in a Reading

- The ability to seize the opportunity, to move ahead and eagerly discover new territory.
- Thinking, speaking, and acting with authority, grounded in reasonableness.
- Maintaining an orderly, stable existence, based on clear thinking.
- The intellect used as a tool to solve problems.
- Straightforwardness.
- Leadership, with superb executive powers; willing to expend a great deal of effort to see the project through to completion.
- The power of the thinking processes used to keep the emotions in check; look carefully without emotional bias.
- Setting boundaries.
- The ego is honorably determined to succeed, never stepping on the sensibilities of anyone else.
- An original, independent, responsible thinker; he is both courageous and compassionate.
- Excellent powers of observation and analysis.

REVERSED

- A domineering, aggressive personality that needs to be vigilant regarding the feelings of others.
- Confrontational, sarcastic, territorial.
- The need to listen to different points of view.
- The cruel streak must be kept in check.
- Impatient, restless.
- Not up to the task.
- Problems in taking charge of the project; management deficiency.
- Disorganized.
- Anxious when events deviate from the plan; trouble improvising.

Meditation on The Emperor

If you find yourself expressing inner pain by going through emotional outbursts devoid of logic, a meditation on the Emperor would be ideal to get you more grounded. If you were wasting energy by letting your life shoot out in too many scattered activities, the Emperor will help give you direction. Also, if you are in need of finding the stamina to see the project through to completion, a meditation on the Emperor will reactivate your innate powers of organization.

Prayer

Awaken my mental vision
crystal sight—
as the window opens to the surging currents.
My thoughts quicken in the breezes!
May the Emperor's flame ignite my perception
and my movements vibrate to the Great Harmony.
But I must remember to drink from the Cup
dipped in the waters that flow from the Moon Temple—
waters that temper my Will with compassion.
And though I struggle to order my world
to reflect Thy Divine Perfection,
I shall not forget my Empress heart.
From the Inner Celestial,
I feel the prodding of the Ram.
He climbs the amber crags,
ordering each layer of thought
with pristine logic.

The Magician watches from below,
knowing he has given clear instruction.
But will vitality and aspiration color the ascent,
or will his steps be rash and ill-tempered?
Are the pathways carefully constructed?
For the wise have learned that faulty routes
detour the Ram to his fall—
where he will surely dash his head upon the stone.

Notes

1. Vera Stanley Alder, *The Finding of the Third Eye* (York Beach, Maine: Samuel Weiser, 1968), p. 33.

Chapter 8

V. The Hierophant
The Voice Behind the Veil

Astrological Correspondence: The steady, maintaining power of Taurus.

Hebrew Letter: Vav ו (meaning "nail" as the implement used to hold the "house" together).

The Inner Atmosphere: The Essence within speaking Truth to our subconscious and, at times, our waking consciousness. Success in life is but a thought away once the seeker becomes dedicated to listening to the Voice of the Inner Self.

Statement: "I am your Inner Teacher, and if you but listen to me, I will tell you secrets."

Quotation: "In eternal life we are far more happy in our ability to hear than in our power to see, because the act of hearing the eternal Word is in me, whereas the act of seeing goes out from me. Hearing, I am receptive." (Meister Eckhart)

The Challenge: The ego, in a stubborn attitude of refusal, ignores the unfolding Truth from within.

Visualization to the Fifth Portal, The Hierophant

Before you looms a huge oaken door.
You are standing on the steps of a massive cathedral,
and when the door to the Fifth Portal opens,
you are stunned by the vastness of the interior.
The ceiling extends upwards into the heavens.
At the altar in front of you,
you see a majestic being sitting on a gray throne—
a holy figure in a red robe and golden tiara.
As Aleph, the Fool, you enter reverently,
and the figure before you raises his right hand
in a gesture of blessing.

"Welcome, Pilgrim . . . come forth . . . into the temple of your mind . . ."
You see two monks at the feet of the Hierophant,
as you, likewise, fall to your knees in supplication.
"Please, Holy Father, I ask that you tell me your secret."
You raise your eyes and see his light-filled countenance.
"I am your Inner Teacher," he says,
"and if you will but listen,
I will impart to you all that is needful."
The monk on the right side of the altar
with white lilies on his vestments, turns around.
"Be sure you approach with purified intent."
Then the other monk faces you, his vestments adorned with roses.
He says, "Prolong your desires,
but see to it that you know exactly what you want."
You hear their advice and sit down in a gleaming mahogany pew,
attuning your consciousness to hearing the Hierophant's message . . .

"Make use of your power to dream, and from these dreams,
imagine what you want to experience for your own good
and the good of others.

Be sensitive to the inner patterns,
and with the force of your will, bring them into manifestation."
You begin to think about his words . . .

He continues: "I am the incarnation of Spirit within you,
and it is through me that you reach the Holy of Holies.
You must be patient and expectant in meditation and prayer,
and then the door will open unto you."

Then his form begins to fade before you . . .

General Atmosphere of the Fifth Portal, The Hierophant

This is Vav speaking, a Hebrew letter meaning "nail," but also used as the conjunction "and" in the language. Vav is the link between Spirit and the ego, and in another sense, the "nail" that holds the "house" of personality together. In Sanskrit, the word for union is *yoga*, referring to the link between self-consciousness and superconsciousness.

The word hierophant means the "interpreter of the sacred mysteries" (ίεροφαντος—*hiero* + *phantos* [verb, *phanein*] is Greek for "to reveal, show"), and the ancients use the Hierophant to represent the frame of mind that accepts a kind of teaching from within.

The seeker is challenged here to still the Emperor's ruling intellect, quiet the fiery energy of Mars, restrain the forward march of Aries: The Hierophant asks the seeker to turn the Magician's power of attention inward, for only there will he or she experience the inner rhythms of the Life-Breath.

At this point in the journey the ego must also adopt the High Priestess' power of memory—along with assuming an attitude of total receptivity to the influence of the inner teachings. Then the power of image-making (the Empress) comes into play, and there is a synthesis of all the previous cards. We could say that here the ego experiences yoga, a union with Spirit, for the Hierophant is the Fool activated in the Physical Plane.

The flaps hanging from the Hierophant's ears (hearing) are in the shape of a yoke, an intimation of connecting oxen, the joining aspect of yoga (also reflected in the yellow "y" on the two monks' garments). The spiritual authority of the Inner Voice is reflected in the blessing gesture of the right hand, while the golden staff symbolizes the four Planes of Existence, with the knob at the top representing the Spiritual Plane.

Astrologically, the Hierophant is associated with the second sign of the zodiac, Taurus, the Bull. As Taurus rules the neck, we can think of it as the link between the head and the rest of the body. In Taurus as Fixed Earth we are reminded of a kind of concentrated practicality. The suggestion here is that listening to the inner teachings of the Hierophant brings a highly practical benefit to the journey. And since Taurus is persistent, the seeker holds to the course and is determined to finish the journey, putting a premium on synthesizing all the previous powers encountered so far.

The Bull is placid, quiet, and receptive. The Moon is exalted in Taurus so we have a great potential for the emotions to become spiritualized in following the inner prompting of the Sacred. Further, we are reminded of the Moon Goddess, the High Priestess: Subconsciousness, memory—and an attitude of receptivity that will lift the veil of the High Priestess and reveal the Mystery.

In the Physical Plane, the realm of matter, Taurus proclaims, "I have." With the Hierophant, the seeker acquires a more refined set of values; the ethics of a situation are accentuated. Taurus is utilitarian and makes use of the realizations gained from quiet meditation, listening to the "still, quiet voice" of God within.

Venus rules Taurus so the Hierophant also indicates an appreciation of the harmony and balance operating in the universe. Attunement to Nature's symmetry will bring a sense of awe and beauty to the journey, and the seeker will be more receptive to God's Voice within.

The Emperor, the Voice of Reason, attuned the seeker to the rulership and orderly unfoldment of Universal Law; the Hierophant, an inner authority, offers a subtle interpretation of the Law. If the seeker can listen to this internal prompting, and respond accordingly, then the journey will yield beneficial, practical results. In meditation, through the sense of hearing, the Inner Self imparts the Secret Wisdom.

At this point in the journey, if we have remained awake, our subconscious has assimilated the previous four powers discussed so far in the Major Arcana: Attention (Beth, the Magician), Memory (Gimel, the High Priestess), Imagination (Daleth, the Empress) and Reason (Heh, the Emperor). But in order to continue, we as the Fool must go beyond even Reason and assimilate the fifth power indicated by Vav, the Hierophant: *Intuition*.

The Hierophant in a Reading

- An invitation to open oneself to the Inner Voice.
- Intuitive feelings brought to bear on the problem.
- A time to seek spiritual guidance.
- A spiritual teacher may enter the seeker's life; be awake for it.
- Harmony in spiritual, emotional, mental, and physical life.
- A practical application of spiritual principles.

- Striving toward integrity at all times will neutralize difficulties.
- The Hierophant draws attention to the moral life.
- A steady, cautious, traditional, nonrevolutionary approach to the problem is called for.
- Patience, forbearance.
- Slow to change, conservative.

REVERSED

- Experimentation, unusual solution needed.
- Not hearing the Inner Voice, rejecting one's intuitive feelings.
- Stubborn, refusing to listen to Reason.
- Impractical.
- Overly extravagant.
- Possessive; obsessed with the fear of losing something.
- Jealous, given to anger.
- Lethargic.
- Out of balance.
- Rigid, unyielding attitude.
- A need to be more easy-going; take life less seriously.
- Stay the course, even though there is a strong tendency to give up.

Meditation on The Hierophant

The ability to open our inner ear to God's holy message is a gift. We need only make the request. Meditation on the Hierophant attunes us to the Inner Wisdom offered continually by Spirit. The challenge is being able to distinguish Spirit's subtle communications from the chatter that continually rattles on in the mind as background noise. Meditation on any of the cards will help you control your thoughts, but the mental state of the Hierophant in particular will help still the mind.

Prayer

The static of the Planes distorts my hearing,
and I soon forget to listen.
I hear only the noise of the world,
in all its random confusion,
fomenting the illusion of chaos.

But in your mercy you still whisper to me
the eternal exactness of the Law.
Oh, and when I do truly hear Thee,
how my life doth change!
So I fall to my knees in gratefulness
at the infinitude of Thy patience.

Chapter 9

VI. The Lovers
The Tree of the Knowledge
of Good and Evil

Astrological Correspondence: The communicative skills of Gemini.

Hebrew Letter: Zain ז (meaning "sword," as the instrument used to cut away the dross to find Truth).

The Inner Atmosphere: When the personality is open to the wisdom of Spirit, choices are made that get rid of the nonessentials. Priorities are put in their proper order, and tasks are approached logically and with renewed vigor.

Statement: "I have seen the need to set the correct boundaries, parameters that protect my energies. Then I can put out the right amount of effort needed. I have developed the ability to penetrate to the core of a situation and cut away the extraneous."

Quotation: "As God is light and love in this delicate communication, He informs equally the understanding and the will, though at times His presence is felt in one more than the other." (St. John of the Cross)

The Challenge: The ego is in disjointed communication with the subconscious, and a chaotic life results.

Guided Visualization to the Sixth Portal, The Lovers

You find yourself walking in a lush rain forest.

You hear birds . . . and rushing streams.

You smell intoxicating fragrances in the air . . . gardenia, jasmine.

Your senses dazzled, you see pink and purple orchids . . .

a waterfall cascading over moss-covered stones.

You feel delicate mists touch your skin.

There is a sensual tension in the air.

A hint of soft, supple flesh against muscled thighs.

As you approach a clearing in front of you,

you walk through the Sixth Portal,

the Portal of the Lovers.

There you behold a stunning sight:

In a golden sky a magnificent angelic being,

raising his arms in blessing,

hovers over a naked man and woman.

However, the male and female figures before you do not touch.

They are in potential.

He looks to her, his arms open for embrace.

She, too, is ready,

but her eyes gaze upward to the golden-flamed Angel, Raphael,

whose arms are extended in a gesture of benediction.

You stand silently in awe and notice

that the woman is standing before a lovely tree with five fruits.

The man stands before a tree with twelve flaming leaves.

The man looks leftward to the woman

and from his eyes,

a golden light streams toward hers.

From her eyes, looking heavenward,
the golden light continues
and meets the golden eyes of the Angel.
The meeting of their three gazes
forms a white fiery triangle in the sky.
Then the Angel looks at you with his gleaming eyes.
In a voice powerful, and yet full of sweetness, he says,
"The root of all desire is the compulsion to experience the soul."
You are then consumed with a prayerful silence,
and in reverence,
fall to your knees.
You ask the Most High to bestow upon you grace and well-being.
Then, suddenly, a second white fiery triangle,
point downwards, descends.
The two flaming triangles meet in the sky above you
and you see a blazing six-pointed star—the Star of David.
The light from the Star quickens your aura,
and you feel its comfort,
drawing upon its loving power.

You rest awhile in this light and then
you can open your eyes when you are ready,
feeling refreshed and awake.

General Atmosphere of the Sixth Portal, The Lovers

The woman stands before a tree with fruits symbolizing the five senses. A snake coils upwards along the tree, reminding us of Eve's sense temptation in the Garden of Eden. The snake is also an intimation of the *caduceus* (the medical symbol of two snakes coiling up a rod). In addition, the Angel Raphael (Hebrew for "God has healed") communicates through the female aspect to the male: Self-consciousness (male-yang), when in a state of intensified awareness, is receptive to the Angel's voice (Intuition) which is heard through the medium of the subconscious (female-yin). The male aspect of our Nature is now in a position to understand absolutely the benefit of right thought, right feeling, and right action in accordance with Universal Law. The energy of the Angel intuiting through the female Substance to the male

Will creates a bonding of the two forces—the Lovers—of our being; it is then that we are made whole.

The man stands before a tree burning with twelve flames. Here is the masculine side, the Magician, naked before God and man, embodying the characteristics of the twelve signs of the zodiac:

Initiative—Aries
Acquisition—Taurus
Communication—Gemini
Feelings—Cancer
Assertiveness—Leo
Scrutiny—Virgo
Equilibrium—Libra
Sensuousness—Scorpio
Inquisitiveness—Sagittarius
Practicality—Capricorn
Altruism—Aquarius
Intuition—Pisces

The purplish-pink mountain between the man and woman is the road to achievement; awareness gained through understanding of the abstract. We climb the mountain using each Tarot card as a sign pointing to the summit.

How do we get there?

Expand our vision, and yet set boundaries. Restrain craving, yet understand—and take care of—our needs. We must then wield Zain, the Sword, chopping through the brambles and eliminating from our lives all that is unnecessary.

If we enter a clear mode of thought embodied in the Lovers, we are endowed with the ability to "separate the wheat from the chaff." When the first humans ate of the fruit, their eyes were opened, and they received the knowledge of good and evil; however, they also became lost to their spiritual innocence. But this process is all part of the Plan. In fact, one of the principal reasons we incarnate in the Physical Plane is so that we can frequently exercise this ability to choose the good from the bad, the wise from the foolish.

In life we are forced to make decisions, and the Lovers show us the way to choose correctly. The man is the self-conscious, and he looks leftward to the woman, the subconscious. She, in turn, looks upward to the Angel, the Inner Self, the Superconscious, the Divine Spark within . . . and we can imagine their gazes forming a fiery triangle in the sky.

When the subconscious receives impressions from the Inner Self, and the lines of communication are open to the Magician, then, point downwards, a second fiery triangle—the triangle of grace—descends.

When the two flaming triangles meet, we see before us a blazing six-pointed hexagon—the Star of David. And it is at this point that the awareness increases.

This "communication" of Superconsciousness through subconsciousness to self-consciousness is also symbolized by Gemini, the Twins, and its ruler, Mercury (the Magician). Perception. Observation. Intelligence. Gemini is versatile, restless, and a highly spontaneous Air sign. Its Mutability gives Gemini an ability to adapt to circumstances, which compliments the Mercurial qualities of interpretation, attention, and expressiveness. Gemini is alert and efficient, intellectual and anxiety-prone. The Twins devour information, interpret it, and disperse it. Gemini is the most curiosity-minded of the signs, exploring the complexities of people and relationships.

However, if afflicted, Gemini can be verbose, indecisive, and unstable. The aware, reasoning mind in its acceptance of accountability helps neutralize the negative traits. Gemini must also remember to nurture the heart vibrations and balance the choice taken with Reason.

The Lovers show the seeker the need to bring the self-conscious and the subconscious into a harmonious relationship. The thoughts of the Magician are refined through the reasonableness of the Emperor and integrated into the subconscious, loving beauty of the Empress and the memory of the High Priestess. Then the Voice of the Hierophant speaks, and Intuition illuminates the seeker.

However, even these powers are not enough. In bringing the Lovers to consciousness we are then able to use yet another ability vital to our progress on the path. When self-consciousness (the Magician) is in communication (Mercury) with the Angel (the Fool, exalted) through the voice of the woman (the subconscious), then the power of Discernment manifests where the seeker can discriminate realistically between the essential and the nonessential.

This is the central theme of the Sixth Portal. Tarot teaches that we must be able to hear the message of the Inner Self and apply the knowledge learned to beneficially affect the circumstances of our lives. We need only to remember to treat the woman with love and kind regard, and she in turn will deliver the Angel's message with preciseness and clarity.

Here in the Sixth Portal we are reminded that the heart of our advancement is desire. We need to formulate desires that are clear and loving, and the floodgates will open, God's grace streaming through consciousness, healing our wounds. Soon the hurtful barriers we have erected with our confused and selfish ego dissolve, and in an act of unique intimacy, the man and woman embrace.

The Lovers in a Reading

- A choice is to be made; dedication, ethical considerations, and clarity of purpose are essential to the happy outcome of the situation in question.
- A loving, committed relationship above all else.
- A healthy outlook on life.
- Clear, perceptive communication will bring a beneficial result.
- Successful partnership due to mutual understanding and appreciation.
- Opening to the spiritual message; celestial influence from above.
- Healing.
- Let go of what is not needed; avoid clutter.
- Adopt a flexible, but logical, approach to the problem.
- Stimulation through variety.

REVERSED

- Undependable.
- Sense temptation leads to selfishness.
- Jumping to conclusions.
- Emotional detachment.
- Faulty communication; static.
- Unclear about emotional needs.
- Misunderstandings.
- Poor character traits.
- A possible unhealthy relationship.
- Harping on others over trivia.

Meditation on The Lovers

You carry on your chores listlessly. The house is a mess. On a cold morning the buzz of the alarm clock painfully jolts you into an unwelcome reality. The walking dead on the 6:10 A.M. bus . . . dirty streets . . . faceless coworkers . . .

Questions to consider:

What areas of my life need improving so that I can enjoy myself again? What do I need to eliminate? Meditation on the Lovers will help reorient you to your subconscious needs. It will help you focus your desires and direct your energies to where they are most beneficial.

When you can have a free flow of information between your self-conscious mind and your subconscious, your heart will open to the Angel and the boredom will flee.

Prayer

Her voice echoes back the words from the lips of the Hierophant,
and I feel compelled to sing his message to the world:
Reflect the Light of the soul in the activities of your life!
I feel the flutter of Angel wings
lightly brushing across my face,
and I pray:
"Oh, Lord, let me always apprehend Thy subtleties."
I will climb the violet mountain
and continue my evolution upward.
Though sensation may distract me,
and clutter my perception with nonessentials,
I will remember the Sword
that the Angel of the Lord rendered unto me.
Then I will decide the route
and not wander these mountain paths
aimlessly lost and staggering as before.
No. I step on the Path of Return,
Sword held high,
and I forge my way back to the Garden.

Chapter 10

VII. The Chariot
The Integrated Personality

Astrological Correspondence: The supporting, nurturing depth of Cancer, with the emotions in perfect balance.

Hebrew Letter: Cheth ח (meaning "fence," as the human personality is a fenced-in, limited field within the Mind of God).

The Inner Atmosphere: This state of mind opens the personality to the influence of the Inner Self, whose image and likeness we are made from. It is the triumph of the personality as it reflects the light of the Inner Self. The emotional self is brought under scrutiny.

Statement: "I am in control, and I hold the reins in on disjointed feelings, erratic thoughts, and an undisciplined body."

Quotation: "In all walks of life it will be proved to the seeker after truth that there is a key to success, a key to happiness, a key to advancement and evolution in life; and this key is the attainment of mastery." (Hazrat Inayat Khan, *Mastery*)

The Challenge: The ego is fragmented and unfocused; this encourages the emotions to dominate. There is a need to organize the contents of consciousness back into its original symmetry.

Visualization to the Seventh Portal, The Chariot

You find yourself standing beneath the gray stone walls
of a medieval town.
The houses and the castles within the walled city have red pointed roofs.
You are also conscious of the golden yellow pulsation
of the Limitless Light permeating the atmosphere.
And here in the Seventh Portal you have come to know this Light
as a loving, breathing Energy in and through all creation.
Now let yourself breathe rhythmically with this loving Light,
the Light of the Life-power.

Feel the Holy Presence infusing your mind,
pulsating within your heartbeat.
And know that you are never alone.
Then, suddenly, before you is the Charioteer,
and from his blonde hair and wreath,
you recognize him as Aleph, the Fool—
now in the Seventh Portal as powerful and triumphant
in his gray-stone Chariot.
He is armored and ready as he wills to leave the known city behind.
Two sphinxes, one white and one black,
are at rest in front of the Chariot.

Politely, you ask, "May I have a ride with you
in your magnificent Chariot?"
"Have you united all the Powers of Consciousness so far presented
in your travels through the previous Portals?"
"Uh. . . I—"

"Tell me, then, do you notice
a perceptible sense of equilibrium manifesting
in the inner and outer circumstances of your life?"
You contemplate his words.
Then he says, "I am in control, and I hold the reins on my emotions,
my thoughts . . . and my body."
"But how do I learn this control, Charioteer?"
"Be friendly to thyself.
And manifest the awe-inspiring Power that hides within you.
Be steady in thy determinations, brave traveler,
and in this thou shalt know mastery."
You thank him for his revelation . . .
and become conscious again
of the golden-yellow Limitless Light . . .
in and through you.
You notice your breathing and keep this awareness . . .
and when you are ready, open your eyes . . .
feeling refreshed and relaxed.

General Atmosphere of the Seventh Portal, The Chariot

Through the Seventh Portal you see yourself as the Fool, only now you are victorious in your Chariot because you have absorbed into your persona all the Powers of Consciousness from the previous six cards:

As the Magician your attention is focused in order to get the project done; as the High Priestess you have come to understand your emotional reactions; with the Empress you exhibit your creative, imaginative Self; as the Emperor your attitude is always reasonable and your approach grounded; in the Hierophant state of mind, your intuitive abilities are heightened; and, finally, with the Lovers you are able to discern which is the most beneficial choice.

In order to emphasize the idea of bringing together all of the previous lessons into the personality, we look to the various symbols in the card of the Seventh Portal.

The Charioteer holds a scepter of dominion and control, which is the Wand of the Magician (self-consciousness). Behind the Chariot we see the blue water still flowing from the robes of the High Priestess (universal subconsciousness). With the green trees, grass, and copper breastplate (copper is sacred to Venus), we are reminded of the creative imagination of the Empress, the personal subconscious. In the center-front of the Chariot we see the flame of Reason and the square gray block and columns of order and measurement (the Emperor). Above the Charioteer we see the celestial canopy, a suggestion of the cosmic influences of Intuition and the Hierophant. The winged golden orb is the opening of the "Spiritual Eye" to the Hierophant's intuitive vibrations. The invisible reins that the Charioteer holds is the focused mind. Here the mind is pictured in control of the senses—the outgrowth of emotions in the Physical Plane (symbolized by the two sphinxes at rest). It is at this point that the seeker is in the sacred moment and is able to make the most correct choice (Discernment and the Lovers).

The Hebrew letter for the Chariot is Cheth, the fence. God has given us our own personal atmosphere—the personality—a "fenced in" area of the Limitless Light (notice the yellow sky behind the Chariot). It is up to us as the Charioteer to fill that atmosphere with goodness and light, vitality and balance. Otherwise, Creativity, Reason, Intuition, and Discernment flee, and the personality becomes a confused energy field of chaotic pain.

The Chariot, as a combination of all six previous Powers of Consciousness, manifests as a special Power itself. Spirit (0. The Fool), awakened to the Examined Life in the Physical Plane, using the Power of self-conscious attention (I. The Magician) and the Emperor's Power of Reason, makes use of the potential of the universal subconscious (The High Priestess) and the personal subconscious (The Empress). This is the Power of Will.

At this point the Chariot's level of awareness prepares the seeker so he or she may clearly hear the Voice of the Hierophant (Intuition). Harmony is reached between the self-conscious and the subconscious (the Lovers) and the Spiritual Eye opens.

The Power of Consciousness represented by VII. The Chariot is the balance achieved between the passive and the active, yin-yang, feminine-masculine, dark-light, magnetic-electric, lunar-solar . . . The integrated personality is receptive and feminine to the influences of the Inner Self and is willful and masculine in its control of errant emotions, thoughts, and sensations.

The astrological sign of Cancer, ruled by the Moon (The High Priestess) and exalted in Venus (The Empress), influences the meaning of the Chariot. The moon-shaped epaulets (one smiling, the other distressed) on the Charioteer's shoulders are Cancerian: We as Charioteer must remain poised between the two extremes of pleasure and pain. The Moon also rules memory (The High Priestess), which in the case of the Chariot suggests that the height of integration reached in the Seventh Portal is a mode of Consciousness which is able to effortlessly remember who and what It is: Spirit incarnating in the Physical, Mental, and Emotional Planes.

The sign of Cancer is activated, highly charged emotion, and when focused, balanced, and selfless, the personality in control is nurturing. The self is truly the vehicle of the Self, the Inner Light streaming forth to warm the hearts of all who enter the Charioteer's aura. There is a sense of cooperation and security in the air. The Cancerian atmosphere is protective.

If, however, the Chariot is reversed and surrounded by stressful cards, the atmosphere turns stifling. The afflicted Cancerian consciousness perceives an emotional vacuum within, and memory focuses on loss and gnawing fear, real or imagined, from the past. The result is a grasping outward in an act of desperate possessiveness—with the Crab's claws holding resolutely to its victim. The Cancerian fear can take the form of jealousy and/or easily hurt feelings, feelings which eventually destroy the relationship.

However, the Chariot is a symbol of the emotions under control. The lower nature has been conquered (the two sphinxes appear domesticated by the Rider). The Charioteer is symbolic of the personality integrated and a uniting of opposites into a cohesive whole.

The Chariot in a Reading

- Control over negative thought patterns.
- Well-disciplined.
- The soul is the driver of a well-balanced personality.
- The male and female energies are in equilibrium.
- The senses under control.
- Moving beyond the known, courageously.
- Sensitive to the feelings of others.
- Receptive to benevolent influence; dominant over habits and subconscious motivation.
- Attentive to pertinent detail.
- Memories put to good use; learning well from past experience.
- Creative solutions to problems.
- Emotions and intellect in balance.
- Intuitive abilities brought to bear on difficulties.
- Discerning choices made.
- Self-mastery.

Reversed

- A highly charged emotional energy characterizes the atmosphere.
- The feeling nature overly dominant.
- Mood fluctuations could alienate loved ones and acquaintances.
- Emotions need better control.
- Need to live more in the present. Past memories overly relied upon.
- Too aggressive or too subservient.
- Fear of moving on.
- Overindulgence in sense pleasure; more discipline needed.
- Matter over mind.

Thoughts for Meditation on The Chariot

If the seeker feels disjointed, out of sorts, and unfocused, a meditation on the Chariot will help unify the thoughts. There is a sense of arrival with this card, a feeling of mastery. In control. The Chariot is symbolic of a unified personality: Poised, aware, imaginative, rational, intuitive, and discerning. The Chariot is ego in perfect balance.

Prayer

I am fenced in,
and I feel Thy protection.
Animate me.
Infuse me with Thy Light celestial,
and I will let Thy blessings pour forth
through me
and to all Thy creation.
I am one-pointed,
always mindful,
inspired,
clear thinking,
listening,
decisive—
I am the Rider
scanning the Landscape
with laser eyes and radar ears
and I am here—now.

The Seven Universal Laws

VIII. Strength to XIV. Temperance

Chapter 11

VIII. Strength
Uniqueness Activated

Astrological Correspondence: The dynamism, courage, and strength of Leo.

Hebrew Letter: Teth ט (meaning "snake," the subtle power within awaiting release; the healing power of the caduceus).

The Inner Atmosphere: The emotions surge, but the Charioteer's force of command is in the air. Consciousness as the feminine side of the Fool awakens to the Power of Spirit; the senses are brought under benign control. The Fire of Life lies dormant, awaiting activation through compassionate understanding of one's human nature.

Quotation: "As soon as a man loses the courage to go through the struggle of life, the burden of the whole world falls upon his head." (Hazrat Inayat Khan, *Mastery*)

The Challenge: Through ignorance the ego is allowed to be devoured by selfish desire; weakness from dissipation of vital energy.

Visualization to the Eighth Portal, Strength

We are still in sight of the great purple mountain,
the challenging climb still before us.
However, we have come far.
We have gained new awareness of our hidden motivations,
of our creative abilities.
We are now more organized,
more comfortably structured.
We can also hear the inner prompting more clearly.
From our encounters with various personages so far,
we are integrating the secrets we have learned from them
into our own personal atmosphere:
Attention . . . Memory . . . Imagination . . .
Reason . . . Intuition . . . and Discernment.
From the awareness of these modes of consciousness,
our personality is better able to reflect the Light
of our true spiritual nature.
So, full of confidence, we move on in our Chariot,
triumphant as we enter the next level of Portals:
The Realm of Universal Law.
Now you find yourself walking on a green and fertile plain . . .
In this next level of seven Portals,
you see before you the Eighth,
and know that you will soon interact with a Law in motion . . .
Become aware of the radiance surrounding you
and flowing through you
the eternal . . . yellow glow . . . of the Limitless Light.
Before you, as you enter the Eighth Portal,
you see a beautiful woman in a luminous white gown.
Like the Magician earlier,
an Infinity sign floats above her blonde hair—
golden curls blooming with flowers.
But you are most struck by what the young woman is doing:

She is ever so gently . . . gently . . .
closing the mouth of a fiery red lion.
And, amazingly, the woman and the lion
are entwined together . . .
within a garland chain of red roses.
You feel compelled to say,
"O, Good Woman, can you likewise
soothe the wildness within mine own breast?"
Before she can answer,
the red lion flashes his flaming yellow eyes at you and growls,
"I do not tame easily, reckless Pilgrim,
and I would just as well devour thee."
But the woman answers in a voice of delicate sweetness,
"Listen carefully to the words of thy animal nature, young Pilgrim . . .
but rest thy thoughts in the warmth of my heart."
And rest you do . . .
again feeling the loving glow of the Limitless Light
in and through you . . . pulsating gently . . . gently . . .
You notice the quiet rhythm of your breathing . . .
soft awareness . . . feel yourself unwinding . . .
into the yellow light of the Life-power . . . gently . . . gently.
You are content as you notice your being softly blending
within the great symmetry of our universe.
Rest quietly in this knowledge,
feeling the loving warmth . . .
and when you are ready, you may begin to come back,
little by little into the room . . .
feeling refreshed and relaxed.

General Atmosphere of the Eighth Portal, Strength

To get an idea of how far you have come on the journey, put the cards we have covered so far down in front of you, face up. In the center top place the Journeyer, Zero, the Fool. Then beneath him in a row, place the next seven cards from the Magician to the Chariot (the Fool should be directly above the middle card, the Emperor). This row represents the Seven Principles of Consciousness.

As Aleph, the Fool entered the First Portal and grasped the secret, the Limitless Light. Tarot calls this state of being the Magician—self-consciousness reflecting the Light of Spirit. Then as the Magician, Aleph, the Fool, sends clear, beneficial direction to the unlimited potential of the subconscious (the High Priestess). Their union produces creativity through the Planes (the Empress). Decisions are made (the Lovers) with great wisdom (the Emperor). And psychic powers expand as we listen to the Voice of the Hierophant.

Finally, at the end of the first series of Portals, we emerge in our Chariot, a synthesis and culmination of the previous cards; as an integrated personality we exhibit great mastery over our emotions, our thoughts, and our deeds. And what is the result of this self-control? *Strength.*

To enter through this Eighth Portal the ancients called Strength, we must exert just the right amount of discipline on ourselves. For as we are cleansed of impurities, achievement of our spiritual goals can only be reached when we show care and lovingkindness to our body/mind. The ancients chose the image of a woman gently closing the mouth of a lion to illustrate this point.

In the Eighth Portal we encounter the first of the seven Universal Laws, and it is therefore important that we have assimilated the secrets of the previous cards so that we can bring these principles into action.

To reach the goal of human existence, the very purpose of our incarnation into the Physical Plane, we must allow the unfoldment of the Light of Spirit in our own life (Aleph, The Fool). Then we must learn to make proper use of the Power of the Life Force, depicted in the First Portal as the Magician. We have been given the ability to direct this Force to help us in our advancement on the path.

When the Power is used for our greatest good and the good of others, then the blossoming of Spirit through the individual persona occurs. We wield this Power only with the greatest awareness, conscious of the practical outcome. But how do we grasp this Power and keep it in our thoughts?

The *rishis*, ancient mystics of India, describe a way, and they illustrate it in the system of spiraling energy centers in the body they call *chakras*, Sanskrit for "wheel." There are seven major chakras located from the base of the spine to the top of the head (see Figure 2), each one spinning within our personal aura (the electromagnetic field of luminous energy surrounding our body).

Through the chakras we receive the subtle energies (*prana*), incorporate them into our personal atmosphere and finally direct them outwards to create our environment.

Seven Chakras
Figure 2

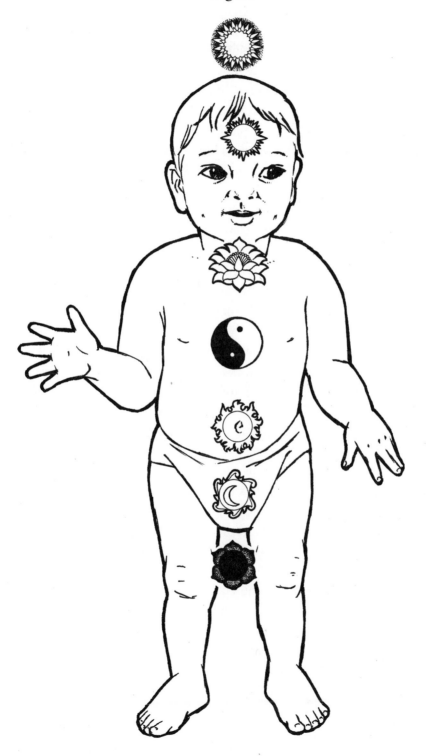

The more consciously we transmit this Power, the more likely we can recreate the Garden of Eden in life.

At the top of the head is the crown chakra, violet in color, where our aura opens to the celestial energies, and we become infused with divine Awareness. It is said to resemble a fountain of golden light flowing upward from the top of the head when this happens. The metal related to the crown chakra (*Sahasrara* in Sanskrit) is gold and the gemstone is amethyst. The gland in the body stimulated by the energies flowing through the crown chakra is the pituitary in the brain.

The sixth chakra (*Ajna*), the Third Eye, is located in the center of the forehead at the pineal gland, and is the seat of Intuition. Its color is deep indigo blue, its metal is silver and its gemstone is lapis lazuli.

Next is the throat chakra (*Vishuddha*), the center for communication and the creative urge, with the color of turquoise. Its metal is mercury and its gem is turquoise. The purpose of the throat chakra is to purify energies at the thyroid gland so that they are free-flowing, enabling us to comfortably speak only what is Real.

Located in the center of the chest is the heart chakra (*Anahata*). Within this center at the thymus we experience love and compassion. Its color is green. The metal is copper and the gemstone is tourmaline.

At the navel, the third chakra is called the solar plexus (*Manipura*). Colored yellow, it is concerned with personal power, the will. This is also where you experience "gut feelings." Its metal is iron, its gem is amber, and it functions at the pancreas.

In the genital area is the splenic chakra (*Svadhisthana*), colored orange. Here in the second chakra is located our vital energy, our desire nature, our etheric self. The metal associated with it is tin and its gemstone is coral.

Finally, at the base of the spine at the adrenal glands, is the location of the root chakra (*Muladhara*). Here churns a vortex of energies, the seat of our basic instincts. It is the place where we exhibit the fight or flight response and our urge toward survival. When there is a freeflow of energy in the root chakra within our aura, we experience the frame of mind of groundedness.

The color of the root chakra is red (metal, lead and gem, bloodstone), and we know from previous cards that red is the color of desire. In Strength the red lion symbolizes the Fire of Will and action. But the woman's unique interaction with the lion suggests a kind of persuasive, measured activity. She is taming the Fire in order to bring Enlightenment into her atmosphere and out into the world.

The rishis called this Fire *kundalini* ("coiled up" in Sanskrit). It is the hidden "nuclear energy" of the aura system, and it is said to be coiled up like a serpent (the Hebrew letter for Strength is Teth, meaning "snake") at the base of the spine—vertebrae resembling figure eights resting on their side like the infinity symbol. As we advance on the path this kundalini energy is released up the spine, energizing all the chakras. The seeker's consciousness is then lifted into the supersensible realms, vivifying the Spiritual Eye. Swami Vivikananda says that as the kundalini "rises step by step, as it were, layer after layer of the mind opens up and many different visions and wonderful powers come to the yogi. When it reaches the brain, the yogi becomes perfectly detached from the body and mind; the soul realizes its freedom."[1]

Freedom. That is the key. But the road to freedom seems long and arduous, and the eventual goal of a mind filled with blissful peace, compassion, and creativity appears far off and inaccessible. It is here on this road, when our mind is disjointed and pessimistic, that we meet the lion. It snarls and drools and extends a slashing claw.

Plato says, "This kind of knowledge is a thing that comes in a moment like a light kindled from a leaping spark which once it has reached the soul, finds its own fuel." Within the psyche, at its lowest, the lion in the Strength card is untamed instinct. The sexual addict, the obese, the enraged—all examples of egos that have been devoured by this "lion."

Along with St. Paul, Strength reminds the seeker not to be overcome by evil, but overcome evil with good. We are cautioned to look at our uncontrolled passions with love, understanding, and an examining mind. It is then that the mouth of the beast closes, and we are calm and aware in the Presence of the Most High. Obsessions in the past and anxiety about the future will begin to lose their dominance. We find a new respect for our body, a new awareness of the feelings of others.

We must never treat our animal nature with disrespect, nor must we allow it to run rampant. It is put upon us to tame this lion, this fleshly vehicle we inhabit. Only with lovingkindness will this body and its instincts surrender benignly; and only through lovingkindness, patience, and sensitivity to its needs will this lion reveal its hidden powers.

The lion then takes on the higher qualities of Leo, the fifth sign of the zodiac, Fixed Fire. With instinct under an enlightened control, Leo blazes forth with courage, confident expectation, enthusiasm, and determination, roaring, "I will!" Leo is vital and channels his power into the proper outlets.

The Leo influence brings out the soul's inner strength, courage, and awesome nobility. When the fiery awareness of Spirit burns in the heart (for Leo rules the heart), humanity reflects God's loving qualities.

Compassion flows outward to all creation, and Leo is content in his open-heartedness. The character of Strength reflects these qualities and more.

When Strength appears in a reading, other leonine virtues add to the picture: Steadfastness, generosity, loyalty. Leo exalted spiritualizes the emotions. And Leo's good heart then influences the subconscious to promote in the ego a variety of desirable reactions, such as creative thinking, ethical behavior, and truthful speaking. It is through Strength that we practice the First Law of Universal Life.

Tarot sees the subconscious as the Eternal Reservoir, God's receptive aspect, forever available to the conscious mind of the Magician (the infinity sign above his head reminds us of his presence in Strength). He attentively uses his tools—Wands, Cups, Swords, and Pentacles—to influence the woman (subconsciousness). And when he uses Mercury's quick intellect in combination with Leo's glowing heart, the subconscious responds in beneficent ways. When the Magician employs enlightened attention to what he wants, and presents to the subconscious his need with a definite sincerity of purpose, the High Priestess becomes impressed with his images—and responds. It is then that she transforms into the creative Empress, bringing about manifestation.

Like the woman and the lion, the interaction between the male and female aspect is benevolent. The Magician does not cajole the High Priestess, but instead uses the first of the Universal Laws, the Law of Suggestion.

The Bible meant this Law when it says, "For as he thinketh in his heart, so is he." (Proverbs 23:7) And, so we too must remember the power of thought, that thoughts are things, things that manifest. If we can make use of the Power of positive affirmation, the awareness of the sacred beauty within, then from this Law we will draw Strength.

Strength in a Reading

- Awareness of the Life-power operating in one's atmosphere.
- Right thinking, acting, and speaking.
- An open heart.
- Patience applied to the matter.

- Examining one's thought processes, motivation, and resultant behavior.
- Generosity of spirit.
- Understanding one's weaknesses.
- Positive suggestion.
- A call for courage, determination, and virtue.
- Taming unruly passions gently and with intelligence.
- Reciprocity.

REVERSED

- Self-indulgence.
- Lack of control.
- Dissipation of energy.
- Wasting time; aimlessness.
- A need to draw on untapped hidden resources.
- Violent domination.
- Self-inflicted torture.

Thoughts for Meditation on Strength

If you are facing a difficult challenge (especially if it involves the body), meditation on Strength will help you connect with the currents of determination, courageousness—and Leo's will to get the job done for all to see. If you want to quit smoking, lose weight, detoxify, meditation on Strength will help you tap into the stamina at Leo's core to combat the power of addiction.

Prayer

Life flows in a spiral
uncoiling
Igniting Fire—
I feel Thy Strength rise
from the Sacred Depth.
And my Eye opens.
Now I know Absolutely
that my Essence

is of Light:
Right seeing, right feeling, right thinking—
My steps reflect the Inmost,
and I can sense
that all ground is holy.

Notes

1. Swami Vivikananda, *Raja Yoga* (New York, N.Y.: Ramakrishna-Vivekananda Center, 1956), p. 50.

Chapter 12

IX. The Hermit
Light at the Summit

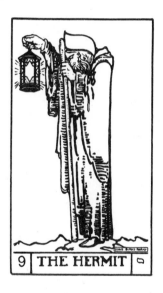

Astrological Correspondence: Virgo's desire to serve.

Hebrew Letter: Yod ' (meaning the "open hand" as a gesture of openness and the offer of help).

The Inner Atmosphere: Only the determination of Will brings consciousness up a long, sometimes difficult path, a road eventually winding to the mountain's pinnacle. Here the highly discerning ego exhibits the power of spiritual understanding.

Statement: "With great humility and with God's grace, I dedicate my life through example to the betterment of my brothers and sisters."

Quotation: "The Mysteries are revealed to the man whose light is shining and he becomes a knower."(Alice A. Bailey, *The Light of the Soul*)

The Challenge: The ego must not fall into a "martyr's" syndrome where the suffering, sacrificing personality is merely a mask for self-indulgence.

Visualization to the Ninth Portal, The Hermit

You find yourself alone, stumbling in the dark,
a pilgrim climbing up an icy, gray mountain.
You shiver from the cold,
but never lose your determination to ascend.
Then, above you, on a snow-covered ridge,
you behold the Ninth Portal.
Atop the mountain you see a lamp glowing—
glowing with a six-pointed star—
and lighting up the mountain's peak.

As your eyes adjust to the brilliance of the lamp,
you focus on an aged, light-filled countenance
looking at you from under a gray hood.

Earnestly you say to the personage,
"Help me, Father, for it seems that I am lost . . ."
Then, in a voice through clinking chimes,
the Hermit says, "My dear one . . .
look at me and see all that you have become—
and cast thy burden into my Light."
"But, Father, I know not how . . ."
"Be who you are, rise above doubt,
and express thyself in abundant joy!"
The Hermit raises his lamp, and with great benevolence,
smiles down on you . . .
"Bring forth thy own Light,
and kindle it with everflowing lovingkindness.
And always remember: You are not lost, my child,
for I will light the Way,
and the Veil of Unknowing shall lift from thine eyes."

Then as the vision of the Hermit begins to fade,
and you feel a new awareness,
your Spirit rises blissfully in the Hermit's diffusing light . . .

When you open your eyes you are relaxed
and feel inexpressible comfort and peace . . .

General Atmosphere of the Ninth Portal,
The Hermit

When Consciousness expresses Itself as the Hermit, the personality is matter-of-factly unselfish, and offers guidance with an open heart. A woman buys a large home with a major portion of her savings, for example, so that she can provide shelter for five divorced middle-aged women living on minimal salaries. She leaves them free to donate for expenses, whatever they can afford that month.

With his or her discoveries in the realm of Spirit, the Hermit, in simplicity and humility, goes about in the world joyfully giving and expressing. In particular, the Hermit shares his spiritual methods with those who seek. The Hermit, in the Consciousness of the Ninth Portal, has delved deeply into the Examined Life.

A psychologist, after a year of meditation and study, decides to volunteer at a small downtown clinic three nights a week. He soon finds himself ministering to drug addicts and prostitutes and other outcasts. He shares of himself and enjoys exchanges with the people.

The pure Consciousness of the Fool as the Magician, the Observer, in the Ninth Portal, reaches a new level of awareness. The ego reflects the Light of the soul, and expands its interest to helping others. Aleph, the Fool is now the "open hand" (the Hebrew letter, Yod) and is filled with grace. We are reminded of this as we observe the Fool's white rose of pure intention transformed into the Hermit's lamp of beacon light. The Wand on which he leans is the Fire of Spirit. In the Ninth Portal the youthful vibrancy of Aleph blends in harmony with the Ageless Wisdom, signified by the Hermit. Likewise, we see a blending of spontaneity with knowledge and enthusiasm with analysis.

Like the Magician, the ego recognizes the power of self-consciousness and becomes an open channel for Spirit. However, in the Ninth Portal, the Magician as Hermit shares the knowledge of how to achieve this openness. Self-conscious awareness is now the Wayshower.

When called, the Hermit heals with the dispensing of his Light. His wisdom illuminates our minds, and we are deeply influenced by his great givingness. In his presence we soon become aware of the generosity waiting expression from our own hearts.

But how does one find this Hermit? He could be hidden within a classic book or poem, or perhaps in a powerful liturgical service. We could even encounter the Hermit in a more literal fashion as a sage we meet. The Hermit is a trigger to our own inner, untapped Wisdom of Things-As-They-Are.

In the Ninth Portal our thoughts rise, and we seek toward higher knowledge. Our mind is filled with inspiration and insight. Through a dedication of Will, the pilgrim has remained steadfast in his or her determination to reach enlightenment at the mountain's pinnacle. With a single-minded purpose the Hermit has attained high powers of centering that allow him to understand duality and the relationship of opposites. Both sides of an issue become clear and the correct choice is made.

To emphasize this, the Hermit is clothed in gray robes. Gray is a color that is a blending of black and white and symbolizes wisdom, achievement, and realization. The Hermit is balanced between the duality of pleasure and pain, positive and negative, hot and cold . . .

The Hermit is poised and confident in his objective point of view as he strives toward an encounter with the Absolute. Of all the signs of the zodiac, Virgo most embodies that pursuit of perfection.

Virgo is feminine, receptive, Mutable Earth with the ability to adjust to any situation. She governs the intestinal tract where energies are assimilated from food. Virgo is symbolized as a virgin gathering wheat, and we can assume she puts what she has gleaned to very good use. She symbolizes harvest time, reaping the fruits of the planting. And what does she say when she has gathered in all the "wheat?" "I analyze."

The atmosphere of Virgo is much less flamboyant than Leo, with the virgin preferring to act outside of the spotlight. In Virgo, talents and skills are brought into focus; she perfects her methods and techniques and preserves her energies. Virgo will sacrifice for family, friends, and even strangers and is known as the servant of the zodiac—as well as the perfectionist. Her very Essence shines through her act of service. Living the virtuous life is at a premium with Virgo, and like the Hermit, she is adept at introspection. Virgo leads a life of purpose and has a high standard of ethics, but she is also intolerant of inefficiency. Virgo is ruled by Mercury: Mental agility, discriminating, and critical.

The purpose of creation was so that self-consciousness could expand until it reaches God-consciousness. The six-pointed star in the Hermit's lamp reminds us of this. The upward pointing triangle signifies humankind's prayer of praise and the evolution of consciousness; the downward pointing triangle is the descent of grace into matter, or involution. The perfect intersection of the triangles, the "Star of David" (See chapter 9, The Lovers), is the moment of revelation and the expression of the Inner Self in the circumstances of our life. The Hermit shows us the way to recognize our true Nature.

In the Ninth Portal we reach a sense of completion, as the number 9 illustrates achievement, accumulated wisdom, reaching a goal, attainment of spiritual awareness. Here we understand that we are of the same substance of the Creative Force of the

Universe, and we are here to bring Its Wisdom, Beauty, and Power into the Physical Plane.

The soul's radiance can shine through the personality, and the Hermit shows us that we can willingly let our ego dissolve into this Light. When this happens the vibration of our aura quickens as we respond to the encouragement of the Inner Self. When we listen and act on the prompting of the soul—which is unceasing—our consciousness expands and evolution continues. Jesus of Nazareth said, "Knock, and it shall be opened unto you." Or in other words, the Second Universal Law, the Law of Response.

The Hermit in a Reading

- Attainment of goal.
- Realization of purpose.
- Perseverance.
- Critical thinking blending with Intuition will light the way.
- Expansion of consciousness.
- Organizing thoughts for an organized environment.
- Providing service to others.
- Good advice.
- Purity of intention.
- Introspection.

REVERSED

- Overly critical.
- Obsessed with detail.
- Cold indifference.
- Not listening to inner guidance, or the guidance of a wise person.
- Misplaced trust.
- Ignorance.
- A need to organize thoughts.

Thoughts for Meditation on The Hermit

We are at a point now where meditation is starting to get more serious. Choose a particular time and place and be consistent so that your High Priestess knows that you are sincere. Ask for heightened receptivity. Candles, soft music, incense . . .

One of the most powerful meditations in the Major Arcana centers on the Hermit: When you are in need of spiritual guidance, or when you want guidance to help others, the Hermit is there to assist you. If you ever feel lonely or isolated, meditation on the Hermit will help you see the benefits of your uniqueness as a Being of Light. If the need to correctly analyze a situation arises, or if you want to stimulate your determination, especially to reach the top, meditation on the Hermit will help you.

With the Hermit several questions can arise from the meditation: How is my Inner Guidance trying to illuminate me? What can I do this week that will best help me be myself? How can I be of service?

Enter the inspirations received in your Tarot Journal. At this point in the journey you could also add any amendments to your Personal Mission Statement that were inspired by your work with The Hermit. What do I consider to be worthwhile enterprises? How can I best share my knowledge (even with a disagreeable person)? How is my sense of purpose doing?

Prayer

I see the flame in your open hand
and I reach for it.
But you stand so far up above me.
How can I overcome this illusion?
I know that between my heartbeats
you await my ascent.
For there you will embrace me in ecstatic union.

Absorb me in Thy Holy Presence,
into the Light of your Being,
where I can best be my Self in service to the Good.

For then I, too, am the Wayshower
holding my lamp aloft in the darkness,
free-flowing and secure in the solitude of my soul.

Chapter 13

X. The Wheel of Fortune
Involution and Evolution

Astrological Correspondence: The expansiveness of Jupiter.

Hebrew Letter: Kaph כ (the "closed hand," in the sense of grasping something).

The Inner Atmosphere: The Wheel inspires us to accept the changing cycles of life and to realize that all the circumstances of our personal experience are for our evolution. Understanding of the Wheel consciousness enables us to "see" into the inner workings of things.

Statement: "I trust in what happens to me—that it is for my good and the good of others. I accept the events and situations of my life as I know they are given to me to help in my education."

Quotation: "Every experience and condition is a useful experience, and these are either made as stumbling blocks or stepping-stones." (Edgar Cayce)

111

The Challenge: The ego gives into despair and blames difficult circumstances on "bad luck."

Visualization to the Tenth Portal, The Wheel of Fortune

Gray storm clouds appear above you,
and you marvel at the flashing, streaking lightning
across the blue sky . . .
You are in a forest at the edge of the Tenth Portal.
As you stand at an opening of trees
you notice an ancient one approaching.
He says in a resounding voice:
"I am the prophet Ezekiel,
and you
will behold living creatures,
behold one wheel upon the earth by the living creatures,
with his four faces . . .
and their appearance and their work was, as it were,
a wheel in the middle of a wheel . . .
Behold!"
Then at the crash of a lightning bolt above you,
in the gray storm clouds,
you see a huge fiery orange Wheel spinning and whirling—
at times a circle, at another moment a glowing orange spiral,
spinning in and out of itself.
Below the Wheel, to the right,
you see one of the creatures that the Prophet Ezekiel spoke of:
A lion speaks to you from the clouds:
"I am Fire, the active Power of God in the Universe."
Then directly above the Wheel, to the right,
you see an eagle rising from a cloud, exclaiming,
"I am Water, the flow of God's Infinite Love in the Universe."
To the left, above the fiery orange Wheel in the clouds,
you see a golden-haired angel:
"I am Air, God's Eternal Wisdom in the Universe."
Below the Wheel, to the left

in the gray storm clouds,
you see a bull.
"I am the Element Earth, God's creation in the Universe."
Then, suddenly, from a cloud,
a wavy electricity descends,
coiling around the left edge of the fiery orange wheel
in the form of a shimmering golden snake.
It says: "I am the descent of Involution,
the Life-power coalescing into matter."
On the underside of the Wheel, curling upwards,
you see the red jackal-headed god Anubis.
He looks at you with a golden eye shaped like a Yod flame.
He says, "I am you, evolving,
as my ears listen to the Voice of the Divine."
Your eyes gaze upwards
as you strain to hear a whispering voice in the distance . . .
"I ask questions," it says softly.
Then above the Wheel you see the most amazing of apparitions.
It is a blue Sphinx holding the Sword of Discernment.
It looks at you directly and says,
"I ask questions, and I must ask you this, brave Traveler:
Are you detached above the whirlings of the Wheel?"
As you stare at the Wheel confounded,
it begins to fade away.
Soon you are looking up into a clear blue sky . . .
The sun is out and you feel its warmth on your skin.
You feel enveloped in peace,
but aware that you have a lot to assimilate.
From what you have just seen,
you feel a sense of well-being,
but you are still a bit overwhelmed . . .
Allow these positive feelings to get stronger and stronger.
Regardless of the stress and tension that may surround your life,
you may now remain more at peace and more relaxed . . .
You are feeling refreshed and begin to come back
feeling alert and awake . . .
When you wish you may open your eyes.

General Atmosphere of the Tenth Portal, The Wheel of Fortune

Whirling. Expansive spiraling. Life gradually unfolds . . . through atoms, molecules, cells. From the microcosm to the macrocosm of spinning planets and vast galaxies, we see Infinity from both directions.

Behind this expression of Life through matter is Consciousness.

Consciousness descends into matter, and as It becomes refined, It ascends, only to continue into Infinity. This ascent-descent is the turn of the Wheel, involution and evolution.

In the Tenth Portal, we have the self-conscious Magician (1), with intent awareness, using the Power of Spirit (0). Ten is the number of cyclic change. Something begins, evolves, ends only to begin again.

Within the Wheel are the whirlings, and we are very much a part of the cyclic activity. However, we are really the Sphinx that sits atop the Wheel, above the whirlings, and like the Sphinx, we are a perplexing entity indeed.

The Inner Self, with the Sword of Discernment, is the embodiment of what the Buddhists call *detachment*. The Inner Self, the mystery of the Sphinx, working through the personality, is able to discern exactly where to expend the energy for the most good; nothing is wasted on trivia. It is colored blue to remind us of the subconscious waters of the High Priestess, guardian of the whirling energies within.

Within the turn of the Wheel are all the activities of Life: Happiness and horror, intelligence and ignorance, wealth and destitution, expansion and contraction, growth and disintegration.

If we enter the Observer mode, the Sphinx above the whirlings, then we can witness that all movement happens cyclically. Which in Tarot is the third Universal Law, the Law of Cycles. Beginning, middle, and end. Then, gaining experience, the pattern continues spiraling upwards to a higher level. We live within a vast ocean of Creative Energy, and as our self-conscious Magician focuses this Power, we gain an understanding of the Law (Kaph, the grasping hand)—and a benevolent turn of the Wheel.

If we move in harmony with the Law of Cycles then we experience well-being in our psyche, and the quality of our lives improves; if, however, we waste energy, and succumb negatively to challenges the Wheel offers, then our psyche experiences turbulence, and we forget that difficult circumstances are also subject to the Law of Cycles—and situations will change.

The ancients, realizing the complexity of this Law, illustrated the Wheel of Fortune rich in symbolism. In the four corners of the card are the four Fixed Signs of the zodiac: Lion (Leo), Eagle (Scorpio), Angel (Aquarius), and Bull (Taurus). They are stationary in spite of the turning cycles of the Wheel.

Leo ("I will!") is Fixed Fire, power gained through spiritual understanding and a passion for enlightenment; Scorpio ("I feel") is Fixed Water, Love flowing to spiritualize the emotions; Aquarius ("I know") is Fixed Air, Wisdom expanding to spiritualize the intellect; Taurus ("I have") is Fixed Earth, manifestation of Spirit as matter and the overcoming of excessive attachment.

The Wheel itself is highly symbolic. The right spoke is Sulphur, the alchemical symbol of Fire and action; the top spoke of the Wheel is the glyph for Mercury, the workings of mind; the left spoke is Salt, or inert matter; and finally at the bottom is the glyph for Water, Dissolution of the pattern to begin again.

In the outer circle of the Wheel are the Hebrew letters YOD-HEH-VAV-HEH, the Holy Name of The Most High, That which was, That which is, That which shall be. It is the One Reality, Consciousness expressing Itself as the Universe.

Also within the outer circle are the letters R-O-T-A (Wheel) and T-A-R-O (Law); if the two words are blended together, they spell TAROT—another way of saying within the cycles of Life are Laws; obey the Laws and experience the harmony of the universe.

Idea—Pattern—Process—Result

The Wheel of Fortune is a mandala of the Eternal Spiral of Creation. The circles of the Wheel illustrate this. 1) The center of the Wheel, the hub, is the Archetypal World, the realm of Idea. Here is Divine Consciousness of the Absolute, the eternal Spirit. It is the innermost nature of the Universal Conscious Energy. The enthusiasm and aspiration of Wands points to this center of Fire. 2) The first small circle is what the ancients called the Creative World, the world of Pattern. Here you choose what you need to get the job done. It is also the realm of Emotion, Imagination, Water, Cups. 3) The second circle is the Formative World, the world of Process. Here you go through blood, sweat, and tears in order to complete the project. It is also the realm of Mentality, Air, and Swords. 4) The outer circle is the Material World of Manifestation and the realm of Result. The senses, Earth, and Pentacles.

The yellow snake at the left of the Wheel depicts the serpent power of Teth descending; involution of the Radiant Energy. It is Light moving in matter, Spirit in the Physical Plane.

The red jackal-headed god Anubis is the evolution of human consciousness, reaching three-quarters of the way to heaven. The ears stick upward, a reference to Inner Hearing.

Jupiter, the astrological correspondence of the Wheel of Fortune, is considered by many astrologers as "the great Benefic," ruling thunder, lightning, storm clouds, and the nurturing quality of rain. The most massive of the planets, the Jupiter vibration is given the qualities of expansiveness and preservation. In psychological terms Jupiter is high spirits, faith, confidence, energy, and openness to the unknown. Jupiter says, "I trust in the turn of the Wheel, because Life offers such rich possibilities."

Jupiter is the Preserver—stability, tradition, equilibrium; tin is his metal. He stimulates aspiration, idealism, tolerance, understanding, vision; he also signifies prosperity and the abundance of Spirit.

The Jupiter Consciousness encourages thoughts like "There is abundance at every turn," "I am powerful and I create my Universe." "I live my life with a sense of freedom," "I expect beneficial opportunities to present themselves often."

Jupiter has a strong grasp of the Law of Cycles and understands how to solve problems regarding duality (i.e., mind and matter). He rules Sagittarius ("I perceive")—outgoing, optimistic, extroverted, independent, freedom-loving. Sagittarius seeks after the spiritual later in life and there gains a better perception about people, places, and things.

The Wheel of Fortune in a Reading

- Growth and expansion of thought.
- Confident expectation.
- Acceptance of circumstances; adapting to change.
- Movement.
- Understanding a situation better through observation.
- Enthusiasm for a project.
- Stability gained through aspiration, love, wisdom, and groundedness.
- Listening to Inner Voice.
- Beneficial circumstances or outcome.
- Generosity.

REVERSED

- Superstition.
- Relying on "luck."
- Not listening to the Inner Voice.
- Stagnation.
- Loving vibrations blocked.
- The project stalls.

- Materialistic thinking.
- Lack of ideas.
- Skepticism, cynicism, ennui.

Thoughts for Meditation on The Wheel of Fortune

A good time to meditate on Kaph, The Wheel of Fortune, is when you want to approach a difficult situation with detachment, when you want to develop a more positive attitude, or be more sensitive to opportunities offered. Swami Paramananda says: "Perchance misfortune's hammering hand strikes its cruel blow. Let it not harden thee. Again when fortune gives her sweet caress, Let it not make thee soft nor rob thee of thine aim."

Certain questions may arise: Am I a good "witness"? How do I handle life's changeable nature? What course am I taking to avoid hurtful, repetitious thoughts, words, and deeds? How can I best be "above the whirlings"? What do I need to "grasp"? Are there any current situations that I am reacting to with excessive emotion, disjointed thinking, and/or selfish attachment?

Prayer

Forgetting the Sphinx,
I am sucked into the whirlings—
waves of emotions,
my own and others.
But in faith I conjure
the image of Thy Mighty Hand
reaching down and pulling me up
to Thy light-filled bosom.

The rotation of the Wheel,
the grip of the Law—
I had better not forget!
For when I insist on blindness
ruled by instinct,
ego marching
my garment soon catches in the Wheel,
and I am dragged
into its jagged mechanisms.
When will I tire of the mangling?

Chapter 14

XI. Justice
What Ye Sow . . .

Astrological Correspondence: The refined balance of Libra.

Hebrew Letter: Lamed ל (meaning "ox-goad," that which prods the ox, Aleph, the Fool, along the path).

The Inner Atmosphere: A belief that we will be given all things needful. Understanding that the Law is always in operation, and if we obey, we will live a life in joyful accordance with that Law. In the Eleventh Portal the Consciousness directs right action.

Statement: "I will be educated in the Way through the circumstances of my life. I will live within the Law and go in peace. For I know that if I must stray off the path, I will be given pain to get me back on course. The choice is always mine."

Quotation: "What proceeds from you will return to you." (Confucius)

The Challenge: The ego refuses to learn from experience and continues to repeat error; emotions become icy.

Visualization to the Eleventh Portal, Justice

You are again standing before a huge temple.
Immediately you are struck by some differences from the Second Portal
that you visited long ago—
the Moon Temple of the High Priestess.

The Temple of Justice, the Eleventh Portal
where you now stand,
is more open to the golden-yellow sky,
airy, breezy,
with the power of the Life Breath.

In contrast, the Moon Temple seemed cool, blue,
and, perhaps,
hiding something.
The Temple of Justice, on the other hand,
is illuminated by fire rather than reflection.

However, when you enter the vastness
of the Temple of the Eleventh Portal,
you know that you are still in the presence of the subconscious.

The Empress has changed into the personage of Justice,
without blindfold—
She sits on her throne,
the central point between two pillars.

In her right hand of self-consciousness
she holds the mighty Sword of Discernment.
In her left subconscious hand,
she holds the golden scales of Cosmic Balance

Rather than the cool blue of the High Priestess,
Justice is dressed in the fiery red of the Magician
and the green of the Empress.

Through the purple curtains of enlightenment
you see the golden yellow of the Life-Breath surrounding her aura.

You approach her presence with great humility.
"I come to you, your grace,
to know what it is that thou must mete out to me."
Then, in a sonorous voice, she says,

"Put the contents of your Consciousness on the golden scales
and we shall see if the bowls must tip."
You are shocked at first . . .
and you shudder at the thought . . .

But before you can answer,
you are alone in the warm golden yellow of the Life-Breath.
You feel the power in the golden atmosphere
and deep within you . . .
you hear the voice of the Hermit.

"You are loved, my child," you hear him say,
"Even at a painful turn of the Wheel.
Never forget that your heart beats at its hub."
Still engulfed in the loving embrace of the Limitless Light,
you lose yourself for a few moments in the Holy Presence . . .
Feel the warmth, feel relaxed, feel at peace.
Now you may begin to open your eyes.

General Atmosphere of the Eleventh Portal, Justice

The modern cliché for it is "What goes around comes around." We can think of the Eleventh Portal as the Third Universal Law, the Law of Karma. Yogananda says, "Whatever energies he himself, wisely or unwisely, has set in motion must return to him as their starting point, like a circle inexorably completing itself."[1]

Justice is the center of the Major Arcana. To illustrate this put the Fool in the center top by himself, then in the first row below him put the next seven cards (the Magician to the Chariot, the Seven Principles of Consciousness); below that row place the next seven cards (Strength to Temperance, the Seven Universal Laws); and finally in the third row, put the last seven cards (Devil to the World, the Seven Levels of Spiritual

Unfoldment). You will then notice that karma (Lamed, the power of the Universal Law that "goads" Aleph, the Fool, along the path) at number eleven is in the very center at the hub of the Wheel of Tarot. Justice is the balance that keeps the flow of energies in sync.

Earlier in the Tenth Portal we encountered Jupiter's attitude toward the turn of the Wheel. In modern terms, Jupiter "keeps the faith." Cosmic Justice ensures that we can trust in the unfailing action of the Law (karma comes from the Sanskrit verb, *kri*, to do). It is up to us to make proper use of this Law because in the Eleventh Portal we learn that we have to answer for our actions.

In the atmosphere of Justice we are face to face with the Law of Cause and Effect. Can we understand the idea that if we focus our thoughts on something, that eventually it will work its way out into the circumstances of our life?

At your job you are bombarded with phone calls. Angry supervisors demand that you explain why the files are incomplete, though these files belong to someone else. You are so busy you forgot to go to the store and a coworker is upset because there's no coffee or milk in the office—your responsibility this week . . .

You could succumb to this onslaught and continue your days in a place electric with anxiety. Or you could dwell on images of escape . . . You see yourself filling out an application for another job, going to an interview, sitting in a new office. The point is, you set the Wheel in motion and prepare yourself for action.

The secret of the Eleventh Portal is to enter a state of creative mind, to imagine yourself in the most wonderful circumstances possible, to really see yourself in an attitude of delight. Dwell on *this*.

The Law of Cause and Effect teaches us that it is folly to focus on future scenes of misery. As for attitude, conjure up the determination to be the best you can be. Why not? Scenes of failure not only drain energy, but they set the stage for a very bleak future scenario. And as the Law of Cause and Effect moves to its inevitable conclusion, you will eventually learn that what you sow, you will reap. You can plant bulbs and get lilies, or you are free to sow seeds that will sprout nettles.

As humans we were given the freedom to choose, and according to the sureness of our thought and the correctness of our decision, we experience contentment or chaos, enlightenment or delusion. We must take what we learned from the Emperor's Fourth Portal, Reason, and combine it with the Discernment of the Lovers' Fifth Portal.

What we think about after experience, what we concentrate on, gets the Wheel of Karma moving. That's why it is very important to be clear about where we direct our interest.

We are given the power to create for ourselves a paradise—or a chamber of horrors. If we identify solely with our body, for example, we set ourselves up for selfishness, which leads to pain. It is only through right action and heightened awareness of our true Self that we can hope to offset any unhappy turn of the Wheel.

The Universal Law of Equilibrium is well illustrated in the seventh sign of the zodiac, Libra, Cardinal Air (potent intellect). She is symbolized by the Scales and says, "I balance." Libra is equilibrium, harmony, and adjustment. Ruled by Venus, she is also refinement (the Sword of Justice's elimination of waste), love of beauty, culture, aesthetics; artistic and charming. Libra functions in an atmosphere of serenity and acts to maintain and protect her inner peace.

Justice in a Reading

- Harmony and equilibrium.
- Fair and balanced outcome.
- Effort pays off.
- Making a correct choice using discernment.
- Poise is called for.
- Prioritizing; elimination of nonessentials.
- Be aware of what you wish for.
- Karma.
- Responsiveness, affection, harmonious relationship.
- A premium on values.

REVERSED

- Wrong choice.
- Injustice; unfair outcome.
- Cluttered thoughts.
- Sloppiness.
- Mistrust.

Thoughts for Meditation on Justice

A good time to meditate on Justice is when you find yourself afraid to take a step, when you feel you must act. Meditation on Justice, Lamed, can also help you to be clearer about the karma you need to face. Some other possible thoughts for meditation are:

Where have I missed the mark? What must I do to redirect my energies in beneficial directions? How can I gain a better understanding of the inharmonious elements of my life? In my recent decision-making have I always taken personal responsibility for the consequences of my actions? Am I comfortable in my faith that all will work out for the good?

Enter your impressions in the Tarot Journal.

Prayer

The pivot on which everything turns,
and the Sword hanging over all our heads, yet,
by a thread, we are in control . . .
Free to hack away at our stability
until we teeter on the very edge of sanity.

Free to crush our neighbor and sneak away
as he lies bleeding in the gutter.
Free to poison the body
until it cries out in the agony of disease.

And, yet, in His mercy, we are free
to become angels.
Burdens and blessings,
the hazards of choice.

Notes

1. Yogananda, Paramahansa, *The Divine Romance.* (Los Angeles, Calif.: Self-Realization Fellowship, 1987).

Chapter 15

XII. The Hanged Man
The Point of View Shifts

Alchemical Element: Water.

Astrological Correspondence: Neptune, where the ego loses its dominance and the gaze turns outward.

Hebrew Letter: Mem מ (meaning "water," the flow of the Cosmic Substance in and through us).

The Inner Atmosphere: Firm in spiritual conviction, the Consciousness is more awake now. One ponders the possibilities of seeking first the Kingdom . . . that is, seeing God at work, both inwardly and outwardly. The more we see the flow of the Divine, the more consciously we participate with God in creating a paradise on Earth.

Statement: " . . . At this stage I am more steadfast in pursuit of the Examined Life; the physical self is less demanding on my attention, which, at this point in the journey, means that I look at the world from an entirely new perspective. I am more and more conscious of the Mind of God as It permeates my being."

Quotation: "Mind is matter in solution. Matter is mind in form." (Phineas Quimby)

The Challenge: The ego experiences a drifting, unmoored lack of direction; absorption in the small self.

Visualization to the Twelfth Portal, The Hanged Man

You are again in a forest, surrounded by a huge canopy of trees.
You walk along creeks where the grass and mosses
grow all the way down to the gently streaming waters.
You toss a pebble into a pool of emerald water
and become transfixed as the ripples form outward.

When you look up you behold a most amazing sight.
A being, with a glowing face,
is hanging upside down, his left ankle tied to a tree
in the shape of the last letter of the Hebrew alphabet, Tav.
He wears red pants with his left leg crossed behind his right.
His top is blue, and both arms are behind his back.
His head hangs between the green grassy banks of a river
where only invisible "water" flows.
Your first instinct is to help him down
from his seemingly painful position on the tree.
But even as he is looking at you upside down,
you are immediately taken in by the splendor
of his wide open eyes and the golden aura around his head.

"Fear not, young Pilgrim," he says as you approach.
"I am relaxing my thought processes . . .
and I am in a spiritual reverie . . . that you, too, should experience.
It is a kind of contemplation that helps you
on your Path of Awakening."
You stop and look at his glowing countenance,
tipping your head to the left a little
in order to get a better look at him.

He speaks to you again,
"I am clothed in the garment of God's Eternal Love
and I am protected.
I fall asleep . . . filled with . . . comforting Peace,
 and I know that everywhere I go
I shall always be bathed in the Light.
My seemingly endless nights of anguish fade
as I surrender myself to the Holy Presence."

As the personage of the Hanged Man
begins to fade from view
you feel strengthened in your faith
that you have been guided and guarded in your long journey.
As you awaken from the dream and reenter your world,
you feel a deep sense of peace
and a heightened sense of colors and light . . .

General Atmosphere of the Twelfth Portal, The Hanged Man

Why is this personage hanging upside down? Our immediate reaction might be—torture, strangulation, death. Wasn't St. Paul crucified upside down? What about Mussolini? Death by blood flooding the brain. Asphyxiation. Lack of breath.

The personage of the Twelfth Portal is hanging by his ankle, and if we look at the expression on his face, we see something mystical, almost beatific. What is really being hung in the Twelfth Portal are the remnants of ego-satisfaction, of selfishness. Me-centered thinking is subordinated. The Twelfth Portal is the realm where we sacrifice our self-preoccupied desire. It is in this position we see that all traces of arrogance have fled.

The world tells us that we must seek personal profit at all costs, and resign ourselves to a life of pain and combat.

The world encourages us to wallow in self-absorption. In the Twelfth Portal we are asked to sacrifice our demanding, ego-centered thinking. In addition we need to sacrifice the desire to create a phony persona, a bloated image of ourselves manufactured for the outside world. This kind of sacrifice goes against the normal thinking and behavior of the human ego.

When we think in terms of sacrifice and concern for others, we are looking at the Physical Plane from a radically new perspective. Unlike many around us, those of us on the path have come to accept certain Truths that we have encountered in the various Portals we have visited.

Can we see the Light of God's Love shining forth in all things? The Hanged Man does. From his perspective, he adopts a more subtle, spiritual point of view that can strengthen our faith in the Intangible as well, if we, too, can adopt it. Our faith will grow with steadfastness, and we will understand that through God's Light we are in touch with all Wisdom, all Beauty, all Goodness. Vast, heavenly—of unthinkable form—the Light emanates from our very Being. The sacred vibration of Love is infinitely distant and yet Omnipresent, hidden in the tabernacle of the heart.

Can we be confident . . . radiant . . . aware, knowing that we do not walk alone, that Spirit is deathless, immortal? This experience of Spirit is what some call Transcendental.

Emerson says, "God is the most elevated conception of character that can be formed in the mind." It is the individual's own soul carried out to perfection. That's why we are told to perceive our own humanness with reverence and awe. Emerson emphasizes that there is a power in the mind greater than the mind. In Transcendental Thought—a form of meditation—is the complete suspension of the intellect.

The Hanged Man is a pictorial representation of suspended mind. Intention is crucial to staying on the path, but if all the activities of the mind can be "suspended," then we enter into a unique act of communication with the Universal Consciousness.

One of the most transcendental thoughts of the Bible comes in Psalm 46: "Be still and know that I am God: I will be exalted among the heathen, I will be exalted in the earth." Transcendentalism sees the Suspended Mind as a point where we allow the Universal Consciousness, the loving intelligence of the Limitless Light, to flow through our own being. It is an act of purification.

If you remember, Aleph was not only the planet Uranus, but also the element Air. The Hanged Man, Mem, is the element Water (as well as the planet Neptune). Water equals emotion, feelings, aesthetic response, appreciation of beauty, receptivity, the power to reflect, memory, the vast potential of the Subconscious, and the infinite underlying substance of the manifested. At the heart of Transcendentalism, this is the kind of Water that Quimby meant. ("Mind is matter in solution—Matter is mind in form.")

Our essential Nature evades words, but the ancients saw us as Spirit individualized within the essential unity of everything—pure Consciousness experiencing what the Physical Plane has to offer. Emerson says, "We are symbols, and inhabit symbols." We are fully alive in the present. We are cognizant of our power to make discoveries, to understand the operation of general causes, and observe general laws.

Emerson said that the world's eye is "unenquiring," but when we are in the state of mind of the Hanged Man, then we walk in the midst of wonders. Herschel, an early spokesman for naturalist philosophy, a primary element of Transcendentalism, said it is "To hope all things impossible, to believe all things not unreasonable." Transcendentalism concentrates on principles over phenomena, but still sees outward phenomena as a source of delight, and believes perfection at the center of everything.

The mind uses Reason to discover Truth; it uses Understanding to see the relation of things to one another, to perceive and comprehend the nature and significance of something. In the atmosphere of the Hanged Man, we are totally focused on the one Reality, and our consciousness becomes altered and expanded.

In the Twelfth Portal we are in an inner state of Superconscious experience, or as the rishis (the ancient sages of India) put it—*samadhi*, a state beyond reason, a state of perfect concentration, where we learn that knowledge is power—where the mind itself eventually becomes the object of perfect concentration.

Another powerful Transcendentalist quotation comes from none other than St. Paul (in Romans 12:2) when he said, "And be not conformed to this world: but be ye transformed by the renewing of your mind—that ye may prove what is that good, and acceptable, and perfect, will of God."

Within the inner realm of Transcendental experience the Consciousness of the Hanged Man is concerned, and focused on, direction of movement in his life. Ethics, morality, attitude, virtue—Truth. He is raising his vibration: Notice the halo around the personage's head. He is in a state of veneration, prayerfulness. He is filled with confident expectation, and he understands the virtue of striving toward excellence. He is steadfast.

In the Examined Life, the Hanged Man insists that character is vital, and there is purpose in the thrust of his energy. He is filled with awe at the complex beauty of the manifested universe. And he is equally in awe of its simplicity. He sees God in everything; he is in a sense a pantheist, and he observes life as an ongoing learning process heading toward enlightenment.

The Hanged Man understands that life is infinite change, and yet at the same time, governed by fixed laws. Emerson says, "We are what we know." We listen to our own intuitions, we trust in our own judgment. We make subtle distinctions. After Transcendental Thought, we are less concerned with the trivial, and we trust in a higher power.

As the Hanged Man we hang there, suspended, and we are purified by our thoughts. We are in a kind of spiritual hibernation, viewing life from an altered, transcendental state. We experience an alteration in values, a change in priorities—our belief system is shaken.

The Law of the Twelfth Portal is the Law of Reversal: Reversal of thought, point of view, attitude. When Truth is realized—self-surrender follows naturally. We allow the

Will of the Inner Self to take over our rigid thinking so that eventually we will become more open to the Guidance of the Holy Presence within.

It's a freely chosen act—submission of the personal consciousness to the direction of the Universal Mind. Surrender. Sacrifice. Giving up something in order to receive something of greater value.

The mind controls the body and the mental vibrations of the Life Breath move more rapidly through the personal atmosphere. As we learned from the Eleventh Portal, your current condition as well as your emotional, mental, and physical being are influenced by what you focus on. The ancients tell us that concentrating on oneness, on the unity and goodness of things, will change your body and environment for the better.

From an astrological perspective, the suspended mind of the Hanged Man is represented in the zodiac by the planet Neptune. Neptune is feelings, appreciation of the mysterious, and reactions beyond the intellectual response. Neptune is the mystical vibration that we surrender to, a connection to the meaning of surrender in the Hanged Man. Neptune is a planet that travels in the outer boundaries of the solar system, the outer dimension. Expanding consciousness; imagination: Neptune is the compulsion to move beyond one's imagined limitations.

We become more in touch with subtleties, the barely perceptible Reality of things. The Neptune mode of Consciousness activates the personal atmosphere with thoughts transcendental: That knowledge of Reality is derived from intuitive sources—reaching beyond—rather than from objective experience.

Neptune knocks the ego off center stage. The egocentric point of view shifts. The lines between self-consciousness and subconsciousness blur, and we find ourselves living a more intuitive existence. We become more aware of Spirit operating in our lives. The shortcomings of constant self-gratification become vividly clear. We lose interest in the trivial, and direct our energies toward more consciously blissful activities.

As Water, Neptune is sensitive, receptive, and reflective. Neptune is mystery and he rules the night—sleep, dreams, and the ethereal. Neptune is also concerned with, and uses, the medium of imagery to bring forth the message. In the atmosphere of the Hanged Man, we contemplate the hidden meaning.

The Hanged Man in a Reading

- A call for sacrifice.
- Surrender to a Higher Power.
- A reversal of attitude, opinion or perspective.

- Priorities change; more other-oriented.
- Firm resolve called for.
- Circumspection.
- Selflessness.
- A time to give something up.
- An act of purification.
- Striving toward excellence.
- A need to stabilize the thoughts.

REVERSED

- Biased opinion.
- Rigid thinking.
- Arrogance.
- A self-centered, materialistic outlook.
- Scornfulness.

Thoughts for Meditation on The Hanged Man

We meditate on the Hanged Man when we want to expand our consciousness, when we are feeling out of touch with the unity of all things, when we are in need of a Transcendental experience.

It is also beneficial to meditate on the Hanged Man when we feel that we need to stabilize our thoughts in the middle of tremendous creative output, or when we feel stuck in a particular point of view that limits our freedom.

If you want to reverse your attitude toward something, such as the perception of yourself as a natural failure in some endeavor like gardening, math, raising children—meditate on the Hanged Man.

If you want to be clear about a sacrifice you are about to make, meditation on the Hanged Man can raise some pertinent questions like: Will the person really benefit from what I am about to do? Why am I resistant to giving up this particular thing?

Other possible thoughts for meditation on the Hanged Man: What recent event(s) have turned my world upside down? Where has a firmness of resolution been of significant help? What have I given up lately that has been replaced by something more beneficial to the well-being of my life? Where have I subordinated my willfulness for a greater sensitivity to another's feelings?

Write your impressions in the Tarot Journal.

Prayer

Stillness,
the pendulum at rest:
I am weary of the bombardments.
Tranquil,
I look at the world upside down
from the peephole in my cocoon.

I hang my hopes on stars
and I look ahead to the ancient ways.
The primordial rivers course through me
as I silently witness the change . . .

Hand me the mirror.

Chapter 16

XIII. Death
Growth and Transition

Astrological Correspondence: The depth and intensity of Scorpio.

Hebrew Letter: Nun ‎נ‎ (meaning "fish" as a noun, and as a verb, "to grow").

The Inner Atmosphere: The imagination is used positively to change the direction of our lives. The old ways of thinking die. The emotional aura is less ego-driven and the consciousness experiences a newness, a reinvented persona.

Statement: "Although I still live in the Physical Plane, I am transforming into a new Being—and I revel in this process of rebirth."

Quotation: "I died as a mineral and became a plant, I died as plant and rose to animal, I died as animal and I was Man. Why should I fear? . . . " (Rumi, *The Ascending Soul*)

The Challenge: The ego refuses to advance and prefers to stagnate.

133

Visualization to the Thirteenth Portal, Death

Move your shoulders a bit
and begin to let go of the tensions . . .
tensions in your neck, your back . . .
Relax your shoulders.
Even the muscles of your face, totally unwind . . .
Feel yourself begin to relax . . .
from the tense experiences of the past week . . .
knowing now that . . . this stress . . .
is from the past . . . remote . . .
remote from you now . . .

Think about Emerson's words,
"Why should we grope among the dry bones of the past?
The sun shines today also."
And in this relaxed state you are floating . . .
peaceful . . . knowing that you are entering
closer and closer . . . to your moment . . .
Feel the tension begin to dissipate . . .
You are feeling more and more comfortable, relax.
Let go of any remaining stress from your week.

Let go . . . of the anxiety . . .
Let go of all the confusion . . .
Now begin to feel warm and content, safe and warm.
Feel warm . . . in your cocoon . . . so warmly conceived . . .
You are at peace here, calm, content . . . and relaxed.
Now notice how much more . . . present you are.
Relaxed . . . conscious and confident,
secure . . . in your own Inner Light . . .
You are secure in the feeling that we are Spirit first . . .
made of love and light . . .
Confident in the vibrancy of our Real Self . . .
Conscious that we are expanding . . .
So much so that you can feel
the cocoon of limitation

tearing at the seams.
You are emerging . . .
Breathe deeply . . .
and on the exhale . . . feel your awareness . . . widen.
Although you are conscious of your Inner Light,
glowing, vital Spirit—
you realize that as you emerge . . .
you are surrounded by darkness . . .
You are alone . . . in the silence . . .
but through the consciousness of your true spiritual nature,
you remember what you learned in the first Portal . . .
and remember that underneath . . .
you are the Magician . . . Observing . . . Silent.
In the distance, you hear the rush of water . . .
a river . . .

And you know that the infinite potential of the High Priestess
is forever near . . .
You follow the sound . . . and hear a waterfall,
remembering the Venusian garden of the Third Portal, the Empress,
and the vibration of creativity . . .
Ahead you notice the light of a sun encroaching on the darkness,
turning the sky red.
You remember the steadiness of the Emperor—
and the discipline to continue . . .
You notice that the ground at your feet
is a rich black loam.
And you are struck by the fresh fragrances.
You also notice the fragrance of rose in the air.
Then, suddenly, you hear a swooshing sound—
Swooooosh!

As the fiery red of the light gets brighter,
you realize that you are at the threshold of the Thirteenth Portal
—the Portal of Death.
And you behold a startling sight . . .
Before you,
you see a glowing white skeleton with a scythe,
cutting through a black field.

Swoooooosh!
You notice two hands reaching
upwards from the black loam.
You then see a foot and another hand.
Also growing up from the ground to the left
you see the head of a blonde woman;
and on the right,
you see growing up from the loam,
a man's head with a golden crown.
The skeleton is walking toward a bush with a huge white rose.
He walks before a river flowing to the rising sun.
A glowing white seed travels in the red sky above you.
Then you notice that the bones of the skeleton
appear almost inside out.
Reversed.

The skeleton then turns his head toward you,
and smiling, says,
"Welcome to the harvest . . .
You've done well to come this far, dear Pilgrim.
You may step along now . . . "
Shuddering you say,
"I . . . I'd rather not . . . thank you."
Then with an even bigger grin he says,
"Don't always believe appearances, my friend.
You never get far around here if you do."
"But . . . I'm not ready to . . . to—"
"To what?"
"To . . . d-die."

"Of course you are—
but the question is, little Pilgrim,
what do you mean by . . . 'die'?"
He begins laughing merrily,
and as he walks away toward the sun,
You think to yourself,
"I wonder why they call him grim . . . ?"
You are actually feeling soothed by his distant laughter

and realize that you have nothing to fear of the unknown

as long as you remember who you are . . .

And after you think about that for a bit . . .

you may begin to come back into the room . . .

feeling refreshed . . . relaxed . . . aware . . .

General Atmosphere of the Thirteenth Portal, Death

At first, as we enter the Thirteenth Portal, we may expect to see a skeleton moving across a field swinging a scythe in a grisly reaping, a place where the living meet their end. The Thirteenth Portal, however, in reality, is the most misunderstood of all the cards—thanks to gypsy fortunetellers who labeled (we should say libeled) the Death card as signifying physical death in the life of the seeker! This is, of course, simplistic and inaccurate.

The ancients, as usual, have hidden meanings operating beneath the first impression you may receive from their imagery.

In the ground, the bones of the skeleton survive for a time after the flesh disintegrates. However, the ancients do want to give you an impression of inevitability, and considering the exactness of the laws so far, the Law of the Thirteenth Portal is no exception. Here they are telling us that, inevitably, as situations, attitudes, priorities, and accumulations age, new ones will evolve and take their place. In other words, things change. But for our purposes on the path, what changes is our growth.

The Hebrew letter *Nun* as a verb means "sprouting" or "growth," and as our consciousness expands, we know that this outward movement is one of the most important aspects of our spiritual, emotional, mental, and physical well-being. The growth we experience on the path, the knowledge we gather, is something we can take with us. The lessons we have learned open us to a special awareness of the Power of the Life Force.

The letter *Nun* as a noun means "fish," in the sense that fish produce in enormous numbers, symbolic of the fertile powers of growth and reproduction. And, of course, fish live in "water."

On the spiritual path we are moving from unawareness to Transcendent Consciousness. As we learned from the Twelfth Portal, our growth takes the form of a shift in focus, a shift in point of view. We are the spiritual center of our universe, and as such, the creator of what happens in this universe. When we realize this, our growth also takes the form of careful thought (Magician), careful speech (Chariot), and careful action (Justice).

In our life we also produce thoughts, words, and actions that make use of the limitless potential of the High Priestess. With the Law of Reversal we saw that we should look at the world in new ways even though it goes against the grain of the status quo. Through examination of the contents of our consciousness, our garden will flower, a new creative, emotional Self will "sprout" up.

We must truly believe that we are Spirit first and manifest this thought throughout our day. We must feel that we are intimately connected with the Absolute, and that when we walk in the Light of Its Loving Guidance, we are the triumphant Charioteer, a personality integrated with Spirit.

In the atmosphere of the Thirteenth Portal we make use of imagery to change the pattern of our thinking so that our lives will change for the better. If you have fear about talking in front of a group, for example, form an image of yourself enthralling the crowd with your presentation, words, and ideas. You see yourself powerfully in control of yourself and events, in command of the atmosphere of your universe. It simply behooves us to be as positively imaginative as possible; it is at the essence of our nature.

A good subject for your Journal is to analyze the transition of your point of view before you began the journey and now. In doing so you will get an idea of what the ancients meant by the death principle. Your old self, your old way of thinking, dies in the consciousness of the Thirteenth Portal. After you have been in the cocoon of the Transcendental Consciousness of Mem, the "Water" of the Hanged Man, your thoughts will change, your mental atmosphere will take on a new vision; and as we will see in the Eighteenth Portal, the Moon, certain aspects of our physical self will die, and we will experience a kind of rebirth even as we still live in the Earth Plane.

In order for us to progress on the Path to Awareness, all obstacles to our purification must also pass away. We are in the midst of the Thirteenth Portal, and we are in the midst of a Law. The urge toward liberation is an inherent human longing. Here we know that we must move beyond the limitations we have imagined for ourselves, consciously dissolving the barriers to growth. We know we can do it because we are not the vehicle we inhabit. Rather, we are a Divine Essence evolving. We are changing, and if we are wise, we are consciously bringing about changes for our well-being and the well-being of others.

As we become less automatic and more aware, we realize that we are the unfoldment of an awe-inspiring Energy. And we know that our movement is a passing from one stage to another, eternally. For this is the Law of the Thirteenth Portal, The Law of Transformation. We are always moving upward and onward. Though we are free to imagine that we are at an impasse, the reality is we are always changing.

Not only must the Thirteenth Portal contend with the misunderstandings of the Death card, but it also must contend with the popular misunderstandings of Scorpio—

sex crazed, lurking in the shadows, with stinger upraised. Although Scorpio rules the House of Death in the zodiac (i.e., the acorn gives up its life so that the oak may be born), the Scorpion can also be viewed in terms of one of its finest qualities: Preciseness.

Of all the signs, Scorpio is a consciousness which expresses its inner realm accurately in the outer realm. Although Scorpio is highly introverted, and much lies below the surface, these expressions are not frequent. "Still waters run deep." That is because Scorpio truly understands her feelings. Scorpio is a feminine, receptive, Fixed Water sign, and says, with confidence—"I create." Of course, Scorpio is sensual. In fact, it rules the organs of regeneration.

If Scorpio can keep her strong personality under control, she can command tremendous inner power. Scorpio people possess the potential for enlightened leadership. On the low end, the symbol for Scorpio is the scorpion. Scorpio can seek revenge for a perceived wrongdoing like no other, and the animal energy can rage within the personality.

The second symbol for Scorpio is the Eagle (remember the Wheel of Fortune) soaring to the heights of spiritual awareness. The third symbol for Scorpio is the Phoenix. Here is Scorpio as the old self dying and eventually rising from the ashes to become an angelic being—far removed from the promiscuous animal of popular misconception.

Scorpio is ruled by Mars as well as the planet Pluto. We will study Pluto in depth in the Twentieth Portal, Judgment. But for now, Pluto is the ruler of Scorpio; think of the god of the underworld in Greek mythology. Pluto dredges things up from the depths, brings them to the surface, and kills off any poisoned unconscious motivations that stand in the way of enlightenment and growth—the Phoenix rising to the sun. It's like making chicken soup: You skim off the fatty foam until the liquid is pure.

Scorpio is also ruled by Mars—and we know there is great power and aggressiveness as in fiery Aries, which Mars also rules (symbolized by the red sky). The difference is that in Scorpio, a Water sign, the activity is in the *emotions*.

Finally, Death can signify a rebirth of the body. Later, when we must discard this physical vehicle, the ancients believe we will return in another body in another time to learn the lessons we missed in this current life. Tarot comes to us in an effort to help us learn as many of those lessons as possible right now.

Death in a Reading

- Transformation of the personality.
- Beginning over; change.
- Renewed hope.
- Discarding old ideas and ways of thinking.

- Old, overwrought emotions dissolve.
- Movement.
- Flexibility.
- Pretensions fade into the background.
- New alignments.

REVERSED

- Afraid to grow.
- Clinging to old ways that have outworn their usefulness.
- Fear of the unknown.
- Stagnation.

Thoughts for Meditation on Death

Are you stuck in a rut? Not moving with the natural flow of things? Perhaps you feel that the limitations you've put on yourself are starting to become a burden. Death, the Thirteenth Portal, is the card to get you moving again. Nun is concerned with your rebirth, your emergence from the cocoon. Are you afraid of the dark? Death shows us that the unknown has an unlimited potential for wonder. Death can also be meditated upon should you have to deal with a great loss in your life, like the actual passing of a loved one.

We move on in our life—or we move on into another dimension. Only our grief-stricken thoughts imagine stagnation, emptiness. Energy is neither created nor destroyed. And at the heart of our nature we are Divine Energy.

Other questions you might ask yourself in the Thirteenth Portal are: Are my inner thoughts reflected in the outer? Or, where in my life can I best direct my powers of imagination? What outmoded attitudes, activities, and/or things are constricting the flow of Spirit in my life? Since I have been on the path, what new insights have added to my growth? These are a few questions that reflect change that exists within the Law of Transformation.

Prayer

I feel the blade of the scythe
slice
through my cocoon.

Oh, the sting of liberation!
Resistance only makes the blade cut

more savagely.
I hang there quietly and observe.

Soon I rise with the river waters to the sky
and my Soul descends in the rain
clear and sparkling—again.

This time, however,
I carved the inlets
as I listened
to the Voice of the Hierophant
whispering in my ear.

Wanna see my garden now?

Chapter 17

XIV. Temperance
Testing the Waters

Astrological Correspondence: The zest and optimism of Sagittarius.

Hebrew Letter: Samech ס (meaning "tent peg," something that props up the dwelling).

The Inner Atmosphere: We test and are tested. As we understand, we break fewer Laws, and are generally more confident now that we have reached the Fourteenth Portal. We're better able to bring into practice what we have assimilated so far. From this point on, we rely less on theory and more on consciously living the lesson of the particular Portal. And because of our new awareness of Universal Law, by the time we have reached this final one, we are also more sensitive to cues and hints. And we further understand that this final Law brings with it impending trials.

Statement: "I will put theory into practice as I bring experimentation into my approach to life."

Quotation: "Trust, but verify." (President Ronald W. Reagan)

The Challenge: The ego gets caught up in analysis; blindly accepts suppositions without using the theories in practical ways.

Visualization to the Fourteenth Portal, Temperance

From your encounter with the intensity of the Thirteenth Portal,
you find yourself feeling a sense of increasing delight
as you walk toward an expanding sky,
a sky glistening like gold metal.
As you approach the Fourteenth Portal
you also see a brilliantly shimmering rainbow in this golden sky
with a color prism like the inside of an abalone shell.
Your heartbeat quickens as you feel the ascending vibrations
affecting your personal atmosphere.
Again you realize how far you have traveled,
wondering if you can absorb it all.
Somehow, though, you know that you are always being guided,
given strength,
and perhaps even recognized,
in some ethereal way,
for your efforts.
At that thought
you notice up ahead
a golden crown shining in the sky over two mountain peaks.
You are immediately filled with a sense of achievement,
and of humbled awe.
But nothing prepares you for the incredible sight you now behold—
it is the most glorious of angelic beings,
the golden-haired Archangel Michael,
luminous and astounding in his beauty.
His wings are fiery red
and he has a solar disk emblazoned on his forehead, his Third Eye.
He is pouring the water from a pitcher onto the head of a lion.

In his left hand he holds a torch.

Behind him we see the yellow Path of the Life-breath

winding up into the blue mountains behind him.

At the sight, you can only drop to your knees—in swooning adoration.

Michael is dipping his right foot in a pool,

while his left foot rests on stones at the water's edge.

Then in a voice both tender and commanding,

he speaks to you.

"I radiate the light of love unto you, O Traveler,

take sustenance from my holy vibrations."

You remain silent as waves of light and love infuse your being.

Then with a smile that could melt your heart,

he says, "Surrender to me your personality, your mind, and your heart

so that I may make you my vessel.

Give me your negativity, your fears, your petty misperceptions,

and cling to me in faith and anticipation."

"But I am so unworthy, my lord," you say, humbly.

"Rise and rejoice, good Pilgrim,

for I am already in residence in the sanctuary of thy heart."

Then you watch him slowly fade.

You are left with a glowing translucent rainbow . . .

and you recognize it as a symbol of attainment.

Feeling secure, you begin to open your eyes . . .

General Atmosphere of the Fourteenth Portal, Temperance

Welcome to the Fourteenth Portal, the glorious ending of the Universal Laws, where we learn that no matter what, as we proceed on the path toward freedom, we are always receiving guidance from within, we are always protected and supported. In fact, the Hebrew letter of the Fourteenth Portal, Temperance, is called *Samech*, the tent peg. This is a reference to the "good news" of God's infinite caring and support for all creation.

One of the secrets of the Fourteenth Portal has to do with the idea of opposites. We are constantly guided by our Inner Self, and nudged to continue increasing our awareness, even though some of the exposure may be unpleasant to encounter. One thing that Tarot has encouraged us to realize is the fact that in order for us to advance, we must take the Examined Life seriously—and yet with a light heart.

In the atmosphere of Tarot we are often presented with polarities. The angel is pouring Water with his right hand and holding Fire with his left. Right to left, left to right. Subconscious to self-conscious. Like the angel, it is up to us to poise ourselves in the middle of the particular continuum. For example, although we must not accept only the outer expression and delve deeply into the complexities that come our way, we must also have a deep appreciation for the simplicity of life as well.

Serious—light-hearted. Complex—simple. Light—dark. Particle—wave. Poised in the center, we are the balance between opposites, and we observe all. At some point in the journey, when we live more in the present moment, it will become quite natural to become detached from energy-draining situations, "above the whirlings." To be in the world, but not of it.

Although we need to keep our thoughts moving in a positive direction, we must never take our blessings for granted, and not get caught up in unbridled, obsessive pleasure for pleasure's sake. Otherwise, when the Wheel turns, the pain will be more severe.

Again the admonition to remain conscious to our inner atmosphere and our outer environment is always operative. From that vantage point, we make observations and draw conclusions about Reality. We then stay balanced in the center by our own lights, like the angel's position between Water and Fire.

Freud saw human nature as hopelessly dominated by instinct—with one exception. He believed the highest expression of the human psyche was the ability of the integrated personality to take the energy of the libido and transform it into artistic expression. He called it *sublimation*.

On the path we try to do something similar, only we call it spiritual sublimation. We take a difficult situation, and through conscious attention, transmute it into an opportunity for growth. To transmute: from the Latin "from one to another." To change from one form, nature, or substance to another.

What do we change? For one thing, our point of view. Self-consciousness affecting the subconscious, and vice versa. Fire on Water; Water on Fire. Enthusiasm and reflection, activity and receptivity.

In the Fourteenth Portal we are constantly being tested. In fact, throughout this interaction of Fire on Water and Water on Fire, the ancients express its dynamics in a double pun: Our "metal" is being "tempered" along with our "mettle." That's what they mean by "Temperance" (not specifically abstaining from alcohol).

Our Great Work on the Path of Return strengthens our mettle—that is, our courage and fortitude. By the time we have reached the Fourteenth Portal we have become a bit more sophisticated, more conscious of our reactions to people and situations; we are more aware of our power to organize our universe. For purposes of the Fourteenth Portal, we are learning more about what works for us. What works. The dominant symbol of this atmosphere is the angel, who is the Holy Guardian Angel, the Angel of the Sun, Michael. The idea is that he is here to help us, for his name means "Strength of God." On his collar he wears the Tetagrammaton (Yod-Heh-Vav-Heh, the Holy Name of God, I AM THAT I AM) to remind us of his divine power as our Inner Self. Over his Third Eye chakra he wears a symbol of the Sun, a symbol of individuality and self-expression. The circle is the infinite manifestation of the Most High; the dot in the center is the divine Essence within everything.

We are evolving as this Essence unfolds in our lives—and because we are giving up our personal willpower more and more to divine guidance. The question is: How willing are we to go along with the sacred prodding?

The seven-pointed star over the Angel's heart chakra intimates the mingling of the creative self (Empress) with the intellectual self (Emperor) in order to reach enlightenment (the seven-sided star is a symbol of mastery). For this to happen, you as a pilgrim on the path need to be tested. And you need to understand what the nature of the test is. The Law of the Fourteenth Portal will then be in operation. It's called the Law of Verification.

In the Fourteenth Portal we are at the final of the Seven Universal Laws and will be involved in a variety of experiments as we move along. We are expected to know more and more of what is true, confirming our beliefs through conscious experience. We have to test out the theories we've learned so far:

1. **The Law of Suggestion (Strength).** Are you conscious of your inner strength? Are you sensitive to your weaknesses? Are you giving yourself positive reinforcement?

2. **The Law of Response (The Hermit).** Are you open to sharing your spiritual knowledge? Are you asking for guidance? Is your life, through example, a beacon light for others to see?

3. **The Law of Cycles (The Wheel of Fortune).** Are you above the anxiety, refusing to be caught up in the "meat grinder"? Are you conscious of your unfoldment? Can you remain optimistic in the midst of difficulty?

4. **The Law of Cause and Effect (Justice).** Are you aware that your thoughts, words, and deeds have a ripple effect throughout your life? Are you measuring the outcome of events? Are you eliminating the nonessentials?

5. **The Law of Reversal (The Hanged Man).** What attitudes, values, and priorities have you reevaluated? What have you sacrificed? What benefits have you received from letting go of negative thoughts?

6. **The Law of Transformation (Death).** What changes are going on with you now? Are there any old emotional patterns that are dying out for the better? Do you fear the unknown? and finally,

7. **The Law of Verification (Temperance).** What in my life needs stabilizing? What are the tests I must pass? What beliefs do I hold that I must verify through experience?

The Law of Verification is a link between what you have learned spiritually and how to use the knowledge in a practical way in your everyday life. The Law of Verification presents you with a trial or a test to see if you can still remain on the path despite challenges to your faith. It is a time for devising new methods in dealing with old problems. It is a time that demands new insights.

In the Fourteenth Portal as we experiment with the knowledge we've learned since we walked through the First Portal, we are encouraged to perfect our skills, our talents, our way of doing things. In gaining some understanding of the workings of Consciousness in the first Seven Portals, to the workings of the Law in the Second Seven, we find ourselves at a turning point. Are we willing to continue the tempering, the purification?

As our character is tested, our attitude toward life itself will be called into play. We become aware of the trial and error involved in our relationships and are given the opportunity to readjust our overall reactions to life's experiences.

And we never really know when our "metal" will be tempered; all we do know is that on this Path of Liberation, trials are inevitable, and if looked at as a means to quicken our advancement, these tests can be seen as a blessing as well.

The astrological correspondence of Temperance is the ninth sign of the zodiac, Sagittarius: Masculine Mutable Fire. He rules the thighs and hips.

Sagittarius is symbolized by a half man-half horse Archer with bow drawn. Again, we are shown the blending of opposites—the animal nature and the human nature. The Archer aims his arrow at a lofty target—for he aspires to attain knowledge over vast areas.

He is adaptable to changing circumstances and will go enthusiastically from project to project—which is what the ancients meant by "Mutable Fire." This aspect reflects the atmosphere of the Fourteenth Portal, for Temperance uses the blending of the opposites of Fire and Water to temper the adaptability of personality.

A positive male sign, the Archer operates from the self-expressive polarity, for Sagittarius is ruled by Jupiter—the most expansive of the planets. Jupiter also accentuates the Archer's optimistic attitude and love of spontaneity. He is imbued with a sense of wanderlust and loves to travel in search of knowledge.

Sagittarius enjoys many friendships and is blessed with Jupiter's happy temperament. However, sometimes the Archer's arrows fly out in all directions, wounding indiscriminately. For Sagittarius lacks tact.

The Archer also wastes time in frivolous dabbling. Sagittarius afflicted is the dilettante of the zodiac. He is highly opinionated about where he should aim his arrows, and can be prideful and overly dogmatic.

Sagittarius afflicted does not take kindly to those who would dissent from those highly held opinions. Their self-expression can turn bitter, degrading those whom they consider inferior. But on the positive end, Sagittarius is almost deliriously independent and adventurous. As they get older, the adventuresome Sagittarian consciousness turns inward, and the Archer becomes the philosopher of the zodiac. Values, ethics, the Examined Life—their interests lean toward the spiritual.

Sagittarians also have an innate capacity to understand the feelings and reactions of people. They are encouraging, respectful, and enjoy learning from others. Sagittarius ruled by Jupiter draws his strength from the power center of the Solar Plexus, symbolized by the horse loins of the Centaur. The upper human half harnesses this power and employs it in his activities in the spiritual, emotional, mental, and physical realms.

As a philosopher, Sagittarius wants to explore new realms and find new meanings. At his best he is disciplined, organized, and reasonable. Sagittarius says, "I perceive."

Although Sagittarius can become fanatically attached to his way of thinking—and its fiery expression, he can be nebulous and illogical in arguing his position. However, for the most part, the Archer is liked for his forthrightness and intuitive qualities.

Temperance in a Reading

- A test is coming.
- The need to verify.
- Adapting to circumstances.
- Showing deference; accommodating.
- Experimentation.
- Idealistic approach, enthusiastic.
- Enjoyment in the search for meaning.

- Gathering facts from far and wide.
- Expanding one's experiences.
- Taking aim at a problem with confidence.
- Balancing alternatives to reach an equitable compromise.
- Tempering one's appetites; moderation.

REVERSED

- Intolerant of opposing opinions.
- Blind faith.
- Opportunistic.
- Insensitive to the feelings of others; self-righteous.
- Restless, jittery need for stimulating experiences.
- Refusing to take the tests life offers; setback and retreat.
- Excess.

Thoughts for Meditation on Temperance

When you feel the need to ignite your enthusiasm, or temper excessive energy expenditure, meditation on Temperance can help you see the areas of your life that need modification. As you are exploring new beliefs about your world, you might want to reflect on how the fresh ways of looking at things are bringing in dividends.

Questions arise:

1. How am I synthesizing opposing forces in my life?
2. How am I being tested on this Path of Liberation?
3. After going through the so-called "Death" experience of the Thirteenth Portal, what characterizes my rebirth in the Fourteenth?
4. Do I take people's word for things too much without verifying the Truth for myself?
5. Of all the Universal Laws I have experienced, with which one do I have the most affinity?
6. Which Law do I violate the most frequently?
7. Why, and what can I do about it?

Prayer

Even though by the solar heat of his breath
he watches over me
and slays my demons,
I am still compelled to wrestle the Angel.
I will not surrender to his tempering fire
and the scorching of my flesh
feels oh so insignificant.
But this needn't be . . .
for surrender is sweet
as he engulfs me
in the consuming power of his Divine Fire.
I have lived the laws,
heard the echoes,
and climbed the holy mountains.
So I am soaring again,
spiraling upwards
to new levels.
I am ready, clear—awake!
And I can hardly wait for the next trial.
What am I saying??

The Seven Levels of Spiritual Unfoldment

XV. The Devil to XXI. The World

Chapter 18

XV. The Devil
The Surface of Things

Astrological Correspondence: The fearful and sensually overstimulated side of Capricorn, the Goat.

Hebrew Letter: Ayin ע (meaning the "human eye," an eye that only sees with the senses).

The Inner Atmosphere: Here we have gained a clearer perspective on the workings of the ego, a better understanding of what's underneath. We have developed a willingness to confront our shadow-self and make amends. From darkness we are inspired to once again face the Light.

Statement: "I bring a sincere, fearless, and diligent attitude toward the project and am able to solve problems with my practical sense. I am not intimidated by my faults and weaknesses."

Quotation: "We intend what is right, but we avoid the life that would make it reality."
(Dallas Willard, *The Spirit of the Disciplines*)

The Challenge: The ego is cold and dictatorial; ruled by the sensual side of life, and therefore blind to the Subtle.

Visualization to the Fifteenth Portal, The Devil

It is quiet and you find yourself groping along in the darkness.
You are not afraid,
but the darkness makes you feel a bit apprehensive.
Then ahead you see a torch pointed downward,
giving off little light and a lot of smoke.
As you approach closer to the Fifteenth Portal,
you hear the flutter of huge wings
and feel the wind from them on your face.
Then you see it:
A beastly-looking creature,
a goat face with horns and red fiery eyes.
It sits atop a half cube with eagle-feather legs and talons.
A white fiery inverted pentagram blazes over its Third Eye chakra.
You are shocked to see a young naked man and woman,
both with hooves and horns.
He has a flaming tail,
and her tail is topped by a clump of grapes.
They have chains around their necks,
and you notice that the chains are attached to the creature's half cube
on which he is weirdly perched.
Then the beast turns and stares at you with its fiery red eyes.
It speaks. "What are you looking at, brave traveler?"
"SSSSatan?"
"Ha-ha-ha—That's your problem!
You are still taking things at face value.
Haven't you already been warned about that?"
"I don't really know what I'm seeing."
"I am your Adversary.
I am here to help you with your spiritual advancement.
But I must give you trials—difficult trials.

That's the Law . . .
Yet you must still overcome me."
"But . . . how?"
"Continue on your way and you will find out."
As we pass by the young man, he says,
"Come join us. Untold pleasures await."
Instead, you reply,
"Thank you for the invitation, but I think I'll—"
As the scene fades away, you hear the flutter of bat wings
And a lot of laughter.

General Atmosphere of the Fifteenth Portal, The Devil

We are now beginning the third and final row of Tarot cards (XV. to XXI.): The Seven Stages of Spiritual Unfoldment. The ancients, who don't usually take our sensibilities into account, make no exceptions for us in the Fifteenth Portal. You would think that the idea of a level-of-spiritual-unfoldment would be gloriously beautiful. However, since we first had consciousness, we allowed ourselves to lose our expression of free spirit qualities. Instead, our conscious reaction to the world around us, almost exclusively, was a result of being unaware of the Subtle. Throughout our earthly existence we were granted free will to use the Power of Consciousness in whatever way we could possibly imagine. Unfortunately, we restricted our awareness of the majesty of our soul Essence, and used our powerful thought processes to think of ourselves as born to limitation.

Therefore, we must begin the third row with a level of awareness that emphasizes our lack of spiritual unfoldment. Instead, we dwell on our imperfections, ignorant of the Power inherent in our being. From the darkness of the Fifteenth Portal, in a striking image which the ancients have named the Devil, we are becoming a little more conscious of our powers within. We might even be able to direct some of it.

At the lowest level before unfoldment, human beings are enslaved to their instincts—and, as a result, suffer blindly in chains. Humankind identifies with the body—thereby living an existence on a lower rung of the evolutionary ladder. Humankind has become prey to obsession and addiction—ignorance—whereby self-consciousness is condemned to swirl within the turbulence of subconscious emotion-thought-sensation.

How often in our lives did we bring to consciousness the sublime, liberating idea that the Loving Limitless Light of Pure Awareness—God—interpenetrates every particle and wave of our being? Anything less, and we live in a world of shallowness.

The Hebrew letter of the Fifteenth Portal is Ayin, which translates as the "eye," the human eye, which can only see the surface of things. The Devil, Ayin, pictured in the Fifteenth Portal, is at the very far reaches of the subtle inner Essence. And the further from the Center we go, the more we indulge in the atmosphere of Ayin— where the Devil perches—portrayed as our ignorance and petty interests.

As we enter the Fifteenth Portal, at the First Stage of Spiritual Unfoldment, we only apprehend the shadow of the Essence. Again, mindful of Ayin, we are urged to change our point of view, to be more objective and try to understand what is beneath the facade.

The scene pictured in the Fifteenth Portal is supposed to be a burlesque of the Sixth Portal, the Lovers, especially as the ancients did not believe in a literal Devil.

The self-conscious male has hooves, horns, a flaming tail, and a chain around his neck. The subconscious female has the same, but the tail is one of grapes—suggesting, perhaps, the idea of Bacchus, the god of wine and revelry.

Now the Superconscious Angel of the Lovers is twisted into the image of a dirty old goat with talons, red eyes, and bat wings. In the Lovers, the sky is golden and the earth is fertile. In the atmosphere of the Devil, however, the background is the ominous darkness of ignorance—and the unknown.

The Devil raises his hand and opens it fully, exposing a tattoo of Saturn. This is in contrast to the gesture of benediction from Vav, the Hierophant (the closed fingers of the Hierophant point to the sacredness of the hidden).

We are not the shadow self, as the card of the Devil suggests. Rather, we have the Kingdom of God in and through us, beyond space and time. Again, we are reminded: Thoughts are things and thoughts are creative. The Devil is our human mind stuck on thoughts of limitation—and limitation on our power of imagination is an illusion. That's why the Fifteenth Portal, at the dawn of Spiritual Unfoldment, is called by the ancients "Bondage."

At our core, the Divine Spark within, is one of purity and Truth, beauty and unconditional love. And the rhythm at our Center is one of perfect harmony and eternal peace. The Devil, on the other hand, is our body, mind, and emotions in chaos. The Devil torments us into a state of mind which creates fear and restriction. We need to remember that with the eye of Ayin we see only the exterior. And then we are condemned to a world of faulty impressions.

When Jesus of Nazareth encountered the Devil of false pride and selfishness, he said, "Get thee behind me, Satan," another way of saying, "I will see the world for what it is with my eyes wide open." Therefore, in the Fifteenth Portal, we learn the nature of the first Level of Spiritual Unfoldment, and that is: As we evolve to an early state of enlightenment, we recognize the fact that our perceived bondage to the material world is unreal.

In the Fifteenth Portal this idea is illustrated by one of the "jokes" in the picture. The chains around the necks of the man and the woman are a phony enslavement. In actuality, they need only lift the chains over their heads to become unbound. All it takes is a moment of awareness.

When your thoughts center on the Divine Creative Power within, you lift the chains of bondage, and your body-mind-emotional self can again resume appreciation of its natural inheritance as a Temple of the Most High.

The eternal Essence within us is the very embodiment of freedom, and the Devil shows us that as humans we usually think about who we are in a narrow way.

The astrological correspondence of the Fifteenth Portal is Capricorn, a feminine, receptive Cardinal Earth sign. Capricorn practices the theories she has learned and is exacting in execution of them; initiating and ambitious. Capricorn is a kind of practicality in action. She says, "I use." The Goat embodies adjectives such as responsible, efficient, patient, perseverant.

Capricorn has great organizing ability and integrity, but can be an isolationist. She can erect a barrier, a wall of aloofness around the Inner Self. If the wall is ever ruptured, Capricorn can become plagued with worries and suspicions. In the atmosphere of the Devil she is stubborn and intolerant—and she can retaliate.

Although exhibiting a quiet exterior, Capricorn is nonetheless attracted to center stage, a need to be recognized for her achievements. Capricorn exalted examines all sides of an issue before deciding the course. She is a planner, and takes her time before coming to a conclusion. She is very serious about reaching her goals and is very result-oriented. She handles herself well in a crisis. She is an excellent counselor and can be conservative in philosophy and behavior.

However, Capricorn afflicted is overly cautious and refuses to take a risk. The Saturn influence holds her back; the darkness of the Fifteenth Portal encroaches on her thoughts, and she encounters her shadow, pessimism.

The Devil in a Reading

- Limited outlook, narrow perspective.
- Reacting only to outer circumstances; danger of mistakes.
- Aloofness.
- Feelings of being shackled to a situation, person, or habit.
- Fear of the real Self.

- The mind is tempted away from listening to the Inner Voice.
- Giving into the animal nature.
- Expending too much energy on illusionary pursuits.
- Dwelling on the material over the spiritual; attachment.
- A preoccupation with the dark side of things.

REVERSED

- Pressure eases.
- Less possessive, less attached.
- Clearer perspective on things; pursuing freedom over bondage.
- Appreciation for subtlety.
- Practical application; more decisive.

Thoughts for Meditation on The Devil

Meditation on Ayin may help bring your weaknesses to the surface. It takes a reasonably well-prepared consciousness, though, to confront inner turbulence. You don't want to let yourself be overwhelmed by feelings of guilt and shame as your mistakes rise up to consciousness. Meditate on The Devil with a detached frame of mind. You need to observe the weaknesses and resolve to strengthen them.

Contemplating the meanings and imagery of the Devil is appropriate if you find yourself in a particular situation where you feel trapped, or you aren't sure exactly what stops you. You can ask yourself: What are the chains holding me down? (fear, anxiety, selfishness, indulgence, intolerance, inflexibility?); Are you having superficial reactions to problems that are causing you serious consequences? Are you misdirecting precious energy by allowing yourself to be consumed by obsessions and fixations? How do you define evil in the circumstances of your life? Do you need to face some unresolved problems?

Prayer

What's that devil inside of me?
crawling
craving
a dribbling beast howling in the night.
I am an animal.
I want to rove the wilderness
searching for my other half.
But I am chained to a stone,
the bondage of my refusal to see.
I am boiling instinct
and I want to devour the world.
But the joke is,

I am also angel
and my Spirit soars beyond all fetters.

I am an enigma, personified.

Chapter 19

XVI. The Tower
Upheaval

Astrological Correspondence: The force of Mars to precipitate action.

Hebrew Letter: Peh פ (meaning "the mouth," our outward mode of expression).

Inner Atmosphere: Consciousness expands as the ego learns from experience. If, however, the ego drifts from the lessons, then in order to return the seeker to the path, the atmosphere of the Sixteenth Portal tends to draw severe tests, crises, and trials.

Statement: "I am receptive, and I will shift my focus to the exciting vibration astrologers call Mars. I am ready for the force that must come my way."

Quotation: "There is something in man which does not belong to this world, something mysterious, holy, serene. It is this that touches and holds him at certain unforgettable moments." (Paul Brunton, *Inspiration and the Overself*)

The Challenge: The ego is traumatized from the tests and trials along the path; inward fixations bring paralysis.

Visualization to the Sixteenth Portal, the Tower

You are shaken, filled with a new awareness of your weaknesses,
but still groping in the dark.
It is evening and you can observe storm clouds in a black sky.
You walk ahead to the Sixteenth Portal
and see a large gray stone tower on a mound of brown rock.
It is topped by a gold crown.
Suddenly there is a crash of lightning,
and the crown is smashed off.
The tower bursts into flames,
and a man and a woman fall from the burning windows
headfirst to the ground below.
Amongst the storm clouds you see several flames—
Yods in the shape of the Tree of Life and the Twelve signs of the zodiac
fall to the ground.
You hear the man cry out,
"We are doomed!
Run away and escape our fate.
Do not come closer!"
You listen, but know that from the Fifteenth Portal
when you faced your shadow,
you have emerged more into the Light.
You have come along far and know that you have no intention
to bottle up your talents and clear thinking in a tower.
You stare at the flames and appreciate the Light,
knowing that after being struck by lightning,
you are more enlightened
and know that you are here for a purpose.
We are here to learn,
to accumulate knowledge of the Sacred
in its complex manifestation as well as in its simplicity.
And you rest in that uncomplicated feeling.
As a result, you are more relaxed now,
feeling refreshed and awake.

General Atmosphere of the Sixteenth Portal, the Tower

The Second Stage of Spiritual Unfoldment is called the Tower. Basically, the Tower is the symbol of the facade we have erected around our true personality. In ancient Greece they wore masks on stage to portray the character. The word "mask" in Latin is *persona*. Our outer expression, our persona, if unreal, conniving, and selfishly founded, is the façade that draws the exploding flash of the lightning bolt.

We have just left an atmosphere where we encountered the Dark Night of the Soul. The Tower is the bondage-ignorance-limitation-illusion of the Fifteenth Portal solidified. The Tower is our rigid ego unyielding, our emotional responses fixated.

In the Bible, at a time when only one language was spoken, man arrogantly tried to build a structure that would reach heaven; God, in turn, confounded them by introducing many languages into their brains, and they fell into mass confusion, babbling. The Sixteenth Portal is also symbolic of this Tower of Babel from Genesis.

In the Fifteenth Portal, in the atmosphere of the Devil, we forgot that the ego is really only a reflection of the True Inner Self. Freud looked at the darker side of human nature, but defined the ego as a "coherent organization of mental processes" and does ascribe a "Magician-like" quality to this ego. He says, "The property of being conscious or not is in the last resort, our one beacon light in the darkness of depth psychology."

The psychological difficulty examined in the Fifteenth Portal is an ego fixated on falseness. Idle or driven, arrogant or mawkish, the ego's outer persona is animated by an underlying unhappiness. Refusing to face uncomfortable truths over the years, the ego isolates itself in a prison, a tower.

We all have spiritual failings as we learned from the realm of the Devil. We are undisciplined and self-indulgent. This focus on the demands of ego—selfishness—is the glue that holds the false structure together.

From the Fourteenth Portal, Temperance, we learned that we have to adjust our rhythms, synchronize the vibrations of our atmosphere with Reality. We need to analyze our plan of action in light of the Laws we have learned, culminating in the Law of Verification (Freud called it *reality testing* and considered the ego the executive of the personality, keeping the instincts under control).

Through reality testing, the well-adjusted ego reasonably assimilates the perceptions and impressions from the outer world. The structure of the Tower is, however, built with repression, ungratified libido tension, fixation, and regression.

The action of the Sixteenth Portal involves the lightning bolt striking the Tower. It is the flash of Truth that shatters the false persona and beliefs that the ego has accumulated from the atmosphere of the Devil.

The lightning bolt can be anything from an "Aha!" to a major upheaval that changes the course of one's life. It is a flash that startles us out of the illusion of the Devil's abode.

When the hidden essence of something is suddenly revealed, the lightning flash is called an *epiphany*. The clarity of the experience brings on awe and a sense of well-being. A Tai-Chi teacher told his class that after working an hour on intense Karate movements, he did something he had never done before: He immediately began to practice the graceful and precise movements of Tai-Chi. The surge of power from the Karate (*yang*) into the subtle atmosphere of Tai-Chi (*yin*) suddenly expanded his awareness of the Universal Energy (*chi*), and he became highly conscious of It flowing through his being.

Here in the Sixteenth Portal we are told to get moving on the path, not to waste our time in foolishness; do not look at the world anymore through the materialistic eye of Ayin. Tarot asks, "Why risk a painful electrocution?"

Our thoughts, words, and deeds set the direction of the Wheel of the Tenth Portal. If the Wheel moves in the direction of delusion, it is only a matter of time before the lightning flash is triggered. Then as the flash shoots across the sky, it screeches the word "Truth!" and destroys the delusion.

If the ego allowed the sudden insight received from the flash to penetrate, it is freed from its self-bondage limitations. As a result, the name of the Second Level of Spiritual Unfoldment is called Awakening. The ego, through ignorance, has blocked the flow of the Life-power. The lightning flash shatters the obstacles which impede the flow. Therefore, if the message of the lightning bolt is properly heeded, it is ultimately an act of salvation.

The ego is not easily disposed to the Examined Life, nor is humility a natural state. But the lightning bolt crashing into the Tower of false structure can awaken the consciousness to both. The idea is to think of the ego as a wave in the great ocean of Universal Consciousness; then the false attitude of separateness from the whole will not hold sway. Yet, individuality and self-reliance remain an integrated part of the ego-wave.

After being struck by the lightning bolt, the ego's perception is purified and expanded. Humbled before the Light of the Life-power, the ego's cunning motivations are exposed.

The Hebrew Letter for the Tower is Peh, meaning "mouth," where we proclaim what we learned during our Dark Night of the Soul.

By this point we have accepted the idea and the power of words: To heal or to destroy. Depending on our level of unfoldment, our experiences are expressed through the mouth of Peh, either with eloquence or with babbling. Peh is the power of the soul to communicate through the human instrument of the mouth.

The personality is at its best when we adopt the technique of right speech, recognizing the true usefulness of words and the sacred power of their utterance.

In the Sixteenth Portal we are shocked into action; Peh stirs up activity, shakes up the status quo, initiates changes. The Crown at the top of the Tower (which is blasted off) is to represent perceived material attainment and ego-worship. Our skewed viewpoint of Reality sets the conditions for the strike of lightning, the inevitable consequence of our ignorance.

With the Universal Consciousness of the Life-power, there is no limitation and no lack. Therefore, if we can consciously express the soul's natural state—serenity, security, harmony, joy, and abundance—then we express the Will of God, and avoid all retribution and suffering.

The lightning bolt is sent from the Inner Self to knock the man and woman from their isolation in the Tower. The man and woman are the two naked people from the Fifteenth Portal, the Devil. From the innocent nakedness of Adam and Eve to the self-consciously ashamed beings cast from the Garden of Eden, they are falling head first because they need to land on their skulls, symbolic of shattering the old ways of thinking.

At the strike of the lightning bolt the self-conscious and the subconscious are in a state of panic. This is Severity on the Tree of Life. This is Life communicating with us through Peh, the mouth. In the Second Level of Spiritual Unfoldment we are shocked out of our inertia. We are shocked out of our disinterest in the subtle expressions of life.

After we recover from the initial trauma, we are more interested in seeing the beauty hidden behind things. We notice the intricate detail on the bark of a birch tree. We notice the deep green of the wild field grasses.

We are also more aware of our missteps—our neglects. This bump on the head hurts, but we like the new preciseness of vision we get. We are awakened and our personality recognizes the animating fire of Spirit within.

Spirit uses our emotions, our mind, and our body for self-expression. When our personality is integrated with this realization, Spirit flowers outwardly from us. Sometimes it takes a sudden revelation like the lightning bolt striking the Tower.

There is a divine light animating our personality and the falling Yods remind us of this. Although no two personalities are alike, we are all grounded in the same light of Divine being, the same Holy Presence, the same infinite Power. We must communicate with this Divinity at our Center, for this experience is the ultimate goal of our journey. And in the next Portal, the Seventeenth, we will learn how.

After the jolt of *Peh*, we are given new insight into areas where we have faltered, and we become more conscious of our frailty as human beings. However, we will then experience a new birth in the mind (Death) and think in different ways. As a result, we can look at our life with enthusiastic expectation, much as we did as children on June 6 at the immanent approach of summer vacation (but as we will see, these extremely positive feelings are more for the Nineteenth Portal, Resh, the Sun).

From an astrological perspective, the Sixteenth Portal connects with the action of Mars, consciousness infused with a kind of dynamic, youthful, enthusiastic energy. It renews our faith in the excitement of life. Mars is decisive, precise, and can be restless and in extreme need of tension release.

Bold, inventive, and physically aggressive, in ancient times he was called the God of War. Mars can be verbally as well as emotionally two-fisted. An activated Mars operates in the extremes and prizes action over sentimentality. As we stated earlier, when the lightning bolt strikes, sensibilities are not taken into account. However, the awakening jolt of Mars can shock us into growth, discarding old worn-out patterns and debilitating habits.

With Mars we synchronize our vibration with a sizzling electric current that stimulates new attitudes and goals. Our continuation on the path accelerates with Mars' fiery dynamism. And with the right attitude, we can experience it as a great blessing when we encounter it—providing we are reasonably prepared for, and conscious of, the "lightning" when it hits.

Mars is a male active current—passionate, competitive, a burning urge to reach conclusion of the project. But Mars in its element can also stimulate conflict, a conflict with the status quo, for Mars can be driven, angry, and violent.

Mars can signify anxiety and nervousness and explosions of energy. It is also the force which shakes up inertia, and it can strike when you least expect it. At first you may find the upheaval upsetting, but its intent is educational. Mars is the urge to accomplish the goal.

Mars consciousness can be self-assertion at its worst, doing whatever we want to do, destructively and with cruelty; at best, Mars is self-discipline and even self-sacrifice. Mars is the struggle toward individuation, ultimately channeling the desire nature into constructive pursuits. Mars is enthusiastic, heroic, fearless, blunt, dominant, and defiant. Mars is vital and electric. With the Tower, Mars shatters falsity.

The Tower in a Reading

- Upheaval: From changing a major in college to quitting a job . . . to quitting a mate.
- A disrupting idea that forces you to reexamine your attitude.
- Sudden change.

- A truth is exposed, sometimes with shattering consequences. Or it could be a remark that forces you to look inside your heart.
- A rupture in a relationship that sheds light on the reality of it all.
- A departure from the traditional approach.
- Heightened awareness after an emotional jolt.
- A more spiritual attitude toward life suddenly eclipses the earlier attitude of indifference.
- The status quo is shaken.
- Caught off-guard.
- Insight after a painful experience.
- The ego is knocked off its pedestal.

REVERSED

- The Truth is not apparent, and the solution to the problem is delayed.
- The awakening is slower as the shock lingers.
- Not learning the lesson well.
- An inconsistent spiritual attitude keeps the seeker in the dark.
- Silent when you should open your mouth.
- Continuing in the illusion.
- Traumatized by events, difficulty in getting the underlying message.
- Apathetic; little interest in finding solutions.
- A need for stimulation.
- A reluctance to face something unpleasant.
- Ideas and beliefs calcify.
- A need to "loosen up," go to a movie, get a massage . . .
- Reevaluate the routine and change it in accordance with love—and the Law in mind.

Thoughts for Meditation on The Tower

In the Sixteenth Portal we are asked, "Are there any jolting experiences going on from which you would like to learn a lesson?" We also need to look at our belief systems. Do any of them need reevaluation? In addition, if we are avoiding certain responsibilities or unpleasant situations that need our attention, the Tower reminds us that we need to draw on Mars' dynamic energy, and put our minds in an attitude of goal-reaching. There is no place for apathy in the Sixteenth Portal.

Finally, we are asked, "Are you reluctant to communicate about something that is unpleasant to face?" As we learned, avoiding certain confrontations can also draw the power of the lightning flash. Meditation on these issues can help ease the jolting affect of sudden awakening.

Prayer

Painful, flashing blast—
My brain reels
in its education.
Where is the relief?
There's not supposed to be any,
so get used to it.
But I'm tired of the endless lessons.
You're never given more than you can tolerate
But I violate laws every day.
Ten thousand violations times ten,
it matters not.
Continue in thy errors
but grasp the essence and move on,
forever spiraling upwards.
Do the steering
and enjoy the ride.

Chapter 20

XVII. The Star
The Inspired Life

Astrological Correspondence: The open-minded compassion and idealism of Aquarius.

Hebrew Letter: Tzaddi ‎צ (meaning "fishhook," the implement that draws the "fish," Nun, out of the "water," Mem).

The Inner Atmosphere: We are more comfortable with our attitude toward ourselves as evolving spiritual beings; within Nature we become better able to detect the fine distinctions around us.

Statement: "I know that I must be mentally agile as well as intuitive about the world I live in. I will turn my well-meaning thoughts to something I can see, feel, and touch."

Quotation: "Holy light! illuminate the way that we may gather the good we planted. Are not our deeds known to you? Do not let us grow crooked, we that kneel and pray again and again." (Isha Upanishad)

The Challenge: The ego focuses on the negative, within and without.

Visualization to the Seventeenth Portal, the Star

At the base of the Tower you pick yourself up from the craggy ground
and gaze off into the distance.
Feeling stronger from the insights received from the Sixteenth Portal,
you are warmly colored from the flash that struck you there,
and with a new, powerful certitude,
you stride off to the land beyond,
this time by your own lights . . .
It is dusk.
You continue walking and come upon a grassy plain
speckled with wildflowers.
The evening sky deepens to an indigo blue,
and when you look up,
you behold a gigantic golden eight-pointed star
surrounded by seven smaller eight-pointed white stars.
You feel yourself aglow with light,
and in gratitude,
fall to your knees in the soft green grass . . .
When you raise your eyes you see a young blonde woman, naked,
pouring water from an orange pitcher with her right hand into a pool;
in her left hand she pours water from an orange pitcher onto the grass.
Her right foot rests on top of the water,
and she kneels with her left on the ground.
You approach her quietly and ask,
"Excuse me, good woman . . .
may I drink of your water?"
She smiles, saying, "You may drink of the water
at any moment you choose.
It is everywhere and belongs to no one."
You cup your hands and sip the water from the pool . . .

Your mind then begins to swirl,

and you feel your weaknesses and faults

rise to the surface of your consciousness.

Calm and filled with the Spirit of Understanding,

you dispassionately observe that which floats before your inner eye.

The light of insight that pervades your being

then disperses the dark pockets of ignorant attitudes and perceptions.

You feel less dominated by thoughts of your weaknesses . . .

You are at peace and contemplate your new self-assurance.

After a few moments, you open your eyes,

feeling fresh and awake.

General Atmosphere of the Seventeenth Portal, the Star

We have moved on from the "Bondage" of the Fifteenth Portal, the Devil, to the "Upheaval" of the Sixteenth, the Tower. We learned that if we don't live in rhythm with Truth, disruption will strike. If we insist on rebuilding the Tower exactly as before (Freud called it *regression*), then the disasters will continue.

Now we enter through the Seventeenth Portal still reeling from the harsh revelations that struck us from the Tower. In the Seventeenth Portal, with the Star, the flash of insight we gained from the sudden awakening of Peh, the Tower, is *sustained*.

There is no place for selfishness or arrogance here, for the ego is illumined, comfortably. The illustration of the Star pictures our inner atmosphere where we are retaining earlier instruction. It is in the Seventeenth Portal that we reach the Third Level of Spiritual Unfoldment.

From the subconsciousness of the High Priestess and the Empress, we are now at the level of Isis Unveiled, where the Goddess of the Moon reveals her secrets. In fact, the Third Level of Spiritual Unfoldment is called Revelation—expressed as a beautiful young woman, *au naturel*.

After the flash of awareness, the Seventeenth Portal offers an atmosphere of internal peace, and like starlight, extends and expands its energy. It results from what Freud called *catharsis*, a condition when the original traumatic experience (lightning striking the Tower) and all the emotions accompanying it, are suddenly brought to consciousness, and the tension and anxiety are released—and relieved.

Hidden emotional stress, an anxiety that works in underhanded ways to make our lives a "vale of tears," needs to be exposed to the sustained starlight of the Seventeenth

Portal. The word catharsis comes from the Greek "to purge or purify." In that sense, after a revelation, we are better able to face who we really are, purged of ignorance; this in turn will eventually lead to a healthier temperament and body.

With her foot resting on the subconscious pool (in contrast to the archangel Michael dipping into the pool), Isis Unveiled is the perfect balance between the emotional realm (Water) and the manifested realm (Earth), bringing about a state of mind that is filled with inspiration and grounded understanding.

Mem, the "Water" of the Hanged Man is "suspended mind," where we are like a pendulum at rest, contemplating the contents of consciousness. In this state of introspection, ideas come into focus, and we are more aware of the power we have to bring these ideas out into the world of appearance. The purpose of the Seventeenth Portal is to enable us to draw Nun, the fish, (Nun, Death, The Law of Transformation) out of the Water (Mem, the Hanged Man, the Law of Reversal).

As a result, we are unhesitating in making use of our talents and skills. We respect our new ideas, we adjust our imbalances, we resolve our conflicts—and the vibrations of the personal atmosphere rise. Further, injurious kinds of actions disappear, and we live more in alignment with the Law.

So what brings Transformation to the surface? Tzaddi, the Hebrew letter of the Seventeenth Portal. Tzaddi is the "fishhook." After we are still in the calm waters of the Hanged Man, we fish in the subconscious to find our enlightenment. We must use the fishhook Tzaddi, which is contemplation, reflection—meditation—to bring about the Transformation of our ego-selves to a pure vessel for the soul (symbolized by the pitchers in the woman's hands).

Now the man and woman who had fallen from the Tower and were chained to the half-cube of the Devil, have been transformed into vessels of expressions for the Creative Force. In her right hand Isis Unveiled pours the self-conscious male energy into the universal subconscious pool. The ancients saw this as a symbol of what we do in meditation, where the waters mingle, and the finest expression of thought, Wisdom, and Understanding of our place in Nature, come to the surface.

From Isis' subconscious left hand she pours the waters of the personal subconscious on the Earth in a gesture that purifies the five senses of the Physical Plane. The green grass reminds us of the fertile garden of Venus, the creative imagination.

After the sustained light of the Star cleanses the mind of negative energy left over from traumatic memories, the ego is then better able to consciously direct the attention to the indwelling Presence of the Life-power. When this happens the large eight-pointed golden Star rises on the horizon of the seeker's atmosphere.

The result is a special kind of enlightenment.

The inventors of Tarot insist that inspiration simply is; what we need to do as pilgrims on the path is to develop the level of consciousness that can discover it. Revelation, when it comes to us, is our Inner Self sending us messages regarding what is true. As we pointed out at the beginning of our journey, we are usually too distracted to hear the Voice.

The question is, are we willing to put the time in to discipline ourselves so that we can hold our thought? to concentrate long enough so that the inner revelations can get through? And for that matter, how do we even know what a revelation is in the first place?

In the meditative state we lose our sense of space and time and enter into the observer mode, intensely alert. The senses have lost their dominion over our attention, and we realize we are one with the majestic All in All. Some of the ancient seers (among them, Patanjali, one of the greatest of the wise men from India) called the process samadhi, where the person meditating becomes one with the Holy Presence. He or she is able to focus the will and become centered, noticing her mind as a transparent channel for the divine Voice. She is then able to bring the message back to use in her everyday life. She has pierced the Reality behind the veil and can perceive the finer vibrations.

She understands the messages because they have to do with her well-being and/or the well-being of others. The revelations are never self-serving and may even be unwelcome because they require a great deal of the seeker, either in terms of performing a valuable task, or giving up something pleasurable, but unwholesome. She knows the Voice of Revelation because It is always loving, even though at times this may be a kind of "tough love."

After feeling comfortable with the messages and adopting meditation as a way of life, it becomes second nature for the seeker to practice harmlessness, contentment, self-control, and Truth-seeking. Faith in the innate Goodness of things is also second nature, along with a healthy respect for the Examined Life. Fears, worries, anger, inertia, possessiveness, lust, and arrogance lose their grip on the self-conscious and are eventually expelled from the atmosphere by the enlightened, personal subconscious.

Balancing the thoughts, words, and deeds becomes an indelible facet of the Ideal, and energy is expended judiciously. In the Seventeenth Portal we are highly conscious of the karma we create—we obey the Law of Cause and Effect, and deliberately, lucidly, visualize the intended effect that will show itself from the original seed idea. This process can be a long one, so we develop and expand our practice of the virtue of patience.

In the picture of the Star we see seven eight-pointed white stars along with a large golden eight-pointed star.

The seven smaller stars are the chakras (which were discussed in chapter 11, Strength, the Eighth Portal):

1. **Root Chakra** (Red, perineum, base of spine, ruby, "fight or flight," survival, grounding, inner stability; Life-Breath manifesting, gravity, Malkuth "Kingdom" on the Tree of Life, Earth, Pentacles).

2. **Splenic Chakra** (Orange, sexual organs, gonads, coral, pleasure, procreation, polarity and attraction of opposites, Yesod "Foundation" or "Vital Life Force" on the Tree of Life, Pentacles).

3. **Solar Plexus** (Yellow, gold, power center, will, dynamic energy, metabolism, Hod "Splendor" and Netsach "Victory" on the Tree of Life, Air, Swords).

4. **Heart Chakra** (Green, emerald, love, relationships, affinity, Tipareth "Beauty" on the Tree of Life, balance, Cups, Water).

5. **Throat Chakra** (Turquoise, creativity, vibration, communication, speech, Geburah "Severity" and Chesed "Mercy" on the Tree of Life, Air, Swords,).

6. **Third Eye Chakra** (Deep blue, sapphire, clairvoyance, imagination, intuition, visualization, perception, lapis lazuli, Binah "Understanding" and Chokmah "Wisdom" on the Tree of Life, Spirit, Wands).

7. **Crown Chakra** (White, diamond, transcendence, clarity, Reality, enlightenment, purified thought, Kether "Crown" on the Tree of Life, Spirit, Wands).

When the energies in the seven spiritual centers are free-flowing, then the Eighth Star appears, and the pineal gland is fully vivified (or as the ancients say, "the Third Eye opens"). In this sense, we don't see with Ayin (the human eye) any longer, but rather with the eye of the soul.

Of course, meditation requires a great deal of the seeker: Besides faith and sincerity, the seeker must also set aside time and space for practice. The mountain in the picture reminds us of the challenge of continuing on in the Great Work, the journey toward Self-Realization.

Regarding the tree with the bird in the picture: The tree is supposed to be the brain and nervous system, and the bird on top of the tree is an ibis, a bird with a hook-like beak for catching fish. The ibis is sacred to Mercury, the intellect, the idea being that in meditation the thought processes are poised in an act of concentration in order for us to hook the fish of Transformation.

The astrological correspondence of the Star is Aquarius. In meditation we tap into the intelligence of Nature and bring its power and knowledge into our own brain. This is called Water. Aquarius is the Water-Bearer, masculine, positive, Fixed Air. He has adopted an attitude where he can bring this Water into his mind. It is then a

Water which represents an infusion of knowledge from the Inner onto the outer world, to be shared with all.

Aquarius is intellectual and communicative. It is Fixed, which is determined and persistent: Aquarius is original, broadminded, helpful. Aquarius wants to pour his knowledge on the head of humanity in a gesture of baptism. The Aquarius glyph looks like water, but it can also be seen as waves of vibration. Aquarians seem aloof because they are mind-oriented individuals. They are friendly, but detached. They are warm, but distant. They may even seem indifferent. Aquarians see the overall picture and want to affect the world by pushing their ideas on the status quo. These ideas can affect the culture, bringing their originality to art, politics, and literature (Mozart, Charles Dickens, Abraham Lincoln, Charles Darwin, Clark Gable, Tallulah Bankhead and James Dean were all Aquarians).

Their minds are analytical and scientific, and they have good powers of concentration. They are philosophical, visionary, idealistic. They are not put off by the strange or unknown, and are fascinated by the unexpected.

Aquarius is ruled by Uranus (Aleph, the Fool), which is the "Awakener" among the planets. It has characteristics such as intuition, perception, reform, idealism, and originality. Uranus can be unpredictable, rebellious, irresponsible, eccentric, impractical and can cause sudden disruption.

Aquarius is highly observant, clear-headed, and objective; he is a progressive thinker, open to the uncanny, independent, and forward looking. Aquarius scorns the petty and focuses on the wide scope of humanity. He is very interested in the welfare of others. He is an optimist and believes in the general goodness of human beings.

The Star in a Reading

- An increase in enlightening experiences; a raise in consciousness.
- Faith in oneself and the goodness of the world.
- Looking forward; excited by the future.
- Spirit shines brighter through the persona; encountering the soul.
- A conscious step closer to the warmth of the Inner Self.
- A peaceful, healthy attitude toward oneself—and in fellowship.
- Comfort with current circumstances.

REVERSED

- Narrow-mindedness; biases interfere with perception of the Truth.
- Pessimistic.
- Sour attitude.
- Loss of faith in a project or a belief.

- A need to be more conscious of the blessings.
- A need to open to the descent of grace.
- More meditation and self-reflection is indicated.

Thoughts for Meditation on The Star

Contemplating the Star can open you to new revelations from deep inside your Inner Self. It can also raise a variety of questions. How has your level of inner concentration improved since you began meditating within *Tarot Awareness*? Are you more comfortable with the inner search, the Examined Life? Are you more confident in your risk-taking? Have you noticed any new energies moving in and through you?

Prayer

Starlight.
How curious
to see such tender glow
on my lightning-struck skin . . .
From below the ragged cliff,
I lift my gaze
and see my soul
reflected back to me
in the evening sky,
whole and shining.
How could it be otherwise?
We fall from grace
only to stare once again
into the eye of God—
I am propelled upward
within the depths
of my brain
to the secret chamber
where my Beloved waits.

Chapter 21

XVIII. The Moon
Into the Unknown

Astrological Correspondence: The receptivity and vivid imagination of Pisces.

Hebrew Letter: Qoph ק (meaning "back of the head," a reference to the medulla oblongata at the base of the brain).

Inner Atmosphere: Body consciousness; the mind apprehends the working of Spirit in and through the personal vehicle. In this atmosphere we see ourselves as evolving body/soul, a reflection of the Holy Presence of the Godhead.

Statement: "I am emerging as I contemplate the unknown. Through my imagination I am sensitive to God's expression in Nature."

Quotation: "What is man, that Thou art mindful of him? . . . Thou hast made him a little lower than the angels, and hast crowned him with glory and honor." (Psalm 8: 4–5)

The Challenge: The ego becomes deluded, fearful of movement, isolated, and lives a life of artifice.

Visualization to the Eighteenth Portal, the Moon

You leave the bright Portal of starlight and walk along a field at dusk.
You feel the green grass at your feet,
and ahead in the evening light,
you see the Golden Path winding to the mountains . . .
Above the path you see a curious Moon
glowing and interpenetrating a magnificent Sun
in a deep blue sky.
You notice from this celestial combination
that Yods rain down on the landscape.
Two towers are in the distance,
and from beyond them you see the Golden Path
reaching into the mountains.
But the most striking feature of the Eighteenth Portal
is a gray wolf and a brown dog baying at the Moon.
From a pool a purple crayfish emerges on the path between them.
Then the crayfish speaks,
"Think ye are a Pilgrim advancing,
struggling through trials and suffering as you continue?"
"Yes, I do. The road has been long."
"You, Pilgrim, are only beginning to understand.
For at this stage of unfoldment,
you are me and no more."
You are at first put off by its words,
but then think about the meaning.
The wolf speaks in a growling voice.
"Does walking beyond the towers frighten you?"
"I am not afraid. Not after all I've seen."
The dog turns around and looks at you.
"Keep going then,
and don't be surprised if your discoveries in the unknown change you."
"For the better?" you ask.
Both the dog and the wolf continue howling at the Moon.

You continue on in the moonlight,
feeling a greater sense of humility,
which is much needed in this Portal.
The howling fades off as you open our eyes,
calm and at peace.

General Atmosphere of the Eighteenth Portal, the Moon

In the Eighteenth Portal we will see that something is born, exists, then dies, then is born again. Throughout the universe, a sun is conceived, and then radiating outwards from the center, planets are created. As the microcosm of our body is a solar system of atoms, molecules, and cells spinning around each other, so is it a reflection of the solar system. Particle and wave, Spirit and body, consciousness and vehicle. One aspect analyzes and plans, the other aspect carries it out. Inductive (Above—self-consciousness) and deductive reasoning (Below—subconscious). As above, the solar system; so below, humankind.

There is a continual expansion outwards, stability, and then contraction inwards; the ebb and flow of radiant currents. Night and day, life and death. Everywhere before us we see the evolution of the manifested world: From mineral (gas, liquid, solid) to vegetable, to animal, to human, all evolving from the limitless void. And within the mix, as evolution advances along the spiral, comes humankind's self-consciousness and free will.

We are given the power to choose, to focus or not to focus, to absorb or ignore. What is the key in the midst of these polarities? Attitude. We need to be clear about this. What is my attitude toward Spirit? toward myself? toward my fellow beings? So much of what we are or what we are not depends on our mental outlook. Is the anchor of our faith a belief in goodness? Or do we believe only what our physical eyes (*Ayin*) tell us? Joseph Campbell says that the key to happiness is to "follow your bliss." Or is it easier to follow your discouragement?

Again, the choice is ours. In fact, basically, we are our choices.

How we think, how we form our attitude will radiate outwards and attract a like vibration into the personal atmosphere. How we feel deep within our emotional self affects our outer environment. If we can feel the Holy Presence of infinite Good within, we will draw on this Goodness to affect our outer life. Fear and uncertainty will evaporate. We can focus our mind on delightful memories from the past, turn our mind to confident expectation in the future, and for the present, enjoy the moment.

An inner attitude of failure will manifest outer failure in our experience. This is a Law.

In the Eighteenth Portal, the Moon, we are aware that there is one Power, one Energy, which manifests as the universe.

In the Seventeenth Portal, we choose to meditate, thereby changing and refining our atmosphere. In the Eighteenth Portal, we experience the effect of meditation on our body. This is illustrated by the Sun and Moon interpenetrating each other in the card.

Our inner atmosphere now reflects the fact that each cell in our body is a conscious entity, and taken as a whole, forms a body of consciousness. The influence of the Moon on the body connects with the energy that holds the body together. The Eighteenth Portal is called Organization, a reference to the body as an organization of atoms, molecules, and celldivision.

The Moon is subconsciousness and from the Moon we see Yods raining down grace on the Physical Plane, that is, the gift of God's love and protection, beauty and sanctification infusing the personal atmosphere. The miracle is that we can use our mental processes to interact with this Organization and increase the rate of vibration within our bodies. In other words, as we progress on the path, and assimilate all we've learned and adopt the proper attitude (such as, life IS worth living), we alter the organization of our body into a finer instrument.

With the Moon, in the Eighteenth Portal, we are supposed to be able to consciously affect what is going on at a cellular level. Our self-consciousness is the Sun in the center of our physical universe, and our body is symbolized by the Moon.

Qoph, the Hebrew letter of the Eighteenth Portal means "the back of the head," which is another way of saying the medulla oblongata located at the tip of the spine. The purpose of the medulla is to accept vibrations from the eye and transmit messages to the rest of the body. It controls breathing, heartbeat, blood circulation, and coordination. The medulla oblongata is the entryway of the Life-Breath, and from its location at the throat chakra, distributes cosmic energy throughout the body.

As we become clear in our desires, perceiving in an unhabitual way (which William James calls 'genius'), the medulla will give these desires form. The vibration of the body changes and a more psychically attuned light-filled vehicle is created. As a result, in the Eighteenth Portal we can become more clairvoyant, telepathic, and supersensible.

Freud said, "The psychic development of the individual is a short repetition of the course of development of the race." Evolution on the Physical Plane is advancing, but the Moon tells us that we can participate in the process with self-conscious attention, and actually bring an acceleration of the body-building activity of the Moon consciousness. Ultimately, the body/soul is like a living, breathing hologram, and is at its core, a whirling of radiant Energy.

The wolf represents our raw animal self, our basic instinctual force, Nature and the subconscious. Both animals look to the light and the descent of grace. The polarity is between being leashed and unleashed. The dog is Nature adapted, civilized, and expressed through art. Henry James said, "It is art that makes life, makes interest, makes importance, for our consideration and application of these things, and I know of no substitute whatever for the force and beauty of its process."

The dog has been transformed from the wolf by his involvement with the mind and heart of humankind. Likewise, as humans on the path spiritualizing our mind and heart, the ancients tell us that our body will experience a new organization of cells that can absorb the more ethereal cosmic energies. As ego disengaged from our real Inner Self, our body was more dense—"wolf-like"—and incapable of taking in the finer vibrations.

What happens as we are able to assimilate the finer vibrations? We become more poised in the center, one-pointed and aware. The lobster crawling out of the pool is evolution from the cauldron of "soup" at creation. It is also the state of our journey of Consciousness so far on the path. The two towers in the background are the last two markers before we head out to the unknown horizon. Before we journey on the Golden Path in consciousness to the beyond, we need certain preparations. Our spiraling through the Tarot has given us some direction, and if we have been meditating and assimilating the information and experimenting with it in our own lives, then our journey could take an amazing turn.

Ernest Holmes in the *Science of Mind* says, "There is nothing wrong with the sum total of Divine Ideas which make up the Real Body, which is Spiritual. Every organ and function of the human body has a Universal Prototype behind it. It is an idea in the mind of God and a Perfect Idea."

When our vehicle is properly prepared, we are supposed to be able to attune ourselves clearly to the Divine Idea behind the particular manifestation. Then we can venture beyond the towers to the top of the mountain where our spiritual destiny waits. In the Eighteenth Portal, the land beyond the towers is what the ancients call the Astral Plane.

We will talk more about this dimension later in the Twentieth Portal, but for now it is important to realize that the Moon also represents the world of illusion, dreams, and delusional experience.

Pisces the Fish, is Mutable Water, feminine and receptive. Pisces rules the feet, a suggestion of our walk on the Golden Path. Venus is exalted in Pisces, which means in the realm of the Moon, the creative imagination reaches its highest manifestation. Pisces is the mystic of the zodiac, and is capable of seeing the divine in everything. Pisces says, "I believe." Here consciousness is entering a more introspective state.

In spiritual pursuits, Pisces are quite unfettered. If they can dedicate themselves to service to humankind, they soar. Some of Pisces characteristics: Unworldly, affectionate, shy, impressionable, perceptive, and intuitive. They seek out Utopias and can live in a fantasy world. Pisces will readily sacrifice for another as their outlook tends to be universally oriented. They will often take an interest in the other person's needs.

The Moon in a Reading

- Emerging; contemplating the unknown.
- The imagination focuses on positive outcome.
- Sensitive to Nature, cultivated, artistic expression.
- Sympathetic.
- Intuitive.
- A message in the dream.
- The body develops according to one's consciousness of Spirit.
- Introspection is called for.
- Situations difficult to fathom.

Reversed

- Deceiving oneself.
- At times comfortable in living the illusion; at other times, distressed.
- Not listening to valuable advice.
- Dangerous activity like alcohol, drugs, or aggressive lust could enter the atmosphere.
- Drifting downstream.
- A need for better self-analysis; facing oneself more honestly.

Thoughts for Meditation on the Moon

A meditation on the Moon might include a question regarding the nature of the activity you are experiencing on the path right now. Are your dreams being affected? Has there been any progress regarding bad habits? Have you gathered more courage in facing the difficulties of a new venture?

Prayer

Moonlight.
I am drawn to it,
a new being—
crawling from the dark pool
to the shining path.
For I am a child of evolution.
Feral and canine creatures bay at my emergence,
a new body forming
from organic cells
reverberating with the one-pointed Light of Spirit.
Now I can feed my imagination
with the nectar of penetrating vision,
and no longer look back into the abyss.
Why should I?
for I need all my energy
for the twists and turns
as I shed my old body
and ascend to the world of dreams.

Chapter 22

XIX. The Sun
Luminosity of the Heart

Astrological Correspondence: The ego transforming into the powerful self-image of the Sun, both as the center of the solar system and the center of the persona.

Hebrew Letter: Resh ר (meaning "face" or "countenance" turned toward the Light, facing the Reality of our own being).

Inner Atmosphere: Enlightenment, as the seeker has taken in the essence of previous instruction and made it a part of the whole personality. Many precepts that have been grasped are affecting the outer circumstances.

Statement: "I am in a state of gratefulness, especially for the better understanding of the relationship I have with my Inner Self. As a result I am filled with faith in the Good and am happy to be alive."

Quotation: "What you feel, what you think, how you behave, what you value and how you live your life reflect the way that you are shaping the Light that is flowing through you." (Gary Zukov, *The Seat of the Soul*)

The Challenge: The pampered ego becomes the center of concern; otherwise little exertion.

Visualization to the Nineteenth Portal, the Sun

The blue sky continues as you walk along the Path.
Ahead you see the Sun blazing before you, illuminating your way.
You are struck by the soft waving radiation
emanating from the shining orb.
Below the Sun on green grass you see a stone wall.
Sunflowers peek over the top.
In front of the wall you see a little boy and girl without clothes.
They are holding hands.
They stand in the center of a circle drawn on green grass.
You stand in front of them, beaming at the scene,
free from care and at peace.
Then the magnificent Sun speaks,
"Follow the Path of the Heart and let my light purify thee."
In tranquil silence,
you raise your arms and feel the rays warm your being . . .
The Sun continues, "What are the qualities that you wish to express?"
At this point on the path you are clear in your thoughts:
"Control of my universe—compassion—and my mind in order."
At these words, you see your face in one of the sunflowers,
golden and smiling.
You are taking in the rays of the Sun,
and are filled with the beauty of the scene.
The Sun's rays are now shining forth from your own aura,
and your atmosphere seems to reverberate with the Light.
Then the little boy speaks, his countenance alive with Light,
"I am a child of the Sun, and so are you."
The little girl smiles and says,
"Beneath your consciousness I dance in delight."
You smile back knowingly and continue on,
luminous with the golden light . . .

General Atmosphere of the Nineteenth Portal, the Sun

So far we have faced many challenges, endured some trials, and adhered to some guidelines. The important thing is, however, we have had these experiences with greater and greater awareness. Or in the words of Tarot, we have been operating in a highly lucid manner from our self-conscious mode, the Magician. As a result, certain blind spots dispersed throughout our lives have been illuminated.

We've observed our weaknesses, worked on them, and moved on to develop important qualities of character. All of this done in an effort to reach a higher degree of self-control. By the time we have finally entered the Nineteenth Portal, when our consciousness reflects the countenance of the Sun, when the vibrations of our personal atmosphere are attuned to its light, our heart is open, our ideals are in the forefront of consciousness, our initiative is fired up, and our subconscious influences are brought out into the open.

From the Sixteenth Portal we have begun the reorganization of the structure of our body, and from meditation on the Moon we have increased our body consciousness. We can feel the energies in our muscles as we stand naked before the Sun.

Striving for health of the body becomes a very important part of the day. We don't want to encourage any thoughts or activities that would harm or weaken our physical vehicle, so we become more conscious of diet, and exercise is added into the meditative atmosphere.

In the realm of the Sun we can look at our faults with more detachment; we are conscious of our self-worth and our God-given abilities. We bring our sense of values to the forefront and properly assess our energy outlay. All of these conditions are aspects of the Sun.

As we enter the Portal of the Sun there is a particular awakening, a certain conviction about our place in the Cosmos. We fully recognize the fact that we are a child of the Most High—we are convinced of it. This acceptance of our Divine Nature brings a sacred joy to the personal atmosphere.

In the Nineteenth Portal we have reached the Fifth Level of Spiritual Unfoldment. The ancients call it Regeneration.

The momentum of our journey shifts again, and in the Portal of the Sun we go through a conscious rebirthing process. Our very being is rejuvenated, especially after our experiences with the Devil and the Tower. As the rays of the Sun fill our Spirit, we feel far removed from our crayfish-like existence in the Eighteenth Portal. We experience a particular harmony of thought, a consciousness enlightened. For we are in the Portal of the Sun, the reward for reaching beyond the two towers of the Moon Portal, the payoff for risking a venture into the unknown. Here we experience a better understanding of the Divine Order. Our spiraling journey through the Tarot has been the matrix of a new and blossoming excitement just in being alive.

We understand that one of our reasons for being is to gather experience, and we have learned to activate more of the kinds of circumstances and situations that WE deem preferable. The awareness within, which has been guiding us in our quest for hidden knowledge, is something we have come to realize is beyond the world, beyond the persona, and even beyond the mind.

When we contemplate the effect of the Sun we see nurturing and growth.

Rather than feel inspiration from the Sun's outer image—fiery gases and immense size—we respond to the image of the Sun on a much deeper level. Its characteristics inspire images of majesty, strength, will, steadfastness . . . In the Sun, we brim with idealism. The Sun is the symbol of self-expression and the ego-self; the Sun is Individuality—who we really are. From the Sun we draw our vital energies. Ultimately, however, the Sun symbolizes God, the Divine Creative Force of our solar system and the universe.

On a personal level, the Sun is the divine spark of life, the Essence within, the nucleus. The Sun also symbolizes one of the major goals of our existence: Self-mastery.

We know now that we have the power to make things happen as we envision them. We know that we can make a difference, that we can affect the acceleration of our own evolution. Through mindfulness, we direct our action and we bring about change through the force of our will, of our blazing internal Sun. The thought of ourselves as a victim of circumstances has become alien to us. Earlier in our journey we had to face our feelings of powerlessness, weakness, and inertia; but now as we drive ahead in our Chariot through the Nineteenth Portal, we ascend to the Sun triumphant—soaring above our ignorance and doubt.

For now we can consciously direct the solar energy to bring comfort and peace, enthusiasm and excitement to our experience. We know what we want and we ask for it. In this sunlight we visualize our needs effortlessly, and know we are worthy of God's abundant grace—because we are loved and wanted, powerful and whole.

This is the awakening of our playful and alive Inner Child. We feel a new sense of freedom, and barriers to our self-expression break down. Just as a plant responds to sunlight, so do our very cells resonate with this inner Sun, and we are regenerated, transformed into a new person.

The four open sunflowers represent the mineral, vegetable, animal, and human kingdoms. They all look toward the children, as though they are controlled by the harmony of the self-conscious and the subconscious. The children, in turn, symbolize the regenerated, spiritualized self—evolution on a higher scale (like the ears of the red jackal-headed god Anubis on the Wheel of Fortune), because Nature wants us to ascend to an ever higher state of consciousness.

The wall symbolizes the barriers we have erected, like the Tower, restrictive and limiting our ability to expand. In the Qabala on the Tree of Life, the Sun is centered in Tipareth, Beauty, the meeting station of the higher and lower energies. It is balance and harmony, sacrifice of the lower self to the Higher. The Portal of the Sun is also the heart chakra, Anahata (the Sanskrit word for "unstuck"). Equilibrium. Resonance. Compatibility. But most of all, the heart chakra is the conduit for the mystery of love.

By now we have learned a great deal about our own weaknesses and where we have allowed ourselves to become misguided. So, as a result, we should have an almost psychic understanding of the vulnerabilities of others. In other words, in the Nineteenth Portal of the Sun, from our inner core, our heart emanates compassion. We radiate all the loving qualities of Spirit—not only to all sentient beings—but most especially to our human self. In the Sun we have refined our self image and feel less inhibited in expressing our worthiness. The straight and wavy lines of the Sun symbolize its subtle activity. The currents are in equilibrium, magnetism and electricity, gravity and radiation. We are in the center of the continuum, where "the sound is made without any two things striking." Here the Magician aspect of our consciousness has developed a very refined one-pointed will. The ability to focus on a situation has reached laser-like precision.

The Examined Life has become an indelible part of our daily experience, and in the light of the Sun, we are living a life of grace. For the Sun's rays envelop all of Life.

The sunflowers rise above the wall, a pictorial way of saying that as we operate in the world as spiritual entities, we transcend our limitations. We are potentially loving beings who express unconditional compassion for all.

The Hebrew letter for the Sun is Resh, which means "the head and face, or countenance." Countenance comes from the French "behavior or demeanor." Our facial expressions reveal our thoughts and emotions. In another sense, when we have "seen the light" our countenance, our persona, is illuminated.

The Fifth Stage of Spiritual Unfoldment is a liberation from the limitations we have imposed on ourselves as sinful, unworthy failures. Instead, in this state we are experiencing a blissful process of personality unfoldment, as the Sun symbolizes attainment, creativity, enlightenment; its rays continually illuminate us as our masculine, assertive, self-conscious side lovingly blends with our feminine, receptive subconscious. And we know that in the Limitless Light of the Sun we are forever supported. The Sun gives us the opportunity to experience life in an unfiltered way, and our energy-draining attachments fade.

At this stage we can sense the light of the soul pouring forth from our Inner Self, our Divine Source. The Bible tells us that we are made in likeness of God, and since God is all-knowing and all-loving, we, too, share in these attributes. Contemplation of the Sun will remind us of this.

The Sun in a Reading

- Consciousness of blessings.
- Knowledge enhanced with compassion; the persona shines.
- Better understanding of one's relation to the Inner Self.
- The heart beats with loving vibrations.
- Innocence and aspiration; optimism.
- Attainment of a body/mind harmony that expresses itself in the outer circumstances.
- Having moved beyond the wall, the barrier we have erected to block our open expression crumbles.
- A general aura of happiness.
- Nurturing encounters.
- The Inner Child comes into play; a delight with existence.
- The Individuality is more "out there" in the world.

REVERSED

- Coldness.
- Erecting rigid structure.
- Discontent.
- Ignorance of certain facts; false impressions not corrected.
- Living in the shadows of the Inner Self.
- Blockage of emotion; the light dims.
- Lack of drive, unenthusiastic.
- Feelings of unfinished business; projects neglected.
- Limited outlook.

Thoughts for Meditation on the Sun

A good time to meditate on the Sun is when we want to recharge our batteries, to gain a new vitality. If the flow of love is restricted, contemplation of the Sun can open the floodgates. If we're feeling stuffy and intolerant, the Sun can bring back that child-like spirit to get things going again. The Sun can also reawaken us to the pulsation of life around us. Contemplation on the Light of the Inner Sun can also help us stimulate our creativity. One might ask questions like, How are we like little children in our approach to the Godhead? What are some of the limitations we still need to face? Are we able at this stage to receive nurturing from our Inner Sun? What is our level of exhilaration? Is a new vigor needed?

Prayer

Where is the swinging scythe?
The painful stretch of the turning Wheel?
I don't even see the descending Sword.
Before me the dissolving Tower refocuses
and I perceive only a grove of towering trees.
No longer am I a crawling thing
emerging from the ooze
peering at the land upside down.
No! It is the world that is fogged up
and out of balance—
For I am lying on the soft grasses,
staring inward,
face to face into the Sun;

and my eyes are burning
from the passions ignited
in my desire
to return to the One.

Chapter 23

XX. Judgement
The Trumpet Call

Alchemical Element: Fire.

Astrological Correspondence: The search for meaning and the power of energy symbolized by the planet Pluto.

Hebrew Letter: Shin ש (meaning "tooth or fang," the Tooth of Fire brought down to purify).

Inner Atmosphere: We become aware that we are on the ceaseless spiral of upward and inward evolution. Our belief in ourselves, our making the best use of our potential is also spiraling upward.

Statement: "I can hear the angel's trumpet call, and I respond with a delighted heart. I am ready to begin again, but now at a higher and finer level of awareness."

Quotation: "When you pay attention to your direct experience of the fire, then you realize just how superficial all the soot and cinders thrown off by that fire really are, and how little they can teach you about the fire itself." (Swami Chetanananda, *The Breath of God*)

The Challenge: The ego travels in the underworld, disinterested in value and quality.

Visualization to the Twentieth Portal, Judgement

How energized you feel from your encounter with the Sun!
You could almost rise from the ground
and blend into the waves of golden sky.
Instead, though, you walk forward on the path,
knowing there is yet another Portal to explore.
The temperature begins to change.
The sudden chill lets you know that the glorious experience in the Sun
is transforming into something else . . .
You notice the sky shimmering from gold . . . to silver . . .
and when you look down at your feet,
you realize you are walking in snow . . .
You are now in a ghostly world . . .
of icy blues and glistening white—
swirling within grays and silvers.
You have traveled beyond the twin towers of the Moon,
deep into the unknown.
You feel that your soul is at last free
as you gently vibrate through blue and white prisms.
You are beyond your imagination into a world
behind our normal everyday waking reality.
In the Twentieth Portal your feet no longer touch the path,
and your soul is in flight to unfamiliar territory.
Although the landscape is new,
you feel welcomed amidst waves of love and acceptance.
You breathe deeply . . . feeling relaxed and at peace . . .
and in this mysterious region
you notice the divine oscillations entering your aura.
Your personal atmosphere is now vibrating to a rhythm
that cleanses your aura with healing Light.

What is this splendor? . . .
You are wonder-struck by the sights and feelings
of this luminescent domain.
Then, in the far distance,
you can hear the faint sound of a trumpet.
In melodious and pleasing flourishes,
the ethereal sounds begin to move through you.
The tone is glistening
and you know you are hearkening to the Music of the Spheres.
The sky is silvery blue
and ahead you see silken white clouds floating above.
You hear the fluid strains of the trumpet coming closer now,
and then . . . in the sky . . .
from a cloud shimmering with waves of light and electricity,
you see him—
the blonde-haired Archangel Gabriel in blue gown and fiery red wings.
He is blowing a gleaming trumpet of gold,
which flies a white square flag with an equal-sided red cross.
And you are awed again at the sights and sounds . . .
Then below the Archangel,
from a cold blue sea surrounded by icy mountains,
you observe a very strange occurrence.
Three stone coffins drifting on the water come into view.
Then to the glorious sound of the archangel's trumpet,
the coffins begin to open.
From the floating stone casket on the right
you see a young man rise,
naked and gray-colored,
gazing upwards to the Archangel.
On the left another naked gray figure emerges.
She is blonde with long hair,
and she raises her arms to the Archangel in an act of praise.
In the center with his back to you, also without clothes,
is a blonde-haired child with his arms raised as well to the Angel.
Suddenly, the Archangel Gabriel opens his eyes to you and speaks,
"So, good Pilgrim, though with love I welcome you to this heavenly clime,
you must not forget that you have never really left it."

This time the man on the right looks passively to the Archangel,
and it is the woman who turns to you and speaks.
"Listen to the trumpet, Brave Traveler,
for ye are always beckoned to partake . . . "
You hear the trumpet again.
As the scene begins to fade and the trumpet sound fades as well . . .
you are relaxed and at peace . . .

General Atmosphere of the Twentieth Portal, Judgement

In the Twentieth Portal, the Archangel Gabriel blows his trumpet, and a new power is brought into the personal aura. In fact, his name, Gabriel, means "Messenger of God." Gabriel is the Fire of the Life-breath brought to consciousness, and we slumber no longer. In fact, the power of the trumpet sound blows us into another almost indescribable depth of mind depicted here in the imagery of the Twentieth Portal, Judgement.

For one thing, the awe and praise we see in the attitude of the three figures in the picture remind us to appreciate the fact that we are more than a body with a brain gifted with the power to think and feel. Instead, it must be remembered that at this point in the journey we are moving far beyond our normal range of thinking: Beneath all impressions regarding our body, our thoughts, and our emotions, we now operate in the Twentieth Portal with the constant knowledge of who we really are—a spiritual being, an ancient Essence—using a fleshly vehicle to get around and enjoy (and/or suffer in) the Physical Plane.

In the dimension of the Judgement Portal, we receive messages. The trumpet is the medium which delivers them. We are told things about Reality that are given to us from beyond our five senses. In terms of *Tarot Awareness*, we might say that the Hierophant—Intuition—sends messages, subtle or otherwise, that tell us things we should do in order to advance on the path. The Emperor—Reason—on the other hand, tells us how to do it. Paul Brunton says in *Inspiration and the Overself* that "Intuition points direction and gives destination. Reason shows a map of the way there."

In the Twentieth Portal we become more convinced about our own particular vision of Reality. At this juncture, the trumpet blow fills us with certitude—and release from the normal, tedious way of seeing and doing things. In addition, we have a better understanding of the functions of the various modes of consciousness from the Magician to the Chariot (self-consciousness, subconsciousness, creative imagination, Reason, Intuition, Discernment, and Integration). Then we ask ourselves: "How often do I follow and maintain the Seven Universal Laws from Strength to Temperance (Suggestion, Response, Cycles, Cause and Effect, Reversal, Transformation, and Verification)?" Then as pilgrims on the path we need to think about our level and frequency of meditation. Therefore, we must ask: What are the impressions I have received so far as I meditated and went through the various Levels of Spiritual Unfoldment from the Devil to the Sun (Bondage, Upheaval, Revelation, Organization, and Regeneration)?"

As we incorporate what we've learned from our studies and our meditations, our thoughts and experience in our everyday waking consciousness should be alive with an energetic imagination (in the language of Tarot we might think of the Empress); a practical positive attitude (Strength), a far-reaching Intuition (the Hierophant) and a mind open to Revelation (the Star).

By the time we have reached the Twentieth Portal of Judgement, we are more attuned to our experience and our self-image as a living example of the Examined Life. Here we strive to become an unencumbered vessel open to instruction from the Inner Light, and then we, in turn, like the Hermit, become a Wayshower for others. The Hermit Consciousness of good-givingness and service becomes for us a natural mode of expression. The inner loving dimension shines outwards through our thoughts, our heart, and our eyes, and we make our "mark" on the world (as we will see in the last Portal of the Major Arcana, the World, with its Hebrew letter Tav, meaning "mark").

As Air belongs to the Fool, and Water is the Element of Mem (the Hanged Man), Fire is the Element of the Hebrew letter of the Twentieth Portal, Shin. It means "tooth" or "fang," and as Paul Foster Case says in his *Tarot: A Key to the Wisdom of the Ages*, Shin breaks down limitation and liberates the energy (as teeth break down food for digestion).

By the time we reach the Twentieth Portal, if we are ignorant of the Law of Cause and Effect (Justice), karma—and we are still unconscious as it operates in our lives—then the Law becomes a punishing tyrant. We are likely to see misery in everything, and the negative outlook will surely show itself in our life as unhappiness (the Wheel of Fortune Reversed).

What we have learned is that through the Law of Reversal (the Hanged Man), we can alter or reverse our use of the Law. The ancients have said that the Law is Mind infinitely moving, and within this Universal Creative Mind we are each a point of Light.

By the time we have reached the Twentieth Portal we have a highly developed sense of analysis and synthesis, inductive and deductive reasoning. We recognize the Magician and the High Priestess operating in our lives. Earlier we saw how our subconscious (High Priestess) is impressed with our self-conscious thought (Magician) in the moment, and how she will automatically follow through with the original thought until manifestation (deductive reasoning). This is the nature of the Law, and it follows a certain pattern. Inductive reasoning, if you remember, is when you reason from a specific occurrence to an overall truth.

For example, if a man compliments a beautiful young woman at a party and she kisses him (an experience), he is likely to give her another compliment so that she will kiss him again. If, however, he ignores her for awhile and there is no contact, he may decide to give a third compliment to see what happens. After he tells her she has beautiful green eyes, and she kisses him again, he could logically conclude that this woman loves compliments (a truth). That is induction.

With *deduction* you start with a premise and follow it through to an inevitable conclusion (plant a sunflower seed and you will get a sunflower, not a pansy).

As we enter the Twentieth Portal beyond reason and emotion, we are now convinced that there is more to us than flesh and bone. In this dimension of Judgement we are beyond what Schopenhauer meant when he said, "Every man takes the limits of his own field of vision for the limits of the world."

With the Law of Reversal (the Hanged Man) we transform our attitude and begin to see the wonder in everything, or at least from time to time, allowing ourselves to become awestruck by the activities within the environment of our life. We then get to see this general optimistic attitude affect the patterns of our life as things move more rhythmically and harmoniously. Thanks to the deductive reasoning of the High Priestess following through on our positive thoughts and accurate premises, we will then tend to have an abundance of fulfilling experiences.

In addition, our atmosphere will emanate certain vibrations, a sureness that we are on the right track, a conviction that the Holy Presence is in, around, and through us. In Tarot, this is the Level of Spiritual Unfoldment known as the Sun, or Regeneration.

We have traveled a long way from the thoughts we once had where we only saw ourselves as victims—where we were once chained in slavery to Ayin, the Devil. Instead, we are now fully aware that our Spirit is guided, and that we remain free and unbound. For at the core of our being we are perfect and whole.

We are more aware that this heightened Reality is also our basic everyday reality as well. We can then be more specific about our needs, and know that we can fulfill them as we become a conduit (Magician) for the Power. But even in this realm of the Twentieth Portal, we must still use the Law of Verification (Temperance).

Gabriel—the Fire of Inspiration—is our Higher Self challenging us to hear the Message, and to make use of it in our daily lives. In the illustration we see the child as our awakening soul on the journey, colored gray as the symbol of blending black and white, yin-yang.

Through trial and error we must discover the Truth for ourselves, as the Law of Verification illustrates. For example, if we accept the idea that love is a cure for all troubles, we need to prove that premise to ourselves in our waking life. We are to use our various states of mind as a laboratory. So a question to ask in this case is, "How can I best make use of the current of love operating in my life?" When a conflict arises, if we can emanate love toward the persons and the situation, moving beyond fault and rancor, moving in a state of mind that accepts the Universal Conscious Energy as an infinitely loving Power, and accepting that balance is the natural state of all things, we can monitor the results and see if showing compassion improves the situation.

As enlightened beings regenerated by the Sun, when the trumpet calls, we know that we are ready to function as instruments of the Power, even though It is something we cannot see with our human eye (Ayin).

In the distance we see the crystal mountains and the potential for clear decision-making, or Judgement. We are reminded that our being is eternal and that our potential is limitless. We are uninterrupted, going forward, and on the spiral we ceaselessly repeat our advancement, each time a rung higher.

Metaphysics as a system of belief is both intriguing and comforting, but if it remains a series of abstract thoughts (the blue mountains in the distance), then we cannot use the knowledge in a practical way—which is one of the main purposes of Tarot meditation and practice.

In St. Paul's Epistle to the Romans (1:20), he said, "For the invisible things of him from the creation of the world are clearly seen, understood by the things that are made." In other words, the visible and the invisible interpenetrate each other, and we can get a sense of the Nature of God from creation. In the fourth dimension, we know this abstract thought as fact.

In the Sixth Stage of Spiritual Unfoldment, the ancients refer to a state of mind they call Realization. As we said before, self-mastery and self-knowledge are the Holy Grail of the Tarot Journey. The ancients told us that if we could but master ourselves, we could master the world. And they gave us many methods to achieve this.

To best benefit from the Examined Life, before going to sleep, the seeker should take a mental inventory of as many thoughts, words, and deeds that occurred during the day. In a detached way, like the Sphinx atop the Wheel (without finger pointing), we can look at the areas where we lost our equilibrium, didn't achieve our goals, or exhibited ignorance of the Law. We may have even deliberately hurt someone else's feelings.

Therefore, it is wise to become sincerely determined to do better the next day, to progress with humility and honor. A good attitude will contribute to burning off some of the negative karma you may have accumulated along the way.

A revitalized spiritual point of view then richly colors our personal atmosphere. We feel more purified, and like the Lovers of the Sixth Portal, our sense of right and wrong is more acute. We are also more discerning in our choices. Tarot is one method that can guide us in the right direction and help us recognize enlightened choices.

If, for example, we were to understand the seven Modes of Consciousness, or cultivate an awareness of the seven Universal Laws (and actually obey them), or feel the unfoldment of a spiritual level—it is conceivable that more complex avenues along the journey could be explored.

Judgement, in particular, offers a very special avenue to knowledge and spiritual encounter: The imagery of the Twentieth Portal suggests a dimension similar to the dream state. In fact, by the time we have reached the realm of Judgement, we may choose to be more conscious during experiences in a supremely vivid "dream."

The key is to remember what you learned and what you experienced. It is therefore good practice to intend to have more consciousness during the dream as you close your eyes. It's also beneficial to bring some clarity to your personal atmosphere before drifting off to sleep. Sometimes we need to ask ourselves about the "bondage" we may have accumulated from the Devil's consciousness of the Fifteenth Portal.

And what constitutes that consciousness? Fear. Anger. Inertia. Possessiveness. Lust. And worst of all, arrogance. Before going to sleep we want our atmosphere to glow with Starlight, that is, enlightenment, and readiness for a very beneficial journey into the world of dreams.

The idea is if we are without the excess baggage of heavy karma holding us down, we can be more conscious as our Essence travels to the finer realms. This is no less than saying that the ancients promise we will be more open to Eternal Wisdom imparted to us in the state of deep sleep.

However, the process needs a second step.

As we awake, it is very helpful to write down in the Journal as much information as possible so that we can remember the best parts of the dream. In this way we will receive a unique education from the realm pictured in the Twentieth Portal.

Sometimes, if we are fortunate, the trumpet call comes in order to awaken us from our inertia. The coffins in the picture are yet another symbol of limitation and confinement, and as we can see from the scene depicted, the coffins are open, intimating a new, unfettered experience of Self-Realization.

In the Twentieth Portal of Judgement, the self-conscious male and the subconscious female actively accept the Message of the trumpet call. And it happens in a realm of experience we usually forget. The Twentieth Portal is depicting a different dimension, the fourth dimension—the astral world. The central idea is that through meditation on Judgement, if we have been sincere and persistent, and have been learning and verifying in our lives all the lessons that have gone before, then the ancient seers tell us that we will, under the right conditions, not only be fully conscious when we are awake, but we can also be fully conscious in the middle of our dreams.

Ultimately, this is what they mean by the Sixth Level of Spiritual Unfoldment: Realization. And under the right circumstances this realization happens during the nightly sojourn in the astral world—where the dream becomes like a classroom. Needless to say, a classroom where the areas of learning are infinite in their scope.

Here in the Twentieth Portal, we could be given information on anything from how to approach various challenges in our lives, how to heal a particular situation, where to concentrate our creativity, how to make correct decisions and adapt to change, or what to do to make life more entertaining.

We, too, like the figures in the illustration, will respond to the Message inherent in the angel's trumpet call.

From an astrological perspective, the planet Pluto rules the atmosphere of Judgement. Pluto was the god of the underworld, and in a sense, that is where we are in the fourth dimension.

Pluto's travel through all the signs of the zodiac takes over 247 years. As Pluto was discovered only in 1930, it heralds the dawning of a new age. From ancient times, Judgement corresponded only to the element Fire, but because of Pluto's discovery, the planet was added to the overall meaning of the Twentieth Portal.

Pluto introduces the idea of a life consecrated to the Eternal and the freedom to continually express one's enlightened nature. Pluto is also the planet of illumination and heavenly light, in spite of being named for the god of the underworld. Actually, the negative aspects of Pluto revolve around darkness, obsession, loss of control, and destruction.

If our existence is one in constant opposition to the Law, then our experience will be a continual struggle in a living hell, the Pluto consciousness at its worst. However, in the realm of the Twentieth Portal, with Pluto we continue our personal regeneration of the Nineteenth Portal of the Sun into an ever more increasing state of awareness.

Judgement in a Reading

- Responding to the message of the Inner Self; hearing the trumpet.
- Seeing clearly, awakening.
- The moment of decision.
- Renewing one's attitude and approach.

- Opening to spiritual influences.
- Freedom from past guilt; a strong desire to improve.
- The ability to see all sides of an issue or situation.
- Inspiration moves the project ahead.

Reversed

- Not hearing the message; ignoring the spiritual side; agnostic.
- The intellect freezes out subtle influences.
- Mistakes made from following wrong advice.
- Refusal to listen to outside opinion; a closed mind.
- Limited outlook.

Thoughts for Meditation on Judgement

Now that we are reaching the end of this rung of the spiral, it's time for some reevaluation: What were some of your most difficult challenges? How did you meet them? What project(s) did you complete during the time of this journey? What card(s) did you adopt as your beacon light? What card(s) did you find hard to relate to? What Portal gave you the most powerful meditation? How does your life currently reflect the Personal Mission Statement? Did any of the cards give you significant dreams?

Prayer

The Angel's trumpet blares the call to decision:
I will refine . . .

Floating on the infinite sea,
the lid on my coffin slides off
and I rise in fiery breath
body-less.

So strange
I feel I've been here before
liberated in the perpetual spiral
in the dimension beyond words—

Limitation discarded,
for even in dream
I am awake.

Chapter 24

XXI. The World
The Cosmic Perspective

Astrological Correspondence: The conscientious self-discipline of Saturn.

Hebrew Letter: Tav ת (meaning "mark or signature," where we are marked by Spirit as we advance).

Inner Atmosphere: Our personal evolution has reached a point where we are given new powers. The harmony of our body-mind-Spirit at this level allows us to see the workings of Nature more clearly.

Statement: "I understand the blueprint of my life, and what I am here to accomplish. I am ready to take on the responsibilities that Spirit wishes to bestow upon me."

Quotation: "But if one can sense—deeply sense—the nonlocal character of the world that God has seemingly built into it, we may find that another view of creation is possible, one in which we are not the end result but active participators in all there is." (Larry Dossey, *Recovering the Soul*)

The Challenge: The ego requires a more mature outlook as it is still confused about its needs and goals.

Visualization to the Twenty-First Portal, the World

You continue on,
energetically moved by the message you received
from the Archangel's trumpet.
Leaving behind the cool, white and blue world of the Twentieth Portal,
you are floating along the Golden Path to the purple mountain heights.
From there you rise into the turquoise-blue sky.
As you enter the atmosphere of the Twenty-first Portal,
the air is electric with Spirit,
and your aura sparkles in the crisscross of vibrating currents.
You are alive to the various Modes of Consciousness,
and you have a better grasp of the Universal Laws
operating in and through you.
From your various meditations along the path
you feel more aware of the influx of boundless divine Spirit in your life.
You stand there and breathe in this awareness of Spirit . . .
You breathe in . . . you breathe out . . .
Slowly . . . you inhale . . . exhale . . .
Think of the Holy Presence as you raise your eyes
to the glistening heavens . . .
Inhale slowly . . . and exhale.
Then, above you,
 you see clouds in the four corners of the sky,
and from each cloud
you behold the four Fixed signs of the zodiac.
In the top right cloud you see the soaring eagle of Scorpio;
from the left you see the golden-haired Aquarian angel.
You notice that the bull of Taurus is in the bottom left cloud,
and the lion of Leo faces toward you from the bottom right.
In the sky above, you see a huge green wreath of victory,

with a red infinity symbol attached at the top and bottom.
In the center of the wreath is a female figure draped in a purple robe.
In each hand the figure holds two spirals . . .
Then the lion speaks to you.
"So, young Pilgrim, has your contemplation of me
made you more expressive?"
"Well, I—"
The lion thunders,
"Have you faced your fear—with my open heart?
Are you more magnanimous now that you have studied me?"
"I like to think that I—"
The eagle interrupts with a huge flapping of wings.
"Can you analyze your emotional state
from a more objective viewpoint?"
"I think I understand my feelings a little better," you say, "but—"
"I want to know," the eagle interrupts,
"if the contact with your new emotional depths
has affected your self-control?
Can you make proper use of the intensity of the new insights?"
You want to speak but are thrown off balance temporarily
by the depth and intensity of their inquiry.
"They seem more interested in posing questions," you think to yourself,
"than in hearing any detailed answers from me!"
Then the angel turns to you and says,
"Good Pilgrim, do you consider yourself a more independent thinker,
and yet tolerant of the other's point of view?
Do you have a vision of the world as it ought to be?
Are you comfortable now that you understand
the vastness of your potential as a human and a spiritual being?"
You almost swoon at all the thoughts bombarding you.
The bull then speaks up.
"I have only one question, and it is beyond the others:
Can you put into practice what you have learned on the path?"
You are speechless for a moment.
The woman in the center of the wreath widens her eyes
and speaks to you.
"I am thy culmination, Good Pilgrim,

thy goal exalted.
Thou hast accumulated much,
and thou shalt accumulate more.
Continue on thy way
and bring thy light unto the world."
You think, "Oh . . . yes . . . I, I will . . . "
And you open your mind to your new environment,
now with a more concentrated, penetrating vision.
You take a deep breath
and on the exhale, say,
"I am now releasing my limitations . . . "
Take in another deep breath,
feeling cleansed and exhilarated.
On the exhale, say,
"I am releasing all my fears . . . "
Then allow yourself to feel relaxed and at peace,
comforted in the Light.
Count slowly backwards, 10 . . . 9 . . . 8 . . .
and when you are finished,
you can open your eyes
feeling refreshed and awake.

General Atmosphere of the Twenty-First Portal, the World

Our travels along this particular road we call Tarot, if nothing else, focus our mind for intelligent inquiry. Our need to know what is true moves to the forefront of our thoughts. As we finish this current rung on the spiral, we are left with many questions, one of which is:

Just how far have I come? Our exploration of the Examined Life will take us in many directions and encourages us to ask of ourselves many more questions. For example, Do I understand the Law of Cause and Effect operating in my life—that through my thoughts, words, and deeds, I am the architect of my fate? Am I more aware of destructive thoughts as they try to gain entry to the Temple of the High Priestess? Do I see only with my physical eye? What is my relationship as a self-conscious entity (Magician) to my subconscious High Priestess? Am I a servant of the Lord? Just Who is the Lord for me?

From the Twentieth Portal, Judgement, a state of mind called the fourth dimension, we reached a point of Self-Realization where we have actually answered the question put to us by the Oracle at Delphi when she says, "Ανδρω, γνοθις σεαυτον" —"Man, Know Thyself."

We see ourselves and Spirit coalesced into a point of consciousness, a mind, a personality, and a body. Joel Goldsmith in *Consciousness Unfolding* says, "When you begin to believe, really believe, that God is the consciousness of you, that all issues from the divine consciousness of you, and not from outside, not from effect, you will be on the first rung of the ladder of spiritual unfoldment."

In the Twenty-first Portal, the World, we enter yet another dimension, the fifth. The ancients hint that this moment exists in something like the center of Now, a state of consciousness that is fully awake in the present. In fact, in Sanskrit, the word for "the awakened one" translates as buddha.

In the fifth dimension we lose all sense of separateness, either from God or from the souls of our fellow beings. The Consciousness of the World is all encompassing and as vast as the limitless galaxies. In the harmony of our body-mind-soul, we become one with the Holy Presence of the Most High. We are present and awake in the eternal creative loving Power of God, and God is present in us.

This thought becomes an indelible part of our personal atmosphere and as Paramahansa Yogananda says, " . . . we do not have to pray that it come to us, that we are not merely near it at all times, but that God's omnipresence is our omnipresence; that we are just as much a part of Him now as we ever will be; all we have to do is improve our knowing."

Our consciousness in the Twenty-First Portal of the World is a moment characteristic for its purity and timelessness. When we have reached this stage of spiritual unfoldment, the seventh and last, Administration, it is our enlightenment, in a sense, that now maintains and supports the universe. We are awakened in an innate way, and we become a willing servant, very rationally accommodating to one and all.

We are exceedingly tranquil, too, with a real affinity for what is true and good. From our center, our expression is mirror-like, reflecting our innate beauty out into the world. In the Twenty-first Portal, through thought, word, and deed, we exhibit compassion and a highly developed communication with the soul-life of our fellow human beings. The movement of our thoughts is rarely disturbed by outside negative influences, and there is little that can deflect us from our mission, which at this point we know with conviction.

In our fully awakened consciousness we are burning off karma and neutralizing our bad habits. The ego-self is more of an observer than a shrill voice with echoes of "me-me-me." In the Portal of the World we are in our detached, objective state, and are quite free to choose, easily deciding to be free from overweening desires.

The importance of the Twenty-first Portal is our relationship to the ever-abiding, unchangeable Truth of What Is, That which is without beginning or end and is always present in the Now. It is our recognition of this Holy Presence which gives us a serenely happy consciousness, a consciousness that heralds tranquillity and helpfulness to the world. There is no prejudice in the atmosphere of the Twenty-first Portal because we are fully aware of our connection to all of creation.

In Tarot, this state of mind is called Cosmic Consciousness, and is represented by the figure in the center of the wreath (which some say is androgynous: Hermes/Aphrodite; Mercury/Venus; the blending of the male and female principles, self-consciousness and subconsciousness; yin-yang).

In an act of free will, the ego allows itself to be subordinate to the subconscious, which has now been cleansed of detrimental karma; the subconscious then influences the self-conscious in highly beneficial ways. She/he is the new body of finer, more luminescent cells formed from the denseness of the old.

At this point since we have grasped who we really are, we are able to use our body-mind-soul to consciously affect the evolution of the race. That's why she is also surrounded by the figures of the Wheel of Fortune, a mandala of the eternal spiral of creation. She is what evolves as the red jackal-headed god Anubis listens to the message of the Most High from his position on the right side of the Wheel. Kaph, the Hebrew letter for the Wheel, is the grasping hand, and in this case, it is the soul "grasping" the message.

We must return to a consideration of the Wheel—the Law of Cycles—because we are now reaching the end of a rotation of that Wheel.

If you remember the four figures represent the four Fixed signs of the zodiac: Leo-Scorpio-Aquarius-Taurus. And if you remember, in the consciousness of the Wheel, we are inspired to continue, to trust life and Nature and realize that all events, circumstances, persons, and things are ultimately harmonious. If we seek, we will get our reward, which is evolving to a higher plane of Consciousness, represented by the figure.

In the Twenty-first Portal, our personal evolution has reached a point where the power of our personal atmosphere, our body-mind-spirit, can actually influence Nature—which is the culmination of the soul's journey in the material plane. After assimilating the meditative state into our everyday waking consciousness, the Universal Power can work freely through the chakras, the spinning wheels of energy which draw the powers of the Life Force into our aura.

The Hebrew Letter for the World is Tav, the final letter of the Hebrew alphabet, meaning "mark or signature." From the fourth dimension of the astral world, the subtle realm of vital energy, of delicate vibrations of sound and color, we have heard the sacred communications of the Archangel Gabriel—and we are marked by Spirit. In another sense, a signature is a distinctive mark or characteristic indicating identity.

The figure of Tav is dancing in the middle of a wreath, forming an ecstatic, but at the same time, disciplined stance. She is moving freely but is still enclosed within. In order to be truly creative, we must understand the Seven Modes of Consciousness, obey the Seven Universal Laws, and meditate as we unfold through the Seven Levels of Spiritual Understanding (7x3=21). We must think, feel, and act in accordance with the Higher Self in order to reach liberation on the Physical Plane.

Now what is the astrological correspondence to Tav, the World?

It is the planet Saturn, the Great Tester, determined to bring us to the "goal of perfection." He brings us to face our strengths and weaknesses through a series of tests. We are challenged by having to deal with thwarted desires, aggressive people, limits on our freedom, grief, debt . . . the list goes on. Rather, it is through this process that we learn that the reason for being in the Physical Plane is not gratification, but to gather experience and fashion our character in light of the virtues of wisdom, humility, compassion, and patience, among others.

Saturn also symbolizes the destruction of what is worn out and useless. The old disintegrates so that better, more adaptable manifestations can come into being. One of the hallmarks of the Saturn consciousness is self-discipline—arrived at through sustained effort and delayed gratification. In the Twenty-first Portal we learn through the Saturn state of mind to gather treasures of wisdom in order to make the correct decisions. From there we gain a sense of the holy, the dependability of Life, and the persistence of the Inner Self to sanctify us.

The Saturn Consciousness encourages us in the Examined Life; we accept delay with equanimity and learn patience from it. Further, we look to Saturn to help us work out our karma and endure the trials that come our way. Then we can exert ourselves to push toward the fullness of Life that awaits us at the end of evolution.

The Saturn Consciousness actually helps us develop our character as a responsible human being. We make the most of our times of solitude and develop trust that things will work out for the best. As we achieve and gain an understanding of the lessons of the Twenty-first Portal and all the Portals, Saturn, of course, leaves us with questions:

1. In what area of life must I learn to move beyond imitation?

2. Under what circumstances will a renewal of self-discipline enrich my experience?

3. Where will my ability to dream and have faith be most severely tested?

4. How can I best improve the structure of my life?

5. Has my adventure through the Portals of the Inner Landscape helped me to focus my Will?

The World in a Reading

- The benefits of self-control are realized; maturity.
- The will is directed with clarity and responsibility.
- Attainment of the goal; finishing the project.
- More conscious of the unity of things.
- Affirming life; a positive attitude.
- An increase in prosperity.
- Good reputation.
- More Truth understood; problems stabilize.

REVERSED

- Plans not yet realized.
- Increased struggle with life's tests; many more lessons to be learned.
- Important principles not grasped.
- More determination is needed; discipline is lacking.
- Overly concentrating on one's limitations and difficulties.

Thoughts for Meditation on The World

As we leave the Twenty-First Portal to continue the journey on a different level through the Minor Arcana, it is useful to ponder some aspects of the knowledge we've gained:

1. How am I grounded in the world, and yet spiritually aware at the same time?

2. Do I have any new responsibilities as I find my consciousness expanding?

3. Have I learned to appreciate at least some form of self-discipline?

4. Can I truly answer the question that Tarot poses, namely, What is it that I want to accomplish?

Prayer:
"On the Way Home"

My upward lifting Soul
meets my Inner Self as it descends—
And I sign my name in shining Light
as this turn on the Spiral ends.
My Inner Self has guided me,
a shuddering Child in fright,
Though I met my shadow on the Way
and fallen from great heights.
I now see the world's appearances
as so much less than they may seem,
For I have heard the Angel's trumpet,
startle me from my dream.
I have learned to form new images
both precise and oh so clear,
so that my dear High Priestess
has nothing more to fear.
Now new vibrations fill my Soul
as another journey has begun,
For I'm the Cosmic Dancer,
and my home is in the Sun.

Part Three

THE MINOR ARCANA

Consciousness
from the Garden to the Battleground

KNIGHT of WANDS.

Chapter 25

The Suit of Wands
Spirit Ablaze

Introduction to the Minor Arcana

The Minor Arcana, which translates "lesser secret," is nonetheless a continuation of the journey into various conditions of earthly existence. First, we will look at different principles and situations occurring in the Physical Plane. Then, in the Court of the Minor Arcana, we will study numerous character traits, attitudes, virtues—and vices.

In the Minor Arcana there are fifty-six cards which include four Aces representing the root of the Elements: The Spirit of Fire (Wands), the emotion of Water (Cups), the intellect of Air (Swords), and the manifestation of Earth (Pentacles). One of the purposes of Tarot is to make you think about these Elements working in and through your personal atmosphere.

In the Major Arcana, the Portals of the Inner Landscape, we studied various aspects of Consciousness with which our soul expresses itself. Our inquiry led us into growth and transformation through a sometimes challenging kind of self-examination. In the Minor Arcana we will see how the soul is engaged in a labyrinth of human experiences. Three questions will dominate the inquiry:

1. How well do you (as an Energy aware of Itself incarnating in order to create and gain experience) understand your purpose (Fire—Wands), emotional make-up (Water—Cups), thought processes (Air—Swords), and physical well-being (Earth—Pentacles)?

2. How well do you understand Universal Law? and,

3. Can you describe your spiritual level of attainment?

Tarot Awareness includes the fact that our personality will reflect the highest ideals of the Spiritual Plane, the lovingkindness of the Emotional Plane, the wisdom of the

Mental Plane, and an integration that leads to paradise on the Physical Plane. Through self-discipline, poise, ethics, and awareness, we will meet the challenges and opportunities for growth offered in the fifty-six situations and personalities of the Minor Arcana. And we will discover that character does indeed count.

In the Minor Arcana we will see the relationship we have to our priorities, our failures and accomplishments, and the nature of our personality characteristics. Obstacles on the path will surely show themselves, and as we meet them, we will conquer our ignorance and weaknesses. As with the Major Arcana, we will continue to gain more confidence and become clearer about our purpose for incarnation.

In the Minor Arcana, through a confrontation with events and people in the seeker's life, certain truths will be revealed if approached honestly.

Although the fifty-six cards of the Minor Arcana were grafted onto the twenty-two cards of the Major Arcana (the Fool plus the twenty-one Portals) much later in the Middle Ages, they can still provide us with vital clues to the overall picture of Reality captured in what we call a "reading" (see chapter 30).

Our modern deck is a direct descendant of the Minor Arcana, with a few exceptions: Wands=Clubs, Cups=Hearts, Swords=Spades, and Pentacles=Diamonds. The modern deck retains the Aces, cards 2–10, Jack (Knight), Queen, and King. However, it eliminates the Pages, bringing the total to fifty-two, and does retain one card from the Major Arcana. The sojourning soul (which Tarot calls Aleph, the Fool) is in search of experience through the Four Levels of Existence, continuing on the path into the situations of the Earth Plane. In the modern deck he is called the Joker.

To begin the Minor Arcana we will consider the First Level of Existence, Wands and the Spiritual Plane. In the spiritual system of Numbers, 1 (or Ace) is the beginning, essence, root, first cause, first manifestation, the self-conscious "I" (The Magician).

The Ace of Wands

Alchemical Element: Fire.

Astrological Correspondence: Aries (Cardinal in the Suit of Fire), Leo (Fixed), Sagittarius (Mutable).

Image: A glowing hand holding a sprouting Wand extends forth from a cloud. In the background we see a castle and a river coursing through fertile land.

Key Phrase: Spiritual power.

Statement: "Here my consciousness gains knowledge to eventually fashion what I have learned into material form."

Quotation: "Nothing great was ever achieved without enthusiasm." (Ralph Waldo Emerson)

Major Obstacle: A tendency to misuse the Power of Fire, initiative twisted for selfish purposes.

The Aces capture the Essence of the Suit they represent, and the Ace of Wands, with its origin in the Spiritual Plane, is basically an alignment with one's Ideal, an enthusiasm for expression, and a sense of adventure. In the Ace of Wands the pioneering soul celebrates in its creative urge. Here the original Idea emanates outward from its fiery center.

Contemplation of the ethereal side of life flourishes, and the consciousness awakens to its spiritual nature as a child of the Most High. The single Wand holding forth from the cloud proclaims this divine heritage, injecting a fiery energy into the reading. The Ace of Wands also heightens the meaning of other cards in its proximity. It brings a focus of the Will to complete the new enterprise.

In its ultimate sense, the Ace of Wands signifies the ability of the seeker to act as an instrument for the expression of the higher virtues: Courage, insight, initiative, fortitude . . .

The major tools employed in the Spiritual Plane are meditation, introspection, and an examination of the contents of consciousness.

The castle in the distance implies a goal to be reached after effort expended on the Spiritual Quest. Enlightenment and generating ideas.

From an astrological perspective, the Ace of Wands incorporates the meanings of the three Fire signs (Aries, Leo, and Sagittarius):

Aries the Ram ("I am"). The soul activated in the first thrusting energies of spring; leadership. Action, adventure, energetic, ambitious, impulsive; a need to climb to the heights.

Leo the Lion ("I will"). Fire of the heart; courageous. Dynamic self-expression, affection, loyalty.

Sagittarius the Archer ("I believe"). Enthusiastic, optimistic, humorous, pointed opinions, Truth-seeking, philosophical.

The Ace of Wands in a Reading

- Beginning of a project.
- Creative energy.
- Beginning the Spiritual Quest.
- New experiences and exploits.
- Spiritual insight.
- The ability to tune into the Higher Power.
- The will to get it done.

REVERSED

- At its worst, a gross misuse of Power gained from the spiritual journey; a Power used for selfish, destructive purposes, setting in motion a tremendous upheaval of bad karma.
- A shadow on the beginning of a new enterprise; delay.
- Doubting one's abilities and a life lived superficially.
- A total acceptance of the surface of things; blindness to the Real.
- Cruel dominance, cowardice, a life without direction, and a denial of one's true Nature.

- Excessive ambition; indiscriminately stepping on people to reach the top.
- Decadence and corruption; a need for spiritual renewal and a rethinking of one's attitude and overall approach to life.

STRATEGY

1. The seeker now brings a colorful, fiery eagerness to the new enterprise, as well as a spiritual, optimistic attitude.

2. Further, an awareness of the invisible in the visible is critical to the success of the project. Blind acceptance of the outer element of a situation is to be avoided.

3. A consciousness that embodies the Ace of Wands operates in the Physical Plane with his or her eyes open, ready to experience what life has to offer—confident, comforted, and faith-filled.

4. A need for spiritual renewal and a rethinking of one's attitude and overall approach to life.

5. This consciousness progresses ahead in creating a new livelihood, a new environment, and a higher set of values, excited by new ideas and ways of interacting with the world at large.

The Two of Wands

"Vision"

Astrological Influence: Mars in Aries (resourceful vitality).

Image: From the roof of the castle in the Ace of Wands, a merchant looks out over a seascape; in his right hand he holds a globe, while in his left hand he holds a Wand. A second Wand is fastened to the parapet next to him. On the opposite, two lilies and two roses cross.

Key Phrase: Energetic enterprise.

Statement: "Drawing on my abilities, I am determined to reach the pinnacle where my decision-making skills will eventually bear fruit."

Quotation: "Mindfulness is like that—it is the miracle which can call back in a flash our dispersed mind and restore it to wholeness so that we can live each minute of life." (Thich Nhat Hanh, *Mindfulness*)

Major Obstacle: The ego is restless and in a continual state of dissatisfaction.

As consciousness travels to the realm of the Two in the Suit of Fire, the seeker experiences a certain balance on the Physical Plane through spiritual understanding and boldness of vision. The balance is between pure motivation (lilies) and the desire (roses) to see the project through to successful completion. The balance of the Two is further emphasized by the merchant's understanding of the infinite potential (globe) of his subconscious interacting with the root idea of his self-conscious (Wand) in order to realize the goal.

The Two of Wands in a Reading

- Clarity of sight.
- The idea sent out to manifest.
- Holding firm to belief in the project.
- Faith that the treasure-laden ship will return.
- Embarking on a new enterprise with courage, fortitude, and a measure of intuition.
- Objective outlook.
- Assertiveness with a good deal of stamina.
- The vital energy of Mars compliments the pioneering spirit of Aries as the seeker leads the way in a new project, another way of saying that "Mars rules Aries."

REVERSED

- Narrowed vision.
- Negative outlook.
- Loss of confidence.
- Superficial observation—faulty decisions.
- Unreasonable expectations that waste valuable time.
- Failure to take risk—missed opportunity (especially with the Four of Cups).
- New enterprise off to a shaky start.
- Impatience (especially with the Seven of Pentacles Reversed).
- Calculating motivations, misuse of power and aggression (Mars in Aries, afflicted).

STRATEGY

1. Never losing faith in one's dreams.
2. Seeing virtue in an attitude of confident expectation; patience.
3. Keeping an open mind regarding one's abilities to visualize success.

The Three of Wands

"The Ships Return"

Astrological Correspondence: Sun in Aries (bold self-expression).

Image: From a hilltop a young man in medieval garb stands between three Wands and watches the return of the fleet he sent out in search of goods.

Key Phrase: Initiative fulfilled.

Statement: "My mind is aflame with ideas, and I count the blessings as they enter my harbor."

Quotation: "They that go down to the sea in ships, that do business in great waters: These see the works of the Lord, and his wonders, in the deep." (Psalm 107:23-24)

Major Obstacle: Energies scattered to the wind.

The Three of Wands in a Reading

- The key to success through effort and foresight; the ability to look beyond the typical (Understanding in the Suit of Fire).
- Perception from a higher level of awareness; astute.
- Direction of the Will brings in the bounty.
- Growth in insight, enthusiastically pursued.
- Physical demonstration of the idea (especially with the Ace of Wands, Swords, and Pentacles).
- Appreciation of progress made.
- Integrity in business dealings assures success in the venture.
- Realization of the dream through practical application.

- Successful collaboration; ingenuity, coordinated effort.
- High-spirited enthusiasm for the project (Sun in Aries).

REVERSED

- Foolish risks (especially with 0. The Fool reversed).
- Illegalities, swindles (see the Five and Seven of Swords).
- Plans not well thought out; enterprise could be derailed if blueprint not corrected.
- Dissipated energies (Sun in Aries, afflicted).

STRATEGY

1. Taking the time to weigh alternatives so that the effort put out will bring in the most dividends without wasting precious energy.
2. The forceful personality directs its vitality toward achievable goals.
3. Listen to the intuitions of the Inner Self regarding the best way to finish what needs to be done.

The Four of Wands

"Completion of an Undertaking"

Astrological Correspondence: Venus in Aries (The love vibration activated).

Image: The Ram, returning home after much energy expended on the enterprise, is greeted warmly with garlands and dancing.

Key Phrase: Blessings after success.

Statement: "I will celebrate the joy of reaching the end of a project and gather the good I have learned from the experience."

Quotation: "No matter how long or how many times he blunders, he has every right to come back to his own spiritual home." (Sri Chinmoy, *Yoga and the Spiritual Life*)

Major Obstacle: Feelings of insecurity affecting the outcome of the enterprise.

The Four of Wands in a Reading

- Reaching a goal.
- Recognition for diligence (especially with the Three of Pentacles).
- Giving oneself permission to rest and relax after hard work.
- Effort rewarded.
- Celebration for completion of a successful endeavor.
- A peaceful atmosphere affects home life.
- Feeling welcome.
- Enjoyment in entertaining visitors.
- An oasis in the midst of turbulence (Venus in Aries).

REVERSED

- Conflict in the home environment.
- A delay in reaching the goal.
- Feelings of insecurity, of not belonging.
- Unwelcome intrusion.
- Inconsiderate words and actions; rudeness (Venus in Aries, afflicted).

STRATEGY

1. From time to time we need to pat ourselves on the back after completing a project. When a lot of energy has been put out, it's fine to rest on one's laurels a bit.
2. After a lot of hard work it's good to take a break, contemplate the successes and where you missed the mark, and celebrate Life for the endless opportunities offered.
3. We also need to recognize the efforts of others and reward them accordingly.

The Five of Wands
"Conflict"

Astrological Correspondence: Saturn in Leo (tension restricts the heart's need to open).

Image: Five young men wield Wands against each other, creating a picture of strife and chaos.

Key Phrase: Misunderstanding leads to turmoil.

Statement: "I refuse to give in to frustration and will try hard to take the other person's point of view into consideration."

Quotation: "My enemies, desire, hatred, and the rest, are destitute of hands and feet; they have no courage or wisdom. How can they enslave me?" (Santideva, *Ways of Enlightenment*)

Major Obstacle: The ego becomes obsessive over injuries inflicted and is determined to seek vengeance for perceived wrongs.

The Five of Wands in a Reading

- The need to overpower others.
- Strife at work or at home.
- Insensitivity; feelings hurt.
- Violent confrontation.
- Fiercely opposing views; draining arguments.
- Confusing events and conversations.

- Open disputes.
- Plans disrupted by meddling.
- Unreasonable demands.
- Aggressive competition.
- Struggle for dominance (Saturn in Leo).

REVERSED

- Underhandedness.
- Possible activity behind the scenes not in the seeker's best interest.
- Deception, treachery.
- Sabotage.
- Stress, anxiety.
- Negative tactics hidden.
- Could also mean the strife is coming to an end.

STRATEGY

1. Stay centered and focused, be productive; don't give in to peer pressure or take the criticism from others to heart.
2. Plan strategies carefully and back up opinions with facts.
3. Do not let emotions get out of control.
4. Forgive those who trespass against you, but don't allow yourself to be tread upon by swine.

The Six of Wands

"Victory After Strife"

Astrological Correspondence: Jupiter in Leo (leadership with heart).

Image: A warrior wearing a victory wreath on his head marches on his horse in front of a cheering throng.

Key Phrase: Efforts to solve difficulties pay off.

Statement: "I have had some hard lessons to learn, but the sense of triumph I now feel in overcoming obstacles made the trials worth it."

Quotation: "A noble soul is always noble in all circumstances." (Swami Paramananda, *Book of Daily Thoughts and Prayers*)

Major Obstacle: The ego glories in false adulation; vanity.

The Six of Wands in a Reading

- Advancement after hard lessons.
- Resolution of an important matter; difficulties overcome.
- Honor unmarred by ego; selflessness.
- Self-confidence brings optimism for long-term goals.
- Self-reliance.
- Recognition for courage and accomplishment (Jupiter in Leo).

REVERSED

- Fear in facing difficulties.
- An obsession to impress others.
- Loss of belief in your abilities to succeed; discouragement.
- Half-hearted efforts not appreciated.
- Disappointing others.
- Scorn.
- Bragging masks insecurity (Jupiter in Leo, afflicted).

STRATEGY

1. Affirm your faith in Life and yourself.
2. Do not give in easily to discouragement.
3. Perseverance energizes aspiration and self-confidence.

The Seven of Wands
"Standing Up for Principle"

Astrological Correspondence: Mars in Leo (valor).

Image: With his Wand, a lone figure holds off aggressive, rising staffs.

Key Phrase: Courage in the face of difficulties.

Statement: "I will not compromise my principles, and I will do my best to lead an ethical life."

Quotation: "If they do not obey the call of conscience the first time, it may become more painful to obey it the second time." (Paul Brunton, *Emotions and Ethics, The Intellect*)

Major Obstacle: Disinterested in forming a philosophy of life; the ego is plagued by weak convictions.

The Seven of Wands in a Reading

- The validity of one's principles is under attack from adversaries.
- The courage to uphold those principles creates advantage.
- Remain at the post no matter what happens.
- Accepting leadership, responsibilities (especially with the XXI. The World).
- Not giving in to peer pressure.
- Refusal to adapt or conform when convictions are at stake; the skill and prowess to resist reaching an unwholesome compromise.
- Successfully standing firm against the infidel.

- Your opinions and convictions anger adversaries.
- Enterprise and initiative meet with resistance; opposing circumstances.
- Individual crusade.
- The situation can come to a climax.
- Inner strength of purpose and determination brought to bear on opposition (Mars in Leo).

REVERSED

- Fear of adversaries, confrontation.
- Weak convictions.
- Cannot hold up positions if vigorously attacked; retreat.
- Intimidation.
- Easily manipulated under pressure.
- Crushed by the negative opinions of others.
- Feeling vulnerable, defenseless.
- Empty, grandiose, aggressive gestures and improbable schemes (Mars in Leo, afflicted).

STRATEGY

1. This is the card that proclaims, "Stand up for what you believe in!"
2. We need to protect what we have worked for, to defend our theories.
3. Tarot always cautions balance and upholding principles without giving in to stubbornness and aggression.

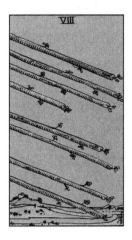

The Eight of Wands
"Sudden Advancement"

Astrological Correspondence: Mercury in Sagittarius (Swiftness).
Image: Eight Wands traverse the countryside, flying in the sky over a river.
Key Phrase: Realization of dreams approaching.
Statement: "I can expect quick results and know that completion is near."
Quotation: "If you dare declare that you are free, free your are at this moment."
  (Swami Vivekananda, *Practical Vedanta*)
Major Obstacle: The ego is distracted and lacks concentration.

The Eight of Wands in a Reading

- The Wands fly past obstacles.
- Great haste.
- Fast results.
- Optimism.
- Action.
- Dwindling resistance.
- Liberation.
- Variety of interests.
- Wanderlust.
- Breezy, adaptable intellect (Mercury in Sagittarius).

Reversed

- Delay; obstacles, interference.
- Aimlessness.
- Not able to cope with swift change.
- Disconnected thoughts and ideas.
- Nerves too tense, restlessness, discontentment, missed details (Mercury in Sagittarius, afflicted).

Strategy

1. Patience pays off (see the Seven of Pentacles); holding strong to one's faith helps develop the virtue.
2. Knowing exactly when action is necessary, however, is also a skill worth developing.
3. Remain confident in a beneficial outcome.
4. Keep a pleasant attitude, especially in the midst of apparent delay.

The Nine of Wands
"Readiness"

Astrological Correspondence: Moon in Sagittarius (highly alert).

Image: A young man, wounded from battle, supported by a Wand, is surrounded in a fortress of eight other Wands.

Key Phrase: Be prepared for the unexpected.

Statement: "I will stand at my station, guarding against negative attitudes, and remain prepared for challenges that might come my way."

Quotation: "The condition upon which God hath given liberty to man is eternal vigilance." (John Philpot Curran, Speech, July 10, 1790)

Major Obstacle: The ego becomes overly suspicious of the motives of others.

The Nine of Wands in a Reading

- Consciousness is in the watchful mode; on guard.
- Being wary after wounds incurred.
- Defensive.
- Principles attacked (Seven of Wands) and now from experience one is ready to defend and enter into battle, if necessary.
- A problem returns as a test and a lesson, but you are prepared this time; the key is to have built your protection comprehensively.
- Strength and readiness in reserve to meet opposition boldly.
- Dedication and resilience.
- Protecting one's reputation.

- Recharging the batteries after a protracted struggle.
- Devotion to one's principles and a determination to make a difference (Moon in Sagittarius).

REVERSED

- In extreme cases, paranoia.
- Mistrust.
- Feeling misunderstood.
- Viewing oneself as an outsider.
- An obstacle returns.
- Letting one's guard down prematurely.
- New adversaries.
- A victim of trickery.

STRATEGY

1. A need to learn from past battles, rather than dredging up only what went wrong. Guard against letting thoughts shift to darkness—otherwise, prepare for anxiety.
2. When you allow yourself to close to your spiritual nature—it is then that you are most defenseless.
3. Seek protection in spiritual thoughts.

The Ten of Wands
"Burdens"

Astrological Correspondence: Saturn in Sagittarius (oppression).
Image: A man is weighed down with ten Wands as he walks across the road.
Key Phrase: Energy drain.
Statement: "I will learn to prioritize and take on a balance of responsibilities."
Quotation: "Cast thy burden upon the Lord, and he shall sustain thee: he shall never permit the righteous to be shaken." (Psalm 55:22)
Major Obstacle: The ego indulges in self-pity.

The Ten of Wands in a Reading

- Burdensome tasks are encountered.
- A person under tremendous pressure.
- Stress.
- A workaholic.
- Impediments to progress; oppressive situations.
- Time not spent on introspection brings on clouded self-perception.
- Free spirit forced into a limiting situation.
- Overcommitment; goals and enterprises not completed.
- Weariness from heavy responsibilities leading to disinterest in spiritual matters; indifference (Saturn in Sagittarius, afflicted).

REVERSED

- Wasting time on feeling sorry for oneself.
- Pressure causes an attitude of self-defeat and jumping to irrational conclusions.
- Violent rebellion to overwork.
- Not fulfilling responsibilities.
- Depending on surrounding cards (i.e., The Star, The Sun), a lightening of burdens.

STRATEGY

1 A need to reevaluate tasks and duties. A time to lighten your load and remove excess baggage from your life.
2. Sometimes trials are necessary to test our mettle, but it is not necessary to invent excessive challenges.
3. A need to delegate work to even out responsibilities.
4. Take care not to overextend yourself.
5. Do not accumulate worries; stay aware during difficult situations.

The Court in the Suit of Fire

The Page of Wands
Basic Trait: Energetic.

Alchemical Element: Earth in the Suit of Fire (aspirations directed at the practical).

Astrological Correspondence: The pioneering nature of Aries, the dynamic personality of Leo, and the directness of Sagittarius.

Image: A youth, dressed in the reds and oranges of the Suit of Fire, looks confidently upward beyond the tip of his Wand. He wears salamanders on his tunic, a symbol of Fire, and on his hat is a red feather looking like a flame. Three pyramids rise in the distance.

Statement: "I intend to fulfill my ambitions in accordance with my individuality."

Major Obstacle: The ego becomes bored and is prone to seek out artificial stimulation.

Consciousness as the Page of Wands brings new spiritual awareness (Wands) to bear on practical matters (Page). He or she is young in experience but likes the idea of taking a risk. Virtues such as honesty, loyalty, and sincerity are part of the character make-up. The Page of Wands is ambitious and is happy in a new venture; can be very competitive.

The Page of Wands in a Reading

- Young, aspiring, spirit of Aries.
- Daring and courageous personality of Leo.

- Expansiveness and sincerity of Sagittarius.
- Outgoing personality.
- This Page can signify a favorable message.

REVERSED

- Indecisive, vacillating, lack of direction.
- Starts off the project in a blaze, but lets the fire burn out long before the venture is finished.
- In extreme cases, unstable, temperamental.
- Insincere.
- The Page of Wands Reversed brings unpleasant news.

The Knight of Wands
Basic Trait: Opinionated.

Alchemical Element: Air in the Suit of Fire (dynamic communication).
Astrological Affinity: The questing, Mutable Fire sign of Sagittarius.
Image: A young Knight rears up on his horse. He wears a fiery feather in his metal helmet; his cape seems on fire as well.
Statement: "I am proud of my opinions and have no problem expressing myself."
Major Obstacle: The ego is rash and impulsive.

As the element Air, the Knight in the Suit of Wands enjoys the give and take of conversation. There is a certain volatility in the personality, and, therefore this Knight is outspoken, with strong opinions. He or she has a certain brashness that gets attention, but is well-liked for the directness and sincerity.

The Knight of Wands in a Reading

- Issue oriented.
- Active—expanding—explosive.
- On the move, traveling.
- Fighter for a cause; principled (especially with the Seven of Wands).
- Confident in pursuit of the goal.
- Enjoys variety.
- Inspired by wanderlust.

- Optimistic.
- Independent.

REVERSED

- Air in the Suit of Fire afflicted stirs up the currents of the thought process and blows wind on the flame. Therefore, the Knight of Wands Reversed is irrationally impulsive (which is also Sagittarius over-activated).
- Very influenced by external pressure.
- Prideful, mean, easily angered.
- In extreme cases, cruelty; otherwise, inconsiderate.
- Self-righteous.
- Refuses to accept the other's opinion.
- Ignores important details.
- Scattered thinking; unorganized (especially with a Reversed Magician).

The Queen of Wands
Basic Trait: Purposeful.

Alchemical Element: Water in the Suit of Fire (the emotions spiritualized).
Astrological Affinity: The self-directed energy of the Cardinal sign of Aries.
Image: A regal looking woman sits on a throne holding a Wand and a sunflower. A black cat sits before her.
Statement: "I am serene. For I radiate outwards the Light of Spirit from the depth of my heart."
Major Obstacle: The ego gives in to anger and loss of self-control.

The Queen of Wands has emotions that embody the dynamic vitality of the Suit of Fire, but they are under control. The example of her life is inspirational, and she shows an understanding of what troubles other people. One of her most endearing qualities is her ability to lift the spirit of others; charismatic.

The Queen of Wands in a Reading

- Benevolent authority.
- Bold in outlook.
- Imaginative.
- Serene and dignified.
- Very aware of where she is going in life.
- Penetrating insight.

REVERSED

- This badly aspected Queen has a sour outlook on life.
- She demands flattery and will never exert herself for anyone else.
- Impervious to the distress she may cause others.
- Intolerant.
- Can savagely attack those who get in her way.
- Suspicious and can lose control of her emotions.
- Crowley in the *Book of Thoth* says the Queen of Wands can have "panic-stricken outbursts of ill-considered fury."
- Self-serving in her treatment of those she considers underlings.
- She expects those beneath her to acquiesce to her every whim.
- The Queen of Wands Reversed might say something like, "Only the little people pay taxes."

The King of Wands
Basic Trait: Zeal.

Alchemical Element: Fire in the Suit of Fire (burning individualism).

Astrological Affinity: The courageous, noble character of the Lion, the Fixed Fire sign of Leo, ruled by the Sun, signifying self-consciousness.

Statement: "I have arrived at a point in my life where I understand the benefits of cultivating an open-minded and trustworthy character."

Major Obstacle: The ego degenerates into megalomania.

The King of Wands is honest, generous, fair, and very much his own person. He values his integrity and is determined to live a productive life. With the warm heart of Leo, the King of Wands gives good advice to those in need.

The King of Wands in a Reading

- Truth seeking.
- Leadership, benevolent authority.
- In control, disciplined.
- Enjoys a good challenge.
- Spiritually aware.
- Enterprising.
- Courageous.
- Will seek center stage.

REVERSED

- Supreme egotist; delusions of grandeur.
- Severe, unyielding, strict.
- Bigoted, brutal, domineering over others.
- Intolerant of anyone telling him what to do.
- He embodies the worst of Leo's Fixed nature: The King of Wands Reversed refuses to budge from the righteousness of his position and considers any challenges a personal affront. His zeal turns to an obsession to destroy any opposition. (Fidel Castro, a Leo, fits this description, as the Cuban exiles in Florida will attest.)

Chapter 26

The Suit of Cups
In the Realm of the Heart

The Ace of Cups

Alchemical Element: Water.

Astrological Correspondence: Cancer (Cardinal in the Suit of Water), Scorpio (Fixed), Pisces (Mutable).

Image: A hand from a cloud holds a golden chalice overflowing with water into a lily pond. A dove is dropping a Communion host into the center of the cup.

Key Phrase: Emotional depth.

Statement: "My consciousness is inspired by love, which flows outwards in a cascade of benevolence and compassion to all."

Quotation: "Love God and do as you like." (St. Augustine)

Major Obstacle: The ego is manipulative and insensitive.

In the realm of the Ace of Cups, the root Essence of the Emotional Plane, we explore feelings and expressions of the heart. We experience aesthetic response to art and Nature as well as the power to visualize. And the Emotional Plane is also the realm of imagination, affection, dreams, and compassion.

The Ace of Cups reminds us that the individual consciousness experiences spiritual energy through the heart. An environment for body-mind-Spirit harmony is created. The dove symbolizes the infusion of Spirit into the emotions, an overflow of grace into the seeker's life. It's an idealized picture of our emotional nature—spiritualized.

From an astrological standpoint, the Ace of Cups incorporates the meanings of the three Water signs:

Cancer ("I feel"): The nurturing, sympathetic, moody, receptive, protective aspects of consciousness.

Scorpio ("I create"): Reserved exterior with intense passions beneath the surface. Scorpio is responsive to another's difficulty and can direct the emotions as an instrument of healing. A very determined consciousness, goal-oriented.

Pisces ("I believe"): Highly sensitive, imaginative, psychic, introspective.

The Ace of Cups in a Reading

- Affairs of the heart.
- The flow of feeling.
- Emotions need to be taken into account.
- The passions can also be involved, but with this Ace they are balanced because of the seeker's spiritual awareness.
- Sensitivity to the feelings of others is one of the great gifts indicated by the Ace of Wands.
- Helping those in need.

REVERSED

- Blockage in emotional expression; the ability to love is erratic.
- There is also the tendency to toy with the emotions of others.
- A smothering, selfish kind of love; possessiveness.
- Emotional upset.
- Vindictiveness, jealousy, resentment.

STRATEGY

1. Feelings and moods can be harmonized through spiritual awareness.
2. There is always a need to be understanding of the emotional state of other personalities in our orbit. The Ace of Cups is there to remind us that we, too, must overflow with compassion for those around us.
3. Appreciation of the beauty of Nature helps harmonize the emotions.
4. The outward stream of love is the greatest of all virtues.

The Two of Cups
"Reciprocity"

Astrological Correspondence: Venus in Cancer (nurturing love).

Image: A young couple exchange Cups in a loving gesture. In the sky above them is a red winged lion head atop a caduceus.

Key Phrase: A mutually beneficial relationship.

Statement: "I am a giving person and I wish to share my heart, mind, and soul. And, under certain circumstances, my body."

Quotation: "As we proceed in our exploration of the nature of love, I believe it will become clear that not only do self-love and love of others go hand in hand but that ultimately they are indistinguishable."(M. Scott Peck, *The Road Less Traveled*)

Major Obstacle: The ego refuses to participate in any give and take; reluctant to commit oneself to a position or another person.

The Two of Cups in a Reading

- Meeting a kindred soul; chemistry.
- Clarity and focus in a relationship.
- The healing power of the passion of love (lion and caduceus)
- Agreement powered by unselfish motives.
- Cooperation; commitment; union based on respect.
- Formal joining of an endeavor.
- Emotional blending; imaginative, charming, sensitive, loving (Venus in Cancer).

REVERSED

- Conflicts in a friendship or partnership.
- Instability, loss of balance.
- Resentments and arguments.
- Inappropriate feelings.
- Jealousy.
- Delusion in a relationship; the infatuation wears off.
- Weak convictions, no commitment (especially near the Seven of Wands Reversed).
- Morbid attachment to love object.
- Overly sentimental, insecure, and gullible (Venus in Cancer, afflicted).

STRATEGY

1. Meeting of the minds increases the chances for success of the enterprise.
2. Each others' sensibilities need to be taken into account; respect for the others' freedom and point of view.
3. It is in the best interests of the relationship to maintain tranquillity in the midst of the action needed to complete the undertaking.

The Three of Cups
"Fraternity"

Astrological Correspondence: Mercury in Cancer (excited emotions).

Image: Three women each hold a Cup aloft as they dance together in a vegetable garden.

Key Phrase: Celebration within the group.

Statement: "I enjoy sharing myself among my family, friends, and acquaintances. I heal and am healed within their atmosphere."

Quotation: "Friendship, like the immortality of the soul, is too good to be believed." (Ralph Waldo Emerson, *Friendship*)

Major Obstacle: The ego, because of antisocial behavior, feels like an outcast.

The Three of Cups in a Reading

- Efforts of individuals brought to a common purpose.
- Solace from belonging to a group; inclusion.
- Brotherhood/sisterhood.
- Beneficial group activity.
- Celebration with friends.
- Relationships grow.
- Communication; views expressed with sensitivity (Mercury in Cancer).

REVERSED

- Disillusionment (with the group).
- Cult activity.
- Emotional pain caused by those close.
- Unexpected harshness and insensitivity from acquaintances.
- Failure to establish agreement.
- Gossip.
- Conflicts with friends; quarrels (Mercury in Cancer, afflicted).

STRATEGY

1. The company of others can be a great source of enjoyment.
2. The Three of Cups emphasizes the idea that "no man is an island."
3. It is important to appreciate those around you; taking people for granted eventually leads to emotional isolation.
4. Activity within the group encourages fellowship, an excellent resource for movement along the path.

The Four of Cups
"Opportunities Offered"

Astrological Correspondence: Moon in Cancer (highly sensitive, warm).

Image: A young man sits cross-legged with arms folded beneath a tree. A hand holding a Cup extends to him from a cloud. Three Cups sit in the foreground.

Key Phrase: Contemplating a decision.

Statement: "I have been passive for far too long and intend to make up my mind in an informed way."

Quotation: "When the superior man gets his time, he mounts aloft; but when the time is against him he moves as if his feet were entangled."(Lao Tzu)

Major Obstacle: The ego indulges in procrastination.

The Four of Cups in a Reading

- Possible refusal to take valuable opportunity offered.
- Not grasping what is in front of you; hesitation.
- Dissatisfaction with conditions and directions.
- Ignoring a situation that should be addressed.
- Not taking valuable advice (especially with a Reversed Hermit).
- Be careful about making rash decisions.
- Overly passive; emotions interfering with rational decision-making.
- Brooding; mood swings (Moon in Cancer, afflicted).

REVERSED

- Action begins.
- Seeking guidance.
- Taking advantage of a good opportunity.
- Reevaluation of goals; new roads taken.
- Kindly, sympathetic, and valuable advice given (Moon in Cancer).

STRATEGY

1. Weighing options is critical to proper decision-making. However, care must be taken not to get caught up in superfluous detail so that the valuable opportunity passes by.
2. One needs to be discriminating when it comes to other people giving advice. Discernment as well as intuition are called for.
3. Since we are in the realm of emotion, one needs to be aware that mood may affect the proper appraisal of the situation. Overemotional reactions do not belong in the same atmosphere with an ego on the verge of making a choice or decision.

The Five of Cups
"Disillusionment"

Astrological Correspondence: Mars in Scorpio (boiling emotion).

Image: A figure dressed in a black robe bows his head in weariness. Three Cups are spilled in front of him, the two upright behind him go unnoticed.

Key Phrase: Blinded to the Good.

Statement: "Rather than dwelling on disappointments, I will move on without regret."

Quotation: "The darksome statesman, hung with weights and woe, Like thick midnight-fog, moved there so slow, He did not stay, nor go; Condemning thoughts, like sad eclipses, scowl Upon his soul. . . "(Henry Vaughn, *The World*)

Major Obstacle: The ego sees negative events as the norm; pessimism.

The Five of Cups in a Reading

- Disappointment in love.
- Remorse over failed relationship.
- Flooded with sorrow over unfulfilled expectations.
- Regret over missed or ignored opportunities from offerings of the Four of Cups.
- Not adapting well to change.
- Feelings of emptiness; depression.
- Not coping well after a trauma (Mars in Scorpio, afflicted).

REVERSED

- Hope and confidence restored.
- Letting go of past pain; rediscovering what's right about your life.
- Redefining purpose.
- New commitments.
- Seeing goodness in the midst of difficulty.
- Determination and focusing ability sharpen (Mars in Scorpio).

STRATEGY

1. You need to remember that you are in the atmosphere of Cups, where the emotions can be purified.
2. It is a time to rediscover your assets and move beyond regrets. It also helps to remember that we are here to experience. And within that experience, Reality has a negative-positive polarity (yin-yang); therefore we can expect that with difficulty always comes relief. Though three Cups are spilled, two cups remain standing.
3. Sometimes suffering is part of the plan; it does us no good to become resigned to sorrow because the Law of Cycles is always in operation.

The Six of Cups
"Nostalgia"

Astrological Correspondence: Sun in Scorpio (self-reflective).

Image: A boy offers a little girl a cup of flowers. Five other cups in the garden where they stand are also filled with flowers.

Key Phrase: A return to innocence.

Statement: "I am content with the humble things in life and have a sense of well-being from happy memories."

Quotation: "Discovering real goodness comes from appreciating very simple experiences." (Chogyam Trungpa, *Shambhala*)

Major Obstacle: The ego regresses into immaturity.

The Six of Cups in a Reading

- Emotions calmed by reflecting on pleasant memories.
- Learning from past experiences.
- Blissful contact with the Inner Self helps balance the disillusionment of the Five of Cups.
- The soul's innocence shining through the emotions.
- Well-being, harmony, purity.
- Respect for tradition; favorable influences from the past.
- Emotional power under control; patient (Sun in Scorpio).

Reversed

- Tendency to hide in memories.
- Morbid clinging to the past.
- Fear of change, fear of aging.
- Childish thoughts and behavior.
- Stuck in a rut; not motivated or hopeful.
- Vengeful, sarcastic reactions; suspicious and cynical (Sun in Scorpio, afflicted).

Strategy

1. Perceived negative past events are not good subject matter for contemplation. Reflection on learning experiences bring more benefit.
2. Calming the emotions can result from pleasant reverie.
3. Taking steps to make one's life less complicated can also lead to tranquillity.

The Seven of Cups
"Excessive Imagination"

Astrological Correspondence: Venus in Scorpio (passion and warring emotions; debauchery).

Image: A darkened figure beholds seven Cups rising from the clouds. Each is filled with an object: a head, a figure beneath a cloth with arms outstretched, a snake, a castle, jewels, a wreath, and a dragon.

Key Phrase: Indolent daydreaming.

Statement: "I will not hold unrealistic views and let my fancies cloud my better judgement."

Quotation: "And his eyes have all the seeming of a demon's that is dreaming, And the lamp-light o'er him streaming throws his shadow on the floor; And my soul from out that shadow that lies floating on the floor shall be lifted—nevermore!" (Edgar Allan Poe, *The Raven*)

Major Obstacle: The ego descends into illusion.

The Seven of Cups in a Reading

- Consciousness falls prey to dreamy thinking.
- Emotions dictate to the intellect.
- Energies unfocused.
- Self-indulgence in pipe dreams; unrealistic views.
- Faulty choices; indecisive (especially with the Two of Swords Reversed).

- Imagination out of control.
- Love of luxury stirred by desire; animal nature demands satisfaction at all costs (Venus in Scorpio, afflicted).

REVERSED

- The imagination is focused.
- Dreams are directed to reaching a particular destination (especially with the Magician).
- Planning is not affected by mood.
- Lightheartedness.
- Spontaneity.
- The strong passionate nature is comfortably under control (Venus in Scorpio).

STRATEGY

1. Consciousness needs to redirect itself back toward the Ideal—with clear thinking and grounded behavior.
2. The seeker needs a creative, practical use of the imagination, intelligent selection, and energy devoted to the proper conclusion of the endeavor.
3. Creative artistic expression helps negate the more unsavory aspects of the Seven. The challenge is to steady the emotions and refocus thought.

The Eight of Cups
"Moving through Emotional Barriers"

Astrological Correspondence: Saturn in Pisces (a serious feeling nature).

Image: A figure crosses a river and begins an ascent up a hill. He leaves eight Cups behind.

Key Phrase: Letting go.

Statement: "I will not stagnate in a situation that stifles my movement onward and upward."

Quotation: "Work out your own salvation with diligence." (Buddha's last words)

Major Obstacle: The ego longs for the return to the emotional equilibrium of the Six of Cups and therefore avoids potentially stimulating relationships.

The Eight of Cups in a Reading

- Retreat from an emotionally painful relationship.
- Letting go of the past.
- Moving away from an impossibly difficult situation.
- Off to the unknown for new experiences.
- Departure from the ordinary.
- A refusal to be smothered and controlled.
- Liberation.
- Tested by having to relinquish a comfortable but harmful situation (Saturn in Pisces).

Reversed

- Refusal to get involved, isolation.
- Abandonment of obligations; guilt to follow.
- Stagnation in a poisoned relationship.
- Emotional entanglements.
- Overly serious.
- Frustration.
- Inhibited expression, blocked flow (Saturn in Pisces, afflicted).

Strategy

1 The figure's upward movement suggests the seeker has put things in their proper order, and the time has come to advance on the path to experience new situations. Sometimes it is beneficial to take the "road less traveled," and journey off on your own.

2. A time to reevaluate current circumstances. Are ideas being compromised? Are you refusing to face a serious problem?

3. The Eight of Cups calls for exploring new possibilities, and trying to look at yourself and life with a sense of humor.

The Nine of Cups
"Well-Being"

Astrological Correspondence: Jupiter in Pisces (inspiring geniality).
Image: A plump merchant sits satiated before a half circle of Cups, his accomplishments.
Key Phrase: Success and good times.
Statement: "I will remember that in order to sustain happiness, one goal must lead to another."
Quotation: "When Fortune's cup into your hands doth pass, think of the headache as you raise the glass!" (Awhadi, medieval Persian mystic)
Major Obstacle: The fattened ego indulges in *la dolce vita* (the sweet life).

The Nine of Cups in a Reading

- Emotional tranquillity.
- The wish comes true.
- Pride in past achievements.
- Sociability.
- Good health.
- Prosperity and growth (Jupiter in Pisces).

REVERSED

- Addiction to food, drink, drugs, sex.
- Energy wasted in pursuit of the sensual.

- Overly materialistic.
- Good intentions gone awry.
- Feelings of insecurity.
- Lazy and a deadbeat (Jupiter in Pisces, afflicted).

STRATEGY

1. Enjoy the good life, but don't get too comfortable. There's always a lot yet to accomplish.
2. Be proud of your successes, but never lord them over anyone less ambitious.

The Ten of Cups
"Joyful Attainment"

Astrological Correspondence: Mars in Pisces (inspired action).
Image: A family rejoices under a rainbow emblazoned with ten Cups.
Key Phrase: Contented bliss.
Statement: "I celebrate Life to the fullest. My heart is warmed by a sense of optimism that everything will work out for the best."
Quotation: "Heaven is where thou standest." (Jacob Boehme)
Major Obstacle: The ego is discontented, searching in vain for rainbows.

The Ten of Cups in a Reading

- Emotional richness.
- Stability; tranquil situations.
- Kindness within the home life.
- Affairs of the heart turn out well.
- A premium on virtue.

REVERSED

- The project disintegrates due to conflict.
- Impermanent relationships.
- Waste and debauchery.

- Emotional strain.
- Disruption.

STRATEGY

1. Do as much as possible to keep the family or significant group intact.
2. Avoid complacency.

The Court in the Suit of Water

The Page of Cups
Basic Trait: Gentle disposition.

Alchemical Element: Earth in the Suit of Water (emotional life balanced by grounding).

Astrological Correspondence: The sensitivity of Cancer, the resourcefulness of Scorpio, the kindness of Pisces.

Image: A fair-looking youth looks at a fish emerging from the Cup he holds. He stands before a waving sea.

Statement: "Love flows freely through my personality, and my emotional well-being contributes to a calm exterior."

Major Obstacle: The ego exhibits a brittle character. A tender, sensitive consciousness, charming and helpful with an appealing innocence (like Forrest Gump). He or she possesses an uncontaminated view of the world. This Page is in the process of exploring his or her feeling nature and can have a calming effect on more turbulent personalities. The Page of Cups signifies what happens when the emotions are entering a more harmonious state.

The Page of Cups in a Reading

- Warm and gracious.
- Soothing, responsive nature.
- Capable of deep feeling.

- A quiet discipline brought to a well organized life.
- If sufficiently introspective, the intuitive sense emerges.

REVERSED

- In an afflicted Page of Cups, the outer persona is weepy, overly sentimental.
- Offers a warning to watch out for emotional outbursts.
- Can signify superficial pursuits.
- Demands for excessive comfort.
- Escapism (very pronounced near the Seven of Cups).
- Shallow display of feelings.
- A facade is erected.
- Lazy, self-indulgent.
- Wastes natural talents on unrealistic goals that lead to a graveyard of unfinished projects.
- The Page of Cups afflicted needs to seriously study the Law of Cause and Effect in his or her life, or a lightning bolt from the Sixteenth Portal (the Tower) could be on the way.

The Knight of Cups
Basic Trait: Idealistic.

Alchemical Element: Air in the Suit of Water (communicating one's feelings).
Astrological Affinity: The introspective consciousness of Mutable Water, Pisces.
Image: Riding a horse, a young Knight with a winged helmet and a graceful aura holds forth a Cup in a gesture of deep emotion.
Statement: "Accept this Cup for I have thought long and hard before presenting it."
Major Obstacle: The ego indulges in excessive imagination.

The Knight of Cups is calm and aspiring and heralds his Ideal. Unlike Air in the Suit of Fire (Knight of Wands), in the Suit of Water the Knight is more reserved. He is receptive and intuitive and can be a Utopian dreamer. But he is also compassionate, intelligent, and on the move. He is charming and optimistic like the Page, though he has more experiences and successes in pursuit of his Ideal.

The Knight of Cups in a Reading

- Skillful communication of the balance, harmony, and beauty of Nature in a multitude of expressions: artist, musician, poet, dreamer.
- Mystical and a visionary as well as an artist.
- Empathetic; receptive.
- The Knight of Cups believes humanity is basically good.
- Comfortable with the subtleties of life.

- On the surface, very tranquil; but in the Suit of Water, can be quite passionate underneath.
- Talents employed in the service of others (Pisces).

REVERSED

- The afflicted Knight of Cups can live in a dream world.
- His airy thought process can turn violent, especially if his deluded fantasy life is ever called into question.
- Idle, brooding, emotional difficulties.
- Unmotivated.
- Unrealistic expectations.
- Will use flattery to deceive.
- He is the Pisces fish in detriment (Mutable Water churning), carried helplessly downstream in a torrent of emotion.
- An afflicted Knight of Cups needs to put less energy on his own emotional aches and pains. If he can concentrate on giving of himself freely from the heart, he will experience less anxiety regarding his own flaws. Isabel M. Hickey in her classic, *Astrology, a Cosmic Science*, says it bluntly: "This is why the spiritual motto of Pisces is 'serve or suffer.'"

The Queen of Cups
Basic Trait: Lovingkindness.

Alchemical Element: Water in the Suit of Water (sensitive feeling nature, both to herself and to the feelings of others).

Astrological Affinity: The nurturing consciousness of Cardinal Water, Cancer.

Image: A beautiful Queen gazes into an ornate Cup, suggestive of the Ark of the Covenant. She is seated on a carved throne at the water's edge.

Statement: "My heart is a channel for Spirit, and I let the tenderness pouring out touch all of Life."

Major Obstacle: The ego is overcome with hysterical reactions.

The Cancer influence gives this Queen a great sensitivity to the moods and dispositions of those around her. She is the embodiment of emotional peace and tranquillity. Because of this highly sensitive and receptive nature, the Queen of Cups is one of the most psychic personages of the Court.

The Queen of Cups in a Reading

- Devoted to the needs of family and friends, and at her best shows them a radiant, compassionate heart.
- Affectionate and motherly.
- She's a dreamer like the other members of Water's Court, and as Queen, she can turn her imaginings into creative activity.

- Like the Knight of Cups, she loves art, music, and poetry.
- Treasures harmonious atmospheres.
- Great emotional depth for those in need (Cancer).

REVERSED

- Morbid worries.
- The feelings percolate hotly through the personality.
- Coming to a wrong conclusion resulting in an outburst.
- Cannot be relied upon.
- Vain.
- Likes to generate phony sympathy and often indulges in a martyr complex.
- Confused, indecisive, the emotions become erratic and explosive; hysteria. (Can be compared to Blanche duBois in Tennessee Williams' *A Streetcar Named Desire*.)

The King of Cups

Basic Trait: Emotional power generating meaningful action.

Alchemical Element: Fire in the Suit of Water (a passionate, spiritual nature).

Astrological Affinity: The intense depth of soul of Fixed Water, Scorpio.

Image: A stately King sits on a throne floating on the sea. He holds a Cup in his right hand, a scepter in his left.

Statement: "I obey Universal Law, and will to understand the feeling side of Life as I turn my Will to the emotions. Then I delight in the energies I discover there."

Major Obstacle: The ego experiences arrested emotional development. The King of Cups is a kind, generous, intuitive consciousness. Like all the Kings of the Court, he offers sound advice, especially in matters of the heart. His power is subtle and he does not interfere in the lives of others. He merely hints at the Truth as he sees it. Like the Knight of Cups, he has a calm exterior over deep emotional passion.

The King of Cups in a Reading

- Sensitive.
- Enthusiastic.
- A creative, quietly vital personality.
- Deeply appreciates the arts.
- Graceful in manner.
- Profoundly cares for the welfare of others.
- As King, he puts a high priority in achieving self-mastery.
- A great deal of energy, determination, and an independent outlook (Scorpio).

REVERSED

- Has difficulty facing his feelings.
- Defensive.
- Thin-skinned.
- Pursues illusions.
- In serious cases, alcohol, drugs, sex abuse.
- Ineffectual.
- Outwardly hostile.
- Inwardly weak and insincere.
- Destructive emotional displays leading to chaotic relationships (Scorpio, afflicted).

Chapter 27

The Suit of Swords
The Air of Thought

The Ace of Swords

Alchemical Element: Air.

Astrological Correspondence: Libra (Cardinal in the Suit Air), Aquarius (Fixed), Gemini (Mutable Air).

Image: Grasping a crowned Sword, a glowing hand extends forth from a cloud. Palm and olive branches hang from the edges of the crown, as six yellow flames (Yods) hover around the hilt of the Sword.

Key Phrase: The power of thought.

Statement: "Here my consciousness breathes the Essence of Air, and I understand what I can accomplish with the workings of my mind."

Quotation: "We mentally conceive the form and then think life into it." (Thomas Troward, *Affirmative Power, Collected Essays*)

Major Obstacle: The ego's domineering selfishness ultimately brings on confused thinking patterns.

The Ace of Swords in a Reading signifies a great thrust of mental energy into the situation, the intellect operating at its most powerful—and glorious—in the life of the seeker. This Ace reminds us of the need to use our will power to overcome the barriers that block our way on the journey (symbolized by the crown). In the atmosphere of the Suit of Air we learn the lesson that we must be unwavering in our determination to lead an ethical, balanced, and reasonable life.

The Suit of Swords signifies that at all times we are bound by Universal Law—and we are supposed to willingly, joyfully accept this fact. Why? Because through observance of the Law our soul lives in freedom.

Besides, we have already learned from the Eleventh Portal, Justice, that if we must compromise our Ideal through ignorance and selfishness, then we must experience the Sword's inevitable, leveling slice.

In the imagery of the Swords, in the Swords' very action, we see a recurring theme: Volatility and the movement toward balance.

To carry this idea further, we can look at the Suit of Swords from an astrological perspective. The root of Swords, the Ace, incorporates aspects of all three Air signs into its overall meaning:

Libra: Balance. Poise. Equilibrium. Harmony. Fairness. Discernment. Impartiality. Concentration and sustained energy focused on the project. Diplomatic. In detriment Libra can be vain and lazy.

Aquarius: Understanding of human nature. Truth-seeker. Open-minded. Independent. Objective. Detached. Unemotional. Rebellious. Individualistic. Loyal. When Aquarius is in detriment, however, he can be cold, detached, and even sadistic.

Gemini: Lively, adaptable, communicative, fast thinking, quick-witted. This personality is inquisitive and versatile. However, since the energy of Gemini rules the nerves of the body, this seeker could become restless and irrationally dissatisfied. And these negative thought patterns could eventually drag the consciousness down into a state of bitterness.

The Ace of Swords in a Reading

- Action, initiating force.
- The rational human mind used as a profound vehicle for propelling the seeker forward on the path.
- Inventive and innovative, the Sword has an energy that brings great power to the seeker's ability to communicate.

- Disciplined thinking.
- Will power used to overcome the barriers that block our enlightenment (symbolized by the upraised, discerning Sword).

REVERSED

- Negative thinking manifests as pain and confusion in outer circumstances; chaotic experiences.
- Anger out of control.
- Obnoxious attitudes.
- Unreasonable expectations of others.
- Extreme need to dominate.
- Brutality.
- A need to reevaluate one's direction, character, and motivation. Regaining poise a top priority. Step back from the distressing situation.

STRATEGY

1. The Ace of Swords teaches us the lesson that principled attitude will lead to a life free from disjointed thinking.
2. Peace of mind and victory over obstacles are ours if we view Life with objectivity, poise, and the search for Truth.
3. Put out the effort to observe the variables of a conflict with objectivity.
4. If the seeker insists on using this Sword with excess, especially to force one's will on another, then weakness and dissipation of the original force will eventually result.
5. With the Ace of Swords Reversed it is well to remember Lord Acton's dictum: "Power corrupts and absolute power corrupts absolutely."

The Two of Swords
"Balance Before Change"

Astrological Correspondence: Moon in Libra (Reflection and objective thinking).

Image: Holding two crossed Swords, a blindfolded woman sits before a moonlit lake.

Key Phrase: Equilibrium between opposing forces.

Statement: "I carefully weigh my decision before acting."

Quotation: "For the object of all this thinking is to awaken within him a mood of soul, a mental atmosphere and even an emotional condition of aspiration towards Truth which will provide an appropriate stage for the entry of illumination." (Paul Brunton, *The Search For the Overself*)

Major Obstacle: The ego experiences uncertainty, vacillation.

The consciousness sits at a juncture, at the center of the continuum, with the two Swords representing the opposite sides of the decision in question. Therefore, the position calls for reasoned judgement in the Suit of Air—because an important choice is about to be made. In fact, the Two of Swords can be viewed as a pictorial representation of the 'moment of decision.'

Notice that the seated figure faces straight ahead, suggesting that the consciousness has not yet decided which way to turn. The blindfold intimates that the decision must be made without external distractions, a decision unaffected by the ups and downs of surface conditions.

The question is, however, can the seeker still be objective if the outside conditions cause considerable pressure?

The Two of Swords in a Reading

- Balance, objectivity, and planning are called for.
- A need to perfect one's strategy.
- Difficult decisions generate stress.
- Unless the seeker is prepared, aware, and in the moment, the choice could be faulty.
- Clear motive and clear goals are essential.
- With the Moon in Libra, the energy of the Scales gives the consciousness balance so that the thought processes are not swayed by an excessively emotional Moon; the Moon energy, however, activates the proper *rhythms* involved in the decision-making process. How will I feel about this particular choice I must make?

REVERSED

- Indecisiveness.
- The consciousness is frozen between two alternatives.
- Distinctions blur, and the lack of decision eventually forces the plates of the balance to tip in the wrong direction; the personality floods with anxiety. The Two of Swords Reversed can mean choice gone awry.
- Still blindfolded, one stumbles in the darkness. And in this state of the error, consciousness can become prey to deceit and manipulation, both internal and external.
- Peace at any price, no matter what the consequences—(Moon in Libra, afflicted).

STRATEGY

1. If the decision has shown to be an incorrect one, then objectivity and detachment from the upheavals of the wrong choice are called for.
2. New perspectives on the problem need to be adopted in order for equilibrium to be restored.
3. The seeker must renew a feeling of expecting the best possible outcome—despite the setbacks set in motion by the wrong choice. Only then can balance return to the Scales, and the Two of Swords turned upright once again.

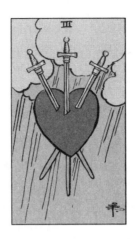

Three of Swords

"Severe Distress"

Astrological Correspondence: Saturn in Libra (afflicted aspect—restrained, one-sided thinking leads to disruption).

Image: Three Swords pierce through a heart suspended in driving rain and thunderclouds.

Key Phrase: The heart tried by pain.

Statement: "Although my decision has caused anguish, I will redirect my attention and use my intellect to transform the distress into a higher good."

Quotation: "And I saw it was filled with graves,
　　　　　And tomb-stones where flowers should be;
　　　　　And priests in black gowns were walking their rounds,
　　　　　And binding with briars my joys and desires."
　　　　　(William Blake, *The Garden of Love*)

Major Obstacle: The ego is overcome with melancholy.

The Three of Swords in a Reading

- The consciousness experiences deep emotional pain, especially from making the wrong decision in the Two of Swords.
- Heart engulfed by sorrow and emotional upheaval, diminishing the ability to think rationally.
- When the consciousness is in this state, a sense of gloominess colors perception, and the world becomes a cold, hostile place; brooding.
- Conflict between thoughts and emotions.

- Divisiveness and thought patterns that engender despair.
- Losing the power to see what's beneath the surface.
- Becoming consumed with one's shortcomings; depression.
- Although Libra is naturally exalted in Saturn, Three in the Suit of Air draws out the detriment: Biased thinking with a stubborn refusal to accept the positive blinds the seeker—and pessimism results.

REVERSED

- Alleviation of sorrow; pain is relegated to past memory.
- The heart tried by pain becomes stronger.
- An apparent loss turns out to be better off gone.
- New insights gained by overcoming grief.

STRATEGY

1. Continually dwelling on the underside of life sours the attitude, and the surrounding atmosphere begins to attract unappealing people and circumstances. Soon the life fills with misery, shifting the consciousness' negative focus to the weakened ego. The unfortunate result is self-pity.

2. The Three of Swords shows what happens when the heart (feelings) and the intellect (Swords) are at war. The seeker needs to develop plans for healing to once again draw peace and equilibrium back into the personal atmosphere.

3. Bring the Magician's concentration to bear on the situation and remember that your personality should be a clear channel for the higher energies. Thoughts should not deviate too far from this.

4. You should draw attention away from the complaining ego to a more worthy subject. Namely, the well-being of others. Burdens lift when we lift the burdens of another. In fact, loving sacrifice will always neutralize harmful thoughts.

5. Three indicates growth, but these Swords bring advancement at a high price. Letting go of the familiar can be a painful process, and if one insists on clinging to the harmful nonessentials, the process can be downright brutal. Hence, the horrifying image of the Three of Swords.

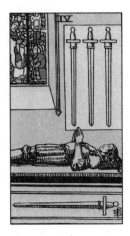

The Four of Swords

"Gathering Inner Strength"

Astrological Correspondence: Jupiter in Libra (Expansive thinking).

Image: A knight, exhausted from the battles fought in the Three of Swords, reclines on a stone slab in a chapel. He is in deep meditation.

Key Phrase: A time of renewal.

Statement: "I will think about the changes that I have experienced and take comfort from the lessons learned."

Quotation: "Pray without ceasing because prayer is the unfoldment of your own consciousness." (Joel Goldsmith, *Consciousness Unfolding*)

Major Obstacle: The ego experiences dysfunctional withdrawal, isolation; over-reaction, anxiety.

The Four of Swords in a Reading

- Quietude and relief from strife and anxiety.
- The embattled consciousness finally agrees to reevaluate the faulty thinking that led to the disaster of the Three of Swords—and in the Four seeks spiritual retreat.
- Reorganizing thought patterns, adopting realistic goals, exerting just the right amount of energy, all help the seeker put things back in their proper perspective.
- The consciousness becomes serene-minded.

- Receptive to the higher energies, the praying knight suggests a deep meditative state of consciousness and may further indicate the end of the conflict.
- Optimistic. Expansive. Refined. Creative. Generous. The seeker has learned the lessons of the anxiety-producing Three of Swords, and for the most part, looks at the brighter side of human nature. Well-balanced (Jupiter in Libra).

REVERSED

- Pathological withdrawal at worst, or in a milder form, procrastination. Instead of meditative, the consciousness becomes fixated; the thinking can revert back to the dismal attitude of the Three of Swords.
- Responsibilities are ignored; laziness (Jupiter in Libra, afflicted).

STRATEGY

1. There is a need to find solace, a point reached where it is necessary to set aside time for rest. Meditation and retreat. Prayer. Seeking to communicate with the Universal Life-power through the Inner Self.
2. Cooperation with others, reevaluation of responsibilities, and an overall self-examination are recommended.
3. In the Four of Swords, the seeker—having faced many challenges—is more sympathetic to the plight of others. The feelings of vulnerability have evaporated and more rational thinking takes over, bringing an atmosphere of tranquillity and concordance.

The Five of Swords
"Opposition"

Astrological Correspondence: Venus in Aquarius (afflicted aspect—the love vibration chills).

Image: A cunning warrior defeats two dejected figures who wander off into a background filled with menacing storm clouds.

Key Phrase: Loss, possibly at the hands of others.

Statement: "I will modify any thoughts that seek to dominate or humiliate other people."

Quotation: "He loves to sit and hear me sing,
> Then, laughing, sports and plays with me;
> Then stretches out my golden wing,
> And mocks my loss of liberty."
> (William Blake, *How Sweet I Roam'd from Field to Field*)

Major Obstacle: The ego gets satisfaction through cruelty.

The Five of Swords in a Reading

- The direct antithesis of the Golden Rule. It shows an individual involved in degrading and cheating others.
- A cunning, unscrupulous personality uses the intellect to manipulate and take advantage of vulnerabilities.
- Lack of conscience.
- The violent clouds in the sky suggest an atmosphere of hostility where the consciousness refuses to recognize the admonition of "doing unto

others," thereby setting up waves of negative karma as he or she insists on a selfish course of thinking and acting.

- The sympathy exhibited in the Four of Swords has frozen into a cold lack of conscience in the Five.
- The Five of Swords also suggests swindle, fraud, lack of preparedness in the face of an adversary, or taking sadistic pleasure in the vanquishing of others.
- Can also mean public humiliation.
- Conflicts caused by others.
- The heartfelt warmth of the Venus vibration is afflicted in the cool Aquarian environment. The emotions chill, and as a result, the consciousness can be icy and self-righteous (Venus in Aquarius, afflicted).

REVERSED

- The hostility is sly and underhanded, and the victim may be unaware of the damage being perpetrated.
- Beneath the surface friendly calm lurks hidden treachery, or from another perspective, this person could injure by a deliberate lack of involvement in helping the seeker. In psychological terms, passive aggression.
- Treachery and cunning.

STRATEGY

1. Feelings of oppression. A need to look at people and situations to see who or what is pressuring you. And *why?*
2. A warning that sometimes we have to stand up to ruthless aggressors rather than adopting a policy of appeasement (i.e., Chamberlain viz. Hitler in Munich).
3. One of the many questions this card poses is whether or not the seeker is the victim or the perpetrator. Surrounding cards will give hints to the answer.
4. The person must realize that in hurting others he or she only poisons the well. The life of the selfish aggressor is doomed to unnecessary strife, illustrating the idea that one who lives by the sword dies by the sword. Only in taking the feelings of others into account can one hope to neutralize negative karma.

The Six of Swords

"Safe Passage"

Astrological Correspondence: Mercury in Aquarius (communication, both skillful and original).

Image: A boatman ferries two figures (burdened by the hostility and humiliation of the Five of Swords) to safer shores.

Key Phrase: Moving to a more secure situation.

Statement: "I will look beyond my feelings of vulnerability and renew my faith in the workings of Spirit in my life."

Quotation: ". . . to be in hell is to drift: to be in heaven is to steer." (George Bernard Shaw)

Major Obstacle: Weakness of resolve to deal with past difficulties.

The Six of Swords in a Reading

- The distressed consciousness experiences movement away from the difficulties experienced in the Five of Swords. The "troubled waters" in the right lower edge of the card remind us of the problems encountered.
- The ferryman can be seen wielding his Wand to calm the waves of negative thinking. He brings the troubled consciousness to a new perspective, to the more tranquil shore on the other side.
- Safe passage in the Six of Swords indicates a dissipation of anxiety and reduction in the feelings of vulnerability generated earlier in the turbulent Five of Swords.

- Rescue from the Five's intense difficulties comes from the renewal of Spirit within, or the rescue can come from a more literal interpretation of the card: The hurting consciousness experiences protection and healing from another individual consciousness (the boatman). A Tibetan Sutra emphasizes the former: "The Bodhisattva helps row living beings to the other shore but in fact no living beings are being helped to the other shore."
- The troubled consciousness, at least temporarily, is given in the Six of Swords a much needed shelter from the previous violent assault of the Five.
- Quick intelligence applied to Truth-seeking, with Aquarius bringing Universal awareness to the mind. Like the mind of the scientist, Mercury is dedicated to helping the world (Aquarius). Mercury is precise and alert, Aquarius is outgoing and humanitarian, a very beneficial combination of characteristics (Mercury is exalted in Aquarius).

REVERSED

- The direction in one's life is off course.
- Suggests meandering, an unconscious deviation into treacherous waters.
- Difficulties are left unresolved, which in turn encourage delays in recovery.
- Further, the consciousness is still trapped in circumstances disruptive to the well-being, staying mired in stagnant attitudes—like the fear of unknown shores.
- This personality remains insecure despite the offer of help from potential rescuers.

STRATEGY

1. This position suggests that a renewal of faith is needed—along with nurturing the flame of adventure. The seeker should find new interests that can spark some enthusiasm.
2. When we encounter difficulties, sometimes the solution lies in the ability to adapt to altered circumstances, to flow with the cycles of change to other climates.
3. A great help in recovery from our earthly traumas is to realize that the problems we experience are tests designed to build our character, to make us stronger so that we can advance even further on the Golden Path. To navigate smoothly through Life's vicissitudes can carry us on the currents to paradise.

The Seven of Swords
"Unstable Action"

Astrological Correspondence: Moon in Aquarius (afflicted aspect—emotional aloofness).

Image: A smug figure sneaks away from an encampment with five of his enemies' Swords, leaving two behind.

Key Phrase: Victimization by the unscrupulous.

Statement: "I will hold Truth as my Sword, integrity as my shield and confront the attacker with patience and deftness."

Quotation: "I shall give you, dusky one,
        Kisses icy as the moon,
        Embraces that a snake would give
        As it crawled around a grave."
        (Charles-Pierre Baudelaire, *The Ghost*)

Major Obstacle: Sabotage affects the ego.

The Seven of Swords in a Reading

- Thievery.
- Plagiarism.
- In extreme cases, unfaithfulness.
- Unprepared and unaware, something of value is stolen. Internally this something can mean discipline, integrity, resolve.

- The seeker then gives in to weakness, laziness.
- Unconsciously, one creates circumstances that are the breeding ground for failure. Or as in the Five of Swords, the seeker becomes the victim of another all over again, only this time, the betrayal is in secret.
- Projects and reputations are undermined.
- In the atmosphere of the Seven of Swords, the precise thought of the Aquarian intellect is used for nefarious purposes. And the Moon influence affects the emotions in unstable ways. The cool aspect of Aquarius can make the personality aloof and detached, while an afflicted Moon can bring emotional eccentricities bubbling to the surface (Moon in Aquarius, afflicted).

REVERSED

- The perpetrator is unmasked.
- The fruit of selfish thoughts, words and deeds ripen for a "bitter harvest."
- The results of past errors, like weeds, choke projects, relationships, and goals.
- Warnings are ignored.

STRATEGY

1. The Seven of Swords can bring distortion to the thinking, whether the seeker is the victim or the perpetrator.
2. It is important to realize that theft and taking advantage of the unprepared gives the consciousness a cynical outlook on life.
3. The Seven of Swords can also be seen as a warning not to leave your "flank" undefended. These acts of thievery are clever, but only to a point. Two Swords are left behind—suggesting carelessness and poor planning—a trail of blood, so to speak. What's left behind points a finger at the perpetrator.
4. This position encourages the seeker to reactivate a course of self-discipline and a thorough review of ethics. Watch for domineering, vain, selfish modes of thought. Reparations may be in order.

The Eight of Swords
"Self-Inflicted Bondage"

Astrological Correspondence: Jupiter in Gemini (negative aspect—inability to concentrate).

Image: A blindfolded, bound woman steps forward with uncertainty. She is surrounded by eight sentry-like Swords.

Key Phrase: Anxiety at every turn.

Statement: "I have blinded myself to the enslaving effect of incessantly concentrating on the painful past. Now, however, I intend to focus my mind and use it as a tool to help loosen the fetters."

Quotation: "When earth is changed into a prison cell,
      Where, in the damp and dark, with timid wing
      Hope, like a bat, goes beating at the wall,
      Striking its head on ceilings mouldering."
      (Baudelaire, *Spleen*)

Major Obstacle: Insecurity and fear.

The Eight of Swords in a Reading

- The seeker is bound in present anguish by dwelling on traumas from the past.
- Powerless to resolve problems and a constant prey to indecision, the person's movement on the path is restricted by fear and self-defeating thoughts.

- Unlike the Six of Swords, this consciousness is unable to become free from seeing only the worst in a situation.
- The bondage is self-inflicted, but the fear of renunciation forces one to stay trapped in mental pain. Psychology calls this the "neurotic paradox."
- Disappointments from the past cause mental disturbances in the present, and the consciousness becomes preoccupied with satisfying the wounded ego.
- The blindfold suggests that the consciousness is incapable of planning for future goals due to the lack of vision caused by painful distractions.
- Scattered thinking. The consciousness can easily be invaded by traumatic pain and bound by gloominess. An atmosphere geared for faulty choice (in Gemini, Jupiter is in detriment).

REVERSED

- The bondage is temporary and the fetters loosen.
- The consciousness realizes the futility of re-conjuring over and over again all the shock of past traumatic events.
- Dismal, obsessive thoughts are no longer given lodging room.
- Energy is prized and expended in more valuable ways.

STRATEGY

1. The Eight of Swords appears in order to remind the seeker that relaxation, pleasant diversions, and some long overdue pampering are called for.
2. A time to take life less seriously.
3. Dwelling in the painful past saps vital energy and can immobilize the seeker. Instead, inner resources should be gathered and prized, to be used later to deal with future challenges.

The Nine of Swords
"A Punishing Conscience"

Astrological Correspondence: Mars in Gemini (afflicted aspect—angry inquisition).

Image: A distraught, sobbing figure sits up in bed in the middle of the night. Nine Swords hang oppressively in the darkness.

Key Phrase: Dark Night of the Soul.

Statement: "I will put my faults in proper perspective and reflect upon the many goals I have reached."

Quotation: "But rather than flagellating ourselves for our obvious lack, we should remember that God always meets us where we are and slowly moves us along into deeper things." (Richard J. Foster, *Celebration of Discipline*)

Major Obstacle: The ego is plagued with incessant fault finding.

The Nine of Swords in a Reading

- Mental anguish due to a guilty conscience. Maybe this consciousness was severely cruel to someone helpless.
- Torture, suffering, loss of sleep.
- The unconscious overwhelms the thoughts with blame for past deeds, causing the ego to feel disgust with itself.
- Self-respect is damaged.
- Doubt, mistrust, uncertainty.
- Worry out of control.

- If near the Three of Swords, grief from loss.
- The Nine of Swords highlights the approaching peak of the problem. If these thoughts are left unchecked, however, depression can result.
- The conscience becomes Inquisitor. Unrestrained cutting tongue. Violent probing. Aggressive thoughts designed to injure. In the Nine of Swords, the aggression turns inward, the target being the enfeebled ego. And the Mars vibrations hone these Swords to a particularly sharp edge (Mars in Gemini).

REVERSED

- Like the Eight of Swords Reversed, the Nine Reversed shows an alleviation of the pressure.
- Despairing thoughts begin to transform.
- A sense of hope returns.
- After living in internal turmoil, feelings of guilt and unworthiness begin to fade into the background.
- The sun comes up, and the consciousness gets a fleeting awareness of the Divine Flame within.

STRATEGY

1. Time is needed to allow for healing. Patience. Faith. The pain experienced in the Nine of Swords takes a long time to neutralize.
2. To begin with, the consciousness must face the fear generated by the past traumas and stay awake with them during the so-called "Dark Night of the Soul."
3. This process is difficult because the consciousness turns numb after continuous assaults, especially from the Internal Inquisitor. It is important to remember, however, that the basic nature of awareness is freedom, and paralysis in the Mental Plane is hell. So in the Nine of Swords the stakes are high.
4. Sometimes recalling Universal Truths aid in the healing process. Jesus of Nazareth gave us a hint when he said, "Know the Truth, for the Truth will make you free." And what Truth was he referring to? That at our Center we are radiant beings expanding outward from the Source.
5. It is also desirable to concentrate on the self-image: Not as a weak sinner (although it's important to be aware of areas where we have

"missed the mark"), but, rather, think about ourselves from time to time as enlightened intelligent beings.

6. Forget the tattered, bloodied robes of the *penitente,* and instead remember our true garment: The radiant robe of immortality. Thinking continually about images of unworthiness or complaining about the rotten side of Life only leads to delay in remembering Truth.

The Ten of Swords
"Delusions Shattered"

Astrological Correspondence: Sun in Gemini (afflicted aspect—mental chaos from strained nerves).

Image: Beneath a blackened sky, ten Swords protrude from a prone figure.

Key Phrase: Hitting bottom.

Statement: "I will no longer blindly accept the superficial, or make shallow choices, and from now on will to view my experiences with utmost clarity."

Quotation: "Whoever undertakes to set himself up as judge in the field of Truth and Knowledge is shipwrecked by the laughter of the gods." (Albert Einstein, Speech, 1953)

Major Obstacle: The ego refuses to face grim realities.

The Ten of Swords in a Reading

- Nowhere to hide.
- The consciousness gropes in ignorance.
- Then when the light goes on, the Ten of Swords, the most horrifying image in all of Tarot, evokes the shock of facing the Truth.
- Virtues ignored, indulgences drive the consciousness to the limit. Health weakens, reputations ruined, family embattled, rampant irresponsibility.
- The breakdown of order.
- The Ten is the end of a cycle, and the consciousness is actually in an ideal position to begin again—from the ground up.

- Ten in the Suit of Air afflicts the Sun in Gemini, or scattered energies and lack of focus stress the nerves. The creative thinking of Gemini is hindered and cannot take hold in the Physical Plane. Excess, a craving for variety, restless anxiety (Sun in Gemini, afflicted).

REVERSED

- The new cycle begins and the Ten Swords fade.
- Eyes gaze upward.
- The Baptism of Fire is over; strength restored.
- One's being fills with the airy power of the Ace of Swords.
- The horizon appears inviting.
- There is a new understanding of the consequences of selfish action and the need to clarify intention.

STRATEGY

1. The Sword of Intellect will now be used for balance and justice, and the Mental Plane once again regains its natural nobility.
2. The consciousness needs to prepare for future upheavals and use the will to accept what may appear on the path to confront the seeker. Then the coming cycle will move in a more positive direction than previously exhibited in the Ten of Swords.
3. Serenity, determination to succeed, awareness of weaknesses all help alleviate the ruinous pain encountered in the Ten. Most of all, it helps to remain reasonably cheerful even though at this time one may only experience setbacks and apparent failure.

The Court in the Suit of Air

The Page of Swords
Basic Trait: Mental agility.

Alchemical Element: Earth in the Suit of Air (practical thinking).

Astrological Correspondence: The adaptability of Gemini, the equilibrium of Libra, and the original approach of Aquarius.

Image: A forward-looking youth holds a Sword aloft in a breezy sky.

Statement: "I activate the Idea in the Mental Plane with inventive, pragmatic thought."

Major Obstacle: The ego uses the Sword to belittle others.

The Page of Swords has a breezy enjoyment of the thought process. The Page is a state of consciousness that begins to bring practicality (Earth) to the Suit of Air (Thinking). Always asking questions, the Page of Swords is diligent in his or her search for the answers. Being earthy, the knowledge gained is sometimes more for upcoming battles rather than for spiritual enlightenment. However, if the Page has an Aquarian temperament, then the thoughts will be more other-oriented, more universal.

The ideal Libra temperament brings equilibrium to the thoughts, while Gemini sends the well-balanced ideas out into the Physical Plane with insight. Although relatively new in gaining knowledge, the Page is quite adept in practical matters. Libra gives the Page charm, Gemini is friendly and outgoing, and Aquarius is humane.

The Page of Swords in a Reading

- A keen, active mind in the pursuit of Truth.
- Opinionated, and in the debate he or she is very well prepared.
- From fact gathering to well-thought-out strategies, the Page enjoys using the intellect to outmaneuver opponents.
- Can mediate well in conflicts—but is also very adroit in starting them.
- When the Page of Swords is near the Two of Swords you could get a quick, well-thought-out decision; with the Seven of Swords: Cunning attack on the unsuspecting; near the Six of Swords the Page becomes a rescuer.

REVERSED

- An instigator.
- A sneak.
- Can rile up controversies and pit one against the other—with much of the mischief done offstage.
- Irresponsible.
- Illogical, and yet arrogant.
- The influence of the Air Signs is afflicted: The finesse of Libra turns uncouth; with Aquarius, the concerns for humanity turn to indifference; and the communication skills of Gemini are directed to humiliating others.

The Knight of Swords
Basic Trait: Volatility.

Alchemical Element: Air in the Suit of Air (turbulence; a tornado).

Astrological Influence: An affinity for the independent, lack-of-restraint thinking of Mutable Gemini.

Image: In a violent storm an aggressive young man swings a Sword from his charging steed.

Statement: "I forge ahead against all adversity."

Major Obstacle: The ego uses the Sword to force thought on others (Mars in Gemini).

The challenge for the Knight of Swords is to learn contentment and reflection, and not to always "rev up" for the joust. He should interfere only when entirely appropriate. He needs to be more comfortable with his mission, for ultimately he is the volatile expressiveness of Mind. In fact, the presence of the Knight of Swords can mean forward movement on the path, even though the road might become more treacherous.

Danger lurks in the bushes, ready to pounce on the preoccupied Knight. He doesn't see it coming, and before he realizes it, he has swept up anger and ruthlessness into his whirlwind. Then in a conflict he becomes frenzied.

The Knight of Swords in a Reading

- Stormy character.
- Courageous, but domineering.

- Skillful thought charging outward for all to hear.
- Center of attention.
- Although impetuous (Air in the Suit of Air), can act on the highest impulse to benefit others.
- Mercury rules Gemini, and therefore this warrior is seriously articulate, albeit with great force. Not always tactful.

REVERSED

- A troublemaker.
- A braggart.
- The Knight of Swords Reversed is a hustler, and an unstable, arrogant one at that.
- Can become obsessed with the need to destroy: property, character, relationships.
- A sociopath.

The Queen of Swords
Basic Trait: Gracefully perceptive.

Alchemical Element: Water in the Suit of Air (a heart both triumphant and pained).

Astrological Influence: An affinity for the refinement of Libra.

Image: A deeply serious-looking woman, sitting on a carved throne, holds a Sword in her right hand, and raises her left hand toward an unseen subject.

Statement: "I rule with clear thinking and bless all whom I encounter."

Major Obstacle: Judgemental thoughts wield the Sword (afflicted aspect—Sun in Libra).

With the Queen of Swords the intellect embodies the energy of the Suit of Air, giving her thoughts originality, subtlety, and accuracy. Well-balanced with a personality touched by Libra's grace, this Queen takes pride in her sense of justice and makes sure that solutions to problems with other people are equitable.

The Queen of Swords in a Reading

- Mentally sharp, quick-witted, this Queen has also known suffering.
- She has triumphed over her pain, however, and her battle scars have faded.
- At times, though, she can exhibit sadness and a stern, cautious nature as residues from her days of strife and confrontation show themselves.

- Nonetheless, the Queen of Wands is a very perceptive and keen interpreter of events; can be a fiercely independent feminist (like Camile Paglia).

REVERSED

- Malicious, deceitful, and intolerant.
- Self-serving in her treatment of those she considers underlings.
- Narrow-minded and impervious to the distress she may cause others. Attracted to the superficial and all forms of artifice, she views only her own interests as pursuit of the highest quality.
- In reality she has no concept of quality and ultimately leads a shallow existence.
- She can be spiteful and will react with savagery, even if it was she who made the faulty decision.
- Does not take responsibility for her wrong-headed actions and will easily blame others.
- Instead of rendering fair judgement, she would rather be judgemental in her decrees.
- Always biased in favor of her own opinions and will rarely consider the other person's point of view.
- Can be vengeful (Euripides' *Medea* is an extreme example of the Queen of Swords Reversed, where the wife of an unfaithful Jason murders their three children in a fit of revenge).

The King of Swords
Basic Trait: Intellectual.

Alchemical Element: Fire in the Suit of Air (communicates his progressive ideas with enthusiasm).

Astrological Correspondence: An affinity for Aquarius' focus of thought. Image: A noble warrior-king, perhaps now retired, sits on a throne sternly holding his sword of many battles.

Statement: "I express Spirit through my intellect, and prize what I have learned from the variety and the intensity of my life's struggles."

Major Obstacle: The Sword cuts with cold exactness (affllicted aspect—Sun in Aquarius).

The King of Swords is a powerful commander, and can be forbidding as he renders his judgement. He is the unfeeling letter of the Law. Determined, productive, rational, but loves to argue. Scoring points in the debate is his *raison d' `etre*, and he is not particularly concerned about the feelings of those whom he may engage.

The King of Swords in a Reading

- Rational; determined.
- Productive.
- Loves to argue.
- Wisdom in action.
- Versatile and exhibits a quick mental agility.

- But he is almost professorial in his demeanor and not very warm in his affections.
- Makes an excellent unbiased counselor in spite of his emotional aloofness.

REVERSED

- Intelligent and cunning, the King of Swords Reversed is ruthless in his demands for power.
- The razor-sharp sarcasm of Aquarius afflicted (George Sanders as nasty theatre critic Addison DeWitt in *All About Eve*).
- A very dangerous personality and cannot be trusted; a hypocrite.
- Anger, violence, perversity.
- Unreasonable and unscrupulous.
- Immoral.
- Will insist his motives are noble as he runs his sword through his victim and has no problem in rationalizing the carnage.
- Worst of all, he becomes implacable if his motives are questioned.

Chapter 28

The Suit of Pentacles
Tangible Earth

The Ace of Pentacles

Alchemical Element: Earth.

Astrological Correspondence: Capricorn (Cardinal in the Suit of Earth), Taurus (Fixed), Virgo (Mutable Earth).

Image: A glowing hand holding a Pentacle extends forth from a cloud. In the background we see a cultivated garden with a path and an archway, through which mountains can be seen off in the distance.

Key Phrase: Power of practical application.

Statement: "Here my consciousness is grounded, and I am firm in my commitment to success in the Physical Plane."

Quotation: "Matter is Spirit at its lowest vibration." (H. P. Blavatsky)

Major Obstacle: The ego is seduced by the material; obsessive greed.

The Ace of Pentacles signifies accomplishment on the Physical Plane. It is the realm of career, business, completed projects, material gain, family...the Idea first conceived in the Spiritual Plane of Wands has traveled through the other Planes and has now become form. The Ace is the forest and the seas, the solid and the stable. It is all that we can touch and taste, see, hear, and smell. Much eagerness, imagination, planning, and hard work went into the formation of the garden pictured in the Ace of Pentacles, reminding us that all those ingredients are required if our garden is to bloom as well.

The mountains in the distance tell us there are more challenges to meet, more situations to experience. The question is: What will be our attitude, our frame of mind, as we approach the new task?

We are in the Physical Plane to do good work and enjoy ourselves while doing it, always widening our perception in the process. We have to use just the right amount of exertion and stay conscious of our purpose—which each of us must define for ourselves.

From an astrological perspective the Ace of Pentacles incorporates into its overall meaning aspects of the three Earth signs of Capricorn, Taurus, and Virgo.

Capricorn: Traditional. Cautious. Determined. Accomplishment through perseverance. Adaptable to surroundings. Attentive to rules and regulations in order not to rock the boat. Practical.

Taurus: Worldly. Reliable. Tranquil. Difficulty in adapting to change. Stubborn. Suspicious. Possessive. Appreciates simplicity.

Virgo: Problem-solving. Critical. Detail-oriented. Perfectionist. Non-extravagant. Shy. Dedicated in their service to others. Methodical. Discriminating.

The Ace of Pentacles in a Reading

- The idea entering the Physical Plane.
- The enterprise begins.
- Skills are in operation.
- The Ace shows us how our efforts produce things.
- The dream takes form.
- An abundance of health and prosperity.
- Common sense.
- Efforts to create an atmosphere of stability.

REVERSED

- Obsessive materialism and greed.
- Selfishness.
- Irresponsibility and laziness.
- When the desired object is not obtained, the consciousness experiences jolts of anxiety.
- Careers are derailed because of carelessness, a life made dull by narrow outlook, an emotional state becomes anxiety-ridden because of a strict adherence to routine.
- The consciousness focuses on the accumulation of things, especially at the expense of others, and in turn, experiences a tainting of the personality and an alienation from the Inner Self.
- If the need for the accumulation of material objects is rigid, the inflow of spiritual aspirations, emotional well-being, and intellectual honesty can become blocked. This is what Jesus of Nazareth meant when he said, "What shall it profit a man that he gain the whole world but loses his soul?"

STRATEGY

1. The basic motto of the Ace is: "Hard work brings practical results."
2. Method and planning are essential so as not to waste vital energy.
3. The Ace of Pentacles signifies stability, especially the solidity of the foundation.
4. The tangible is the outer veil of the ethereal.

The Two of Pentacles
"Balance Amidst Change"

Astrological Correspondence: Jupiter in Capricorn (willing to take a risk).

Image: A young man in a tall hat juggles two Pentacles encased by the infinity symbol. He stands before a choppy sea.

Key Phrase: Keeping track of many "irons in the fire."

Statement: "I can focus in the moment, stay centered, and make the correct decision in spite of the opposition surrounding me."

Quotation: "Yesterday we honored false prophets and sorcerers. But today Time has changed, and lo, it has changed us too. We can now stare at the face of the sun and listen to the songs of the sea, and nothing can shake us . . ." (Kahil Gibran, *The Sons of the Goddess*)

Major Obstacle: Life out of balance.

Here the consciousness maintains a certain equilibrium in the middle of opposing forces and turbulent surroundings. When confronted with a situation that requires change, the ego remains poised—and adaptable. The consciousness in the Two of Pentacles can see both sides of a complex issue and render objective judgement for a sometimes ingenious solution to the problem.

The infinity symbol reminds us of the endless cycles of change, and that sometimes Life is a balancing act. The old yin-yang. Pain and joy. Peace and interruption. Time, budget, career, family, health, and recreational considerations can hit us all at once, sometimes forcing us to make choices per minute.

The Two of Pentacles in a Reading

- The ability to maintain a certain rhythm between the spiritual and material, the self-conscious and the subconscious.
- When this card appears, think of polarities, opposite ends of the spectrum. Activity—inertia, virtue—vice, prosperity—poverty.
- Although there is a conflict in energies, and in Capricorn, Jupiter is in its fall, with the Two of Pentacles this combination brings a much needed caution to the situation. Capricorn's discipline helps modify Jupiter's negatives of impracticality, indulgence, and gullibility.

REVERSED

- Rigidity.
- Refusing to accept the inevitable.
- The balance shifts in an unexpected direction; caught off guard.
- Wrong decisions are made due to confusion from stress and carelessness.
- Long held positions can no longer be defended, and the consciousness is easily rattled when confronted with Life's many challenges.
- Anxiety in the face of change.
- An inability to handle conflict or several situations at once; panic.

STRATEGY

1. The Two of Pentacles teaches the lesson that since Life is cyclic, for better or worse, we will always experience transition.
2. The challenge is to adapt to change cheerfully and methodically. To do otherwise is likely to bring failure and unhappiness.

The Three of Pentacles
"Hard Work Recognized"

Astrological Correspondence: Mars in Capricorn (expressive, persistent energy).

Image: A young craftsperson works on the inside structure of a cathedral. Two figures in the foreground stand in approval.

Key Phrase: Skills appreciated.

Statement: "I discover the hidden quality of the object and bring out its inherent elegance."

Quotation: "There is no more beautiful experience than when the world expands beyond its accustomed limits." (Deepak Chopra, *Quantum Healing*)

Major Obstacle: The ego is content with mediocrity.

The Three of Pentacles in a Reading

- The consciousness operates diligently and skillfully in the Physical Plane.
- Those in authority recognize and appreciate the work performed.
- This consciousness uses the Earth confidently and with considerable talent.
- Material increase often results.
- Growth; completion of a project.
- A person entering the consciousness signified by the Three of Pentacles will find great joy in mastering the craft.
- Professional approach to a task.

- Quality for Quality's sake
- Constructive use of one's skills.
- The cathedral represents the Ideal, and in this atmosphere the consciousness works to rectify motive, speech, and behavior.
- The Three of Pentacles conjuncts beautifully with the exalted position of Mars in Capricorn. In this case Mars jolts Capricorn with a dynamic, expressive energy. Capricorn brings persistence to the effort. Mars in Capricorn is a very earthy, ambitious thrust, and in the atmosphere of the Three of Pentacles its major characteristic is practical skills.

REVERSED

- Drudgery in one's job.
- A situation that needs to be remedied because the consciousness can drift into aimlessness and lack of ambition.
- At best, a mediocre product results; in this state of mind, the seeker can lose his or her usefulness to a critical, demanding supervisor.
- Your disinterest in your work leads you to not bother finishing what you've begun, leaving assignments for others to finish.
- Blaming others for your errors.

STRATEGY

1. Although we are in the Physical Plane (Pentacles), the Three becomes a force for virtue. In the Mental Plane (Swords) we experienced suffering, chaotic thinking, sorrow, defeat, humiliation; in the Emotional Plane (Cups) we used our imagination with varying degrees of success, and experienced loss and missed opportunities, or on the other end, tranquillity; in the Spiritual Plane, we experienced either a debilitating sense of boredom or perhaps an exalted state of grace. In the Three of Pentacles, if you learned the lessons from the previous cards, your vision will be far-reaching and you will see the blessings received in doing quality work.
2. The cathedral in the card reminds us that there is sanctity in good work; the Three of Pentacles shows us that there is no reason to settle for the ordinary. Things are always more interesting when we stretch.

The Four of Pentacles
"Efficient, But Consuming Work"

Astrological Influence: Sun in Capricorn (security achieved through endurance).

Image: A noble figure sits on a stone cube with a city in the background. Each foot rests on a Pentacle; he clutches one and has one perched atop his head.

Key Phrase: Concentration on material gain.

Statement: "I am intently focused and work for success in my dealings with the world."

Quotation: "The ancients knew something which we seem to have forgotten. All means prove but a blunt instrument, if they have not behind them a living spirit." (Albert Einstein, Speech, 1939)

Major Obstacle: Money on the brain.

The Four of Pentacles in a Reading

- His consciousness is firmly grounded in the Physical Plane, but does not derive a great deal of satisfaction from that state of mind.
- It must be noted that the motivations involved are not necessarily selfish, just that concentrated effort and skill are needed to achieve the particular material goal—but at a huge expenditure of energy. Whether it's worth it or not depends a great deal on his attitude.
- Are other important duties neglected in the pursuit of the material goal?
- Is the character dulled? Is the love of luxury becoming too dominant in the person's life?

- The Sun in Capricorn emphasizes that excellence in performance is a must; Capricorn prizes her integrity and stability. She is ambitious, goal-oriented, efficient, and hard working.

REVERSED

- In the Four of Pentacles Reversed the consciousness identifies itself with things.
- Greedy (especially with a Reversed Ace of Pentacles).
- Money troubles.
- Success in business thwarted due to unsound investments and poor financial decisions.
- IRS.
- A lack of concentration leads to instability of purpose and weakness.
- Impetuosity resulting in debt. Errors in judgement.
- Capricorn in detriment can bring insecurity leading to a tyrannical, emotionally detached personality. Neurotic, driven, and constantly "stressed out" from overwork.
- Reaching the goal can become so consuming that the person will step on others in order to achieve. And he or she can be quite cold and unscrupulous in doing so. Capricorn's Saturn ruler brings a severe discipline to the enterprise that can make the person anxious.

STRATEGY

1. There is a need here to be tolerant of others and to slow the pace down from ambitious overdrive.
2. The power of discernment needs to be revived.
3. Shift the emphasis to blending the spiritual with the emotional and the intellectual again and away from the dominance of the need to overachieve.
4. The lesson in the Four of Pentacles is to be capable, calm, and caring in the little things. Build the foundation sturdy and symmetrical, and success will follow naturally and without strain.

The Five of Pentacles
"Affliction"

Astrological Correspondence: Mercury in Taurus (plodding, insecure communication).

Image: Two destitute people trudge along in the snow past a cathedral window.

Key Phrase: Awareness of another's difficulties.

Statement: "Although I am challenged, I will not let circumstances get the better of me."

Quotation: "There is a hunger for ordinary bread, and there is a hunger for love, for kindness, for thoughtfulness; and this is the great poverty that makes people suffer so much." (Mother Teresa, "Saint of the Gutters," Calcutta, India)

Major Obstacle: Accepting the role of victim.

The Five of Pentacles in a Reading

- An indication to the seeker to be mindful of the needs of others.
- There is a call for spiritual guidance here, as the figures in the card pass by the sign offered to them (the cathedral window which seemingly floats in the dark).
- The personality is anxious, and in the Five of Pentacles shows itself in the Physical Plane, perhaps by unpaid bills, credit card problems, or in certain extremes, abject poverty.
- Health could also be a problem affecting the imbalance of the Five.
- This card carries with it the admonition to care for the sick.

- A refusal to help those in trouble, exploitation of the unfortunate, or taking advantage of another's weakness will only bring misery to the perpetrator. Very severe near the Five or Seven of Swords.
- Five in the Suit of Earth brings inertia and stubbornness. The slow, lumbering nature of Taurus slows Mercury down. Ponderous, dull. The desire to possess things comes to the fore. In the Five of Pentacles Taurus panics as security is lost.

REVERSED

- Despairing thoughts, instability; spiritual guidance is scorned.
- Financial strain and struggles along the path continue.
- There is a danger of a loss of faith in Life's benevolent nature.
- Dwelling on what's gone wrong; forgetting that Life moves in cycles.
- Worries and lack of initiative create an atmosphere of misfortune.
- Martyr complex (especially near IX. The Hermit Reversed).

STRATEGY

1. The Five of Pentacles suggests the need for renewing one's caring nature; charity.
2. The Five of Pentacles encourages the seeker to "walk in the other person's shoes."
3. Or if the seeker is the victim of the Five of Pentacles, he or she must take responsibility to alleviate the dire conditions, the inertia, as well as accepting temporary assistance from others.
4. Personal initiative is crucial to solving the problems presented by this card.

The Six of Pentacles
"Generosity"

Astrological Correspondence: Moon in Taurus (charming business sense).

Image: A rich merchant holding a scale distributes alms to two unfortunates.

Key Phrase: Joy in giving.

Statement: "I live a life with many blessings, and it is my duty to share my bounty with others."

Quotation: "A gift is a gift of integrity when it is given at the right place and time to the proper person, To one who cannot be expected to return the gift—and given merely because it should be given." (*Bhagavad Gita*)

Major Obstacle: The ego is determined to take advantage of the vulnerable.

Six of Pentacles in a Reading

- A balance to the acquiring of wealth and the enjoyment of it, a balance of the spiritual and the material.
- Sensitivity to the plight of others; philanthropy.
- Tithing.
- Earning capacity enhanced.
- Beneficial return from proper investment.
- Intelligent preparation for financial situations in the future.
- Generosity is repaid through material prosperity, the reward for fulfilling the admonitions of the Five of Pentacles (helping the unfortunate).
- Good karma.

- Excellent business sense. Resourceful. A pleasant personality. Venus, the ruler of Taurus, brings sensuality and the love of beauty. Secure in the present; Taurus also prepares for what's to come. Taurus strives for simplicity and is content with the basics. Six in the Suit of Earth is highlighted by a straight forward, direct Taurus, while at the same time exhibiting an appropriately fun-loving Moon (The Moon is exalted in Taurus).

REVERSED

- Self-indulgence.
- Extravagant.
- Poor investments.
- Not planning for the future.
- Overly materialistic.
- Inconsiderate.
- Intolerant of the weaknesses of others.
- Inflexible attitudes.
- Exploitation of the gullible.
- On another level the Six of Pentacles Reversed can indicate bribery, gifts given for selfish reasons.
- Refusing to listen to the admonition of Jesus of Nazareth not to let the left hand know what the right hand is doing.
- Avarice.

STRATEGY

1. Actions directed in the service of others set up a rhythm whereby countless blessings return.
2. Giving as second nature creates an example for those not activated toward generosity.
3. Sharing of yourself, even in small ways, makes a difference—enough to change the world.
4. In this way you can enjoy all of God's abundance in the form of success, comfort, and material prosperity.

The Seven of Pentacles
"Patience"

Astrological Correspondence: Saturn in Taurus (discipline in letting go of the useless).

Image: A young man leans on his hoe after toiling in his garden. Seven Pentacles grow on a vine next to him.

Key Phrase: From the seed to the plant to the flower.

Statement: "I am not dissuaded from completing my tasks, even though the time involved may be longer than I expected."

Quotation: "For ye have need of patience, that, after ye have done the will of God, ye might receive the promise." (St. Paul's Epistle to the Hebrews, 10:36)

Major Obstacle: Disappointment from hard work unrewarded.

The Seven of Pentacles in a Reading

- Encourages the seeker to cultivate the virtue of patience, to persevere in one's endeavors.
- Growth will occur with effort and hard work—even if the results are not always tangible.
- Exerting energy with determination toward a worthy goal always brings dividends.
- If the energy becomes focused without the modifying influence of heart and mind, however, the consciousness can develop obstinate attitudes. And should the consciousness become overly attached to the fruits of his labor, he turns possessive.

- In the Seven of Pentacles we're simply supposed to experience conscious effort. It's our choice whether or not the effort is enjoyable.
- In addition, the zodiac contributes another nuance to the meaning of Seven in the Suit of Air—the influence of Saturn in Taurus is multilayered: Not only does the Seven of Pentacles have the Bull's earthy practicality and persistence, but it also has the discipline of Saturn, ever striving for perfection. Although the earthy sensuality of the Bull can conflict with Saturn's stern attitude, Saturn in Taurus brings a disciplined, humble, and ever-advancing determination to the consciousness in the Seven of Pentacles. Spirit uses the Saturn vibration to show us that the useless must make way for the new, even if in the process we experience the pain of letting go. In turn, Saturn also asks, as does Albert Brooks' film *Defending Your Life*: "Have you faced your fears?"

REVERSED

- Unproductive, sloppy, abandoning the goal.
- Dissipation.
- Aimlessness and ennui.
- Loss of faith.
- Dissatisfaction with the work.

STRATEGY

1. In order to reestablish contact with the virtue of the Seven of Pentacles, the consciousness needs to visualize eventual gain.
2. It also doesn't hurt to periodically engender feelings of gratitude. For starters, we can be thankful that Spirit gave our consciousness the ability to think, plan, evaluate, and, most importantly, the power to bring the Idea into Physical Plane manifestation.
3. The Seven of Pentacles also counsels us to remember past accomplishments, and not to forget that in the Physical Plane we are bound by time. There is no use losing patience with it.
4. If we want to bring forth fruit, we must properly tend the soil and plant a fertile seed. In other words, form a clear goal and use the most effective means to get there.
5. Saturn turns the Seven of Pentacles into a test: Can you bring the sheer joy of being alive to your work? Do you insist that what you experience with your five senses is the only criteria for Reality? Does your need to finish the project encourage you to equate delay with failure?

The Eight of Pentacles
"Productivity"

Astrological Influence: Sun in Virgo (efficient, detailed work).

Image: A young craftsman works diligently making Pentacles. He displays his finished product on the wall next to him.

Key Phrase: Pride in one's creative output.

Statement: "I will work hard and continually strive for Quality in whatever I do."

Quotation: "It is (humankind's) privilege to learn the harmonious relations of all the chords of life and to arrange them on the staff of existence with such masterly art that no discord can be detected." (Charles Filmore, *The Twelve Powers of Man*)

Major Obstacle: Laziness.

The Eight of Pentacles in a Reading

- Stresses a healthy perfectionism.
- Striving "to be the best you can be."
- Encourages a self-directed, finely-tuned consciousness that lives up to its potential.
- Further, the Eight encourages pride in the Quality of the product.
- As in the Three of Pentacles, those in authority recognize the seeker's worth, and services are justly compensated. The consciousness works for constant betterment through advanced study, training, and performance.
- Great problem-solving abilities brought to the situation.

- Virgo's critical sense puts emphasis on turning out a valuable product, thereby fulfilling Virgo's role in the zodiac as the practitioner of superb craftsmanship.
- A consciousness engaged in working with the materials of the Physical Plane to bring about a result conceived from an Idea originating in the Wands.
- The Will is concentrated, meticulous (Virgo), and determined.

REVERSED

- Sloth, laziness.
- The consciousness considers the work involved to be too strenuous, so the project is abandoned.
- Passive, numb to responsibility, lack of ambition.
- Important details ignored.
- Shoddy workmanship.
- Discontent with one's job.

STRATEGY

1. The Virgo point of view gives the person a certain preciseness and an industrious utilitarianism, well-illustrated in the Eight of Pentacles.
2. Why not make the work time something special? Pat yourself on the back when you fulfill your responsibilities on the job—even if no one else notices your contribution.
3. Modify the complaining attitude. Do your best to change the condition constructively.

The Nine of Pentacles
"Accomplishment"

Astrological Correspondence: Venus in Virgo (loving and conscientious).

Image: In a fertile garden, a wealthy-looking woman holds a falcon in one hand, rests her other hand on Pentacles growing on a grapevine.

Key Phrase: Appreciating the harvest.

Statement: "I enjoy the fruits of my success, but resist becoming satiated."

Quotation: "The great Law of the Universe, however, is just this—that what you think in your mind you will produce in your experience." (Emmet Fox, *The Sermon on the Mount*)

Major Obstacle: Self-indulgence amid the good life.

The Nine of Pentacles in a Reading

- Suggests contentment in the Physical Plane, although the achievement may be temporary.
- Indicates physical well-being.
- Enjoyment of the good things in Life; positive outlook.
- Personal goals achieved.
- Pleasure from one's accomplishments.
- A state of consciousness that is willing to struggle. The danger comes if the mind becomes too critical (Virgo's fall). Then the consciousness is never satisfied. With the Nine of Pentacles comes a real balancing act: On one hand the card says don't become too complacent; on the other, don't become too unappreciative (Venus in Virgo).

REVERSED

- Erecting of a facade.
- Self-deception.
- Self-indulgence.
- The consciousness is fixated on the material.
- The needs of the soul are neglected.
- Boredom.
- A jaded attitude.

STRATEGY

1. The Nine of Pentacles does carry a warning, however. It is important that the consciousness does not become overly enamored with the activities and pleasures of the Physical Plane.
2. Success runs in cycles. The fertile garden can dry to a barren desert. Famine can consume the harvest at any time.
3. Always fill your thoughts with gratitude for the good things because the Law of Cycles decrees that new challenges wait around the corner.

The Ten of Pentacles
"Contentment"

Astrological Correspondence: Mercury in Virgo (a well-ordered mind).
Image: A family rejoices beneath the archway to a castle.
Key Phrase: A happy environment.
Statement: "I am secure in the belief of my spiritual origin, and my world reflects God's benevolence because of this faith."
Quotation: ". . . Go to your bosom/Knock there and ask your heart what it doth know." (Shakespeare, *Measure for Measure*)
Major Obstacle: Instability.

The Ten of Pentacles in a Reading

- Shows that efforts are successful because of an enduring belief in one's innate goodness.
- With the painstaking advance along the Golden Path, mindful of the lessons learned in the process, the consciousness has used intelligent practicality to bring results.
- The mind is tranquil and focused, logical and perceptive; common sense prevails. Curious and analytical, Mercury in Virgo brings a certain thoughtfulness to the personality. Mercury in the Mutable Earth sign of Virgo is inventive. Virgo's restraint helps calm the mind when appropriate, and Mercury compliments Virgo's curiosity about how things work. For example, the frame of mind you are in right now is curious about Tarot. Mercury exalted in Virgo gives this curious mind the tendency to

find out how Life works. This search is Aleph on the Golden Path. When his Mercury is "exalted" in Virgo, Superconsciousness (the Fool) is highly individualized, another way of saying that Spirit coalesces into self-consciousness (the Magician).

REVERSED

- Some important lessons still need to be learned.
- The life situation is not quite on course because some character-building challenges have not been met. They will have to be faced in the next cycle.
- The self-consciousness still needs more practice in using his or her tools.
- He's not yet clear about his purpose in Wands, doesn't fully control his emotions in Cups, and sometimes his thinking is confused in Swords.
- Unfortunately, these imbalances get reflected in the Life experience on Earth (Pentacles). Lack of enthusiasm, strains in important relationships, communication difficulties, or financial problems can result.

STRATEGY

1. Remember the garden of the Magician. The magical youth wearing the red of desire and the white of sincere intention draws power from the Air of the Life-Breath. Then, in the field of experience he deftly orchestrates the energies with his tools: Wands, Cups, Swords, and Pentacles. In Wands he wants to communicate with his Inner Self. In Cups he wants to understand his emotional reactions, while in Swords he wants to monitor his thoughts. And when these elements work together in concert, along with the Will to achieve, the Magician becomes clear in what he wants to happen in the Physical Plane (Pentacles).

2. At this point along the path, self-consciousness has become highly sensitive to Spirit as It expresses Itself in the Physical Plane. In the Ten of Pentacles, with Mercury exalted in Virgo, this awareness culminates in a stable, secure earthly environment. Prosperity, prestige and, as pictured in the card, a happy family milieu.

3. At the Ten of Pentacles it is probably a good idea to reexamine the structure and content of consciousness so that the Fool is more prepared as he steps on the next rung of the spiral.

4. The positioning of the Ten of Pentacles in the picture is in the form of the Qabalists' Tree of Life (See chapter 3 for an explanation).

The Court in the Suit of Earth

The Page of Pentacles
Basic Trait: Inquisitiveness.

Alchemical Element: Earth in the Suit of Earth (the perpetual student).

Astrological Correspondence: The perseverance of Capricorn, the prudence of Taurus, and Virgo's pursuit of perfection.

Image: A youth in a green flowering field reverently holds a Pentacle aloft. He is surrounded by the yellow sky of the Life-Breath.

Statement: "I am idealistic, and will explore all possibilities toward the achievement of my goal."

Major Obstacle: The ego can use the Pentacle unwisely and lose power from too much self-indulgence.

In interacting with some of the Personages of the Major Arcana, the experiences of the Page are enriched. If in the reading the Page appears near XV. The Devil (Capricorn), you know he must face his attachments; if he appears near IX. The Hermit (Virgo), it signifies a potentially enlightening encounter.

Should the Page conjunct Taurus in the reading (V. The Hierophant), we might expect an important spiritual message coming from the Inner Self. The seeker should listen for it.

Astrological influences play a further role in the makeup of the Page of Pentacles' character: The consciousness is benefited by Capricorn's ambition. And as Earth in the Suit of Earth, the Page is well-grounded. Saturn rules Capricorn, and therefore the Page is disciplined, responsible, and diplomatic.

1. Saturn is the Challenger, so in order to continue his walk along the Golden Path, the Page must be tested. For example: "Why am I bored?" (Wands). The Cardinality of Capricorn can help him energize indifference with renewed interest.

2. "How come she seems so distant this morning?" (Cups). Taurus can help him steadfastly watch his emotional state so that he doesn't lash out in unconscious ways at his girlfriend.

3. "Why do I keep thinking about my boss's cutting remark?" (Swords). The Mutability of Virgo encourages him to properly adapt to the situation and attend to the project fully. The quality of the product takes on an all new importance; the opinions of others fade more into the background.

4. "I can't believe I owe over $2,000 on my credit card!" (Pentacles). Capricorn helps him understand his standard of living. Taurus shows him the benefits of using his resources wisely. And Virgo makes him more methodical.

The Page of Pentacles in a Reading

- Alert, inquisitive, and practical.
- He loves learning things; in the Court of Pentacles, the Page is the natural student.
- Always willing to work hard.
- He is optimistic and sure of what he can accomplish.
- He wants to understand the world around him.

REVERSED

- Missed learning opportunities.
- Exaggerated self-image.
- Disorganized.
- Overly critical of others (Virgo afflicted) to hide one's own deficiencies.
- The Page of Pentacles Reversed is an oaf on one extreme (especially near 0. The Fool Reversed), and a hedonist on the other (near XV. The Devil). If he's near a reversed Hierophant, he listens to the messages of his emotions, intellect, and/or body rather than the whisperings of the Inner Self. With his Taurus afflicted he needs to acquire as many "toys" as possible. He craves luxury, although he lacks the means to live such a life. Here Capricorn's practicality could turn to cunning, especially near the Seven of Swords.

The Knight of Pentacles
Basic Trait: Diligence.

Alchemical Element: Air in the Suit of Earth (intellectual and practical).
Astrological Correspondence: Affinity for the industriousness of Mutable Virgo.
Image: An armored young man on a rigid black horse holds a Pentacle in front of him. Like in the Page's card, the sky is the yellow of the Life-Breath.
Statement: "I will carefully proceed to fulfill my responsibilities."
Major Obstacle: The ego leans toward slothfulness.

The Knight of Pentacles represents a consciousness that concentrates on character building. At his best the Knight dedicates himself to serving others, patiently, efficiently. As Air in the Suit of Earth, this Knight thinks carefully about his goals, and then sets up realistic, practical steps to achieve them. He works in the world using his mind as his chief tool. When the Fool, the Air of Consciousness, takes on thoughts that reflect the Knight of Pentacles, he adeptly uses his mind to find solutions. In the Suit of Pentacles the problems he may encounter will involve the tangibility of the Physical Plane. "What's been a recent success for me?" is a question the Pentacles' environment might stimulate him to ask. Or: "What are my obligations?"

If the issue involves a relationship, then the Knight's emotions are engaged. Several Wands in the reading could change the environment of the question to fiery and impassioned. If he's surrounded by Cups, he might get his emotions over-activated and let them interfere with his thinking processes. In the Mental Plane, if he's still not thinking clearly, he could turn a critical eye on himself. With a preponderance of

Swords in the reading, his thoughts take on a sharper edge. Or if there are a lot of Pentacles, maybe this Knight has learned many lessons.

The Knight of Pentacles and IX. the Hermit are both compatible with Virgo: The Hermit has analyzed Life and holds his beacon lamp for all to see. The Knight accepts the Hermit's guidance and ascends the mountain to the Light.

Near the Eight of Pentacles the Knight is prudent; near the Nine of Pentacles, the Knight is enjoying the fruits of his labor; and with the Ten of Pentacles he shows financial acumen.

As the Knight's consciousness becomes more aware, Air in the Suit of Earth offers him certain lessons:

1. Planning and hard work lead to achievement. The Knight of Pentacles says, "I need to invent my own program. This one doesn't make sense." He's adopting the Mutable Virgo point of view. When the Knight's original software program eventually does flash on thousands of computer screens (Pentacles), then the Knight has achieved his goal in the Physical Plane. It can be said that his "Mercury, the ruler of Virgo, is exalted." In other words, he used his head brilliantly.

2. How do his thoughts (Air) blend with his emotions (Cups)? Does he show weakness? ("I feel rotten because I don't think she cares about me"). or, Vitality? ("I have too much to get done to worry about her opinion of me.")

3. The lesson of the Swords involves his thought processes. "Do I let my job stress me out?" or "I like political debate, and like to see the phonies 'get caught in the crossfire.'"

4. What do I manifest? Pentacles is the Plane where physical activity comes into play. "Is my behavior responsible and efficient, or boorish and sloppy?"

The Knight of Pentacles in a Reading

- An astute observer with emotions calm, mind expectant.
- He uses Virgo's efficiency to bring out the best in his work.
- He will often ponder the yin-yang of a situation: Female—Male, Receptive—Active, Negative—Positive. Before getting to the Truth, the Knight of Pentacles likes to explore the details and understand the polarities. Hot—Cold; Strength—Weakness; Value—Irrelevance; the point is, the Knight of Pentacles thinks about things.

REVERSED

- Energy not well directed.
- Depletion.
- Laziness.
- Idleness.
- A cheat.
- A lethargic contempt for the world at large.
- Shattered idealism.
- The Knight of Pentacles Reversed can be aggressive in an attempt to defend untenable positions.
- Demands more than he is worth.
- Shady contracts.
- Virgo afflicted can cause financial miscalculations.
- Mercury afflicted causes verbose communication, irresponsibility, indecisiveness.

The Queen of Pentacles
Basic Trait: Sensible.

Alchemical Element: Water in the Suit of Earth (affectionate and hard-working).
Astrological Correspondence: An affinity for the pragmatism of Cardinal Capricorn.
Image: A queen holding a Pentacle sits on a throne carved with goats. She is surrounded by a fertile garden and yellow sky.
Statement: "Through good common sense I will get all that I need."
Major Obstacle: The ego gets bored too easily.

As Queen, the consciousness has learned the lessons of the Elements. From Wands she has achieved spiritual awareness, from Cups control of her emotions, and from Swords clear thinking. In Pentacles she enjoys her growth in the Physical Plane.

In the Pentacles environment she might ask something like, "How much energy do I need to devote to my career?" Near the Eight of Wands she would need to put out the effort immediately. Near the Four of Cups she needs to be aware of opportunities offered. And near the Four of Swords she's put out too much energy and needs a rest.

In her relationships the Queen of Pentacles gives strength to those around her. She is the original 'Earth Mother', and encourages people to lean on her.

Capricorn gives the Queen the tendency to take her responsibilities seriously. She is efficient and in control. In fact, the Queen expresses her Inner Self through the proficiency of her endeavor. She is steadfast, reliable, honest.

Saturn, the ruler of the Capricornian Goat, tests her constantly. As a result she is cautious, self-restrained, and disciplined. The Queen creates a secure environment for those around her, and she is admired for her ability to withstand the pressure from difficult situations. She uses her common sense to solve problems and fulfill her ambitions.

The Queen of Pentacles in a Reading

- Stable.
- Trustworthy.
- A consciousness steeped in altruism, especially devoted to family and friends.
- The physical being glows with a healthy, joyful desire to advance upward.
- A beautiful generosity of Spirit exhibited by the Queen of Pentacles inspires all who enter her sphere.
- Intelligent, highly practical. Can also be a very successful businesswoman, loved by those she "governs."

REVERSED

- Obstinate and excessively fearful of taking risks, yet perpetually discontented.
- Often jaded, the Queen of Pentacles can be cold and haughty.
- A dull personality weighed down with a pessimistic outlook, the Earth Queen in detriment is often gloomy.
- Or she can be obsessively ambitious, neglecting loved ones, and to get her way, will take advantage of the weakness of others.
- Condescending.

The King of Pentacles
Basic Trait: Mastery.

Alchemical Element: Fire in the Suit of Earth (practical ambition).

Astrological Correspondence: An affinity for Fixed Taurus' ability to concentrate energy.

Image: A king adorned with an abundance of grapes contemplates the Pentacle on his raised knee. His throne is carved with bulls.

Statement: "I will use my skills in the ways of the world to benefit myself and others."

Major Obstacle: The ego must face its tendency toward possessiveness.

The King of Pentacles is a master at what he does, especially in business and financial matters, and always exhibits an inspiring maturity. He is a preeminent leader and provider. Like the Queen, he is mindful of his spiritual nature, is emotionally stable, and a fine thinker. As the King of Pentacles he enjoys his station in life and is able to bring his ideas into Physical Plane manifestation.

If he is near the Seven of Pentacles, his persistence to complete the task is even more accelerated; near the Five of Pentacles, the King is asked to use his skills to help others in need; near the Three of Pentacles, the King could be acclaimed for his achievements, leading to more important projects.

The abundance of the King's garden reminds us of his love of Nature and his affinity with Taurus. He is a sensualist like Taurus and likes the touch of things.

The King of Pentacles in a Reading

- Patient and understanding.
- High sense of ethics.
- Admired for his skills, but keeps his achievements in perspective.
- His temperament is steady.
- As with all the personages of the earthy Suit of Pentacles, the King is practical, industrious, and reliable.
- Creative with an innate sense of Art, the King sees to it that his world reflects beauty, as Venus is the ruler of Taurus.
- He is a patron of the arts.

REVERSED

- Greedy and materialistic, the King of Pentacles in detriment can treat those around him as possessions.
- He can become involved in shady deals and unfulfilled contracts; imprudent, he can be saddled with debt.
- Lazy, idle, self-indulgent.
- On the other hand, he can become obsessed with his work and burn himself out (and those around him).
- Can be very out of touch with his emotions; not easy to figure out what he's thinking.

Part Four

Tarot in Practice—
Reading the Cards

Chapter 29

Proximity

WHAT EXACTLY IS A TAROT "READING?" IT IS A PRECISE, INTUITIVE ANALYSIS of a particular moment in time illustrated by a seemingly random selection of Tarot cards. The resulting combination of meanings and symbols will then trigger a "story" in the mind of the reader, which he or she will relate to the seeker; the degree of a reading's success will depend on how relevant the information is to the seeker's healing and/or enlightenment. It will also depend on the reader's spiritual attunement and his or her knowledge and experience of the various levels of the Tarot system.

Several factors need to be in play as the reader prepares to interpret the cards. First of all is *sensitivity to the Inner Voice*. Your ability to intuit the message the combination of symbols imparts is of paramount importance (in chapter 30 we will look at methods to help in this preparation). Secondly, *a working knowledge* of the meanings of the Major and Minor Arcana will give you a springboard into your own unique depth of meaning for the cards. And, thirdly, you need to know *how the various meanings of the cards enhance each other* as they occur simultaneously in a reading.

When we take into account the meanings of cards that surround the card or cards in question—and how they relate to one another—we refer to this conjunction of meaning as *proximity*. A kind of meeting of the minds (plus hearts and souls) occurs as the Tarot moment is analyzed and interpreted; when a second card is then drawn from the deck, it is said to "enter the atmosphere" of the previous card. Awareness of its proximity to other cards enriches the interpretation of the reading.

Since the possible combinations involving the seventy-eight cards of the Tarot deck are virtually endless, in this chapter we will look at several examples using short impressions that vividly illustrate the concept of proximity.

To be more receptive to the meanings of the card combinations, it is a good idea to get yourself in the proper attitude and approach (See chapter 30, "Preparation for Reading the Cards"):

341

Let yourself feel relaxed, light a candle, and enter into your own private Tarot atmosphere, however you conceive that to be. Then for each sample given, put the cards in question before you on the table or desk that you use for Tarot; write some of your thoughts from the experience in the Tarot Journal.

0. THE FOOL

1. If the Fool should fall near the Two of Wands ("Vision"—From the top of a castle, a merchant holding a globe and a Wand looks out over the sea) in a reading, it could indicate *taking a chance* (0. The Fool) *on a new business opportunity* (Two of Wands).

2. 0. The Fool Reversed in conjunction with the Seven of Cups ("Excessive Imagination"—Where a startled figure beholds seven Cups floating in a cloudy blue sky; each Cup has unusual and even bizarre images emerging from them) suggests that 0. The Fool made a *thoughtless, faulty choice* because of *an imagination out of control* (Seven of Cups).

3. With the Ten of Swords ("The End of Delusion"—Ten Swords pierce a prone figure), the Fool brings *new opportunity and the possibility of a clean slate* to the series of problems plaguing the seeker.

4. Near the Eight of Swords ("Self-Inflicted Bondage"—A woman, blindfolded and bound, is surrounded by eight Swords), the Fool might suggest that the seeker *lighten up a bit*, be *more spontaneous* (0. The Fool) and *less pessimistic about one's predicament* (Eight of Swords).

5. 0. The Fool Reversed and the Three of Wands Reversed ("The Ships Return"—A merchant looks at his cargo enter the harbor) is a difficult combination; it suggests *foolhardy risk-taking.*

I. THE MAGICIAN

1. In combination with the Two of Swords ("Balance Before Change"—A blindfolded woman sits with two crossed Swords) suggests that *decisiveness is called for* (Magician), especially if the Eight of Wands ("Sudden Advancement") is included in the reading.

2. With the Seven of Wands ("Valor"—A man holding a Wand is defending six Wands behind him), the Magician *bolsters the seeker's confidence to stand up to adversity* (Seven of Wands).

3. With the Ten of Wands ("Oppression"—A man burdened with a heavy load of ten Wands), the appearance of the Magician might suggest that the seeker *needs to plan better, reorganize priorities, and direct his or her efforts to pursuits that will relieve stress.*

4. With the Three of Pentacles ("Hard Work Recognized"—An artisan is working on a cathedral with his employers looking on), a Magician Reversed might indicate *a lack of follow-through* or *disorganized* working habits interfering with completion of the project.

II. THE HIGH PRIESTESS

1. With the Nine of Swords ("A Punishing Conscience"), the High Priestess brings *hidden influences that add to the seeker's anguish.*
2. In conjunction with the Eight of Pentacles ("Productivity"), the seeker is encouraged to use his or her *unlimited potential to get the job done.*
3. With the Five of Wands ("Conflict"), the High Priestess indicates that *subtle methods need to be used in order to defuse the conflict.*
4. With a High Priestess Reversed, the treachery found in the Five of Swords ("Lack of Conscience") is *underhanded and hidden from view.*
5. A Reversed High Priestess, combined with a Seven of Cups and XVIII. The Moon, would certainly get Edgar Allan Poe's attention.

III. THE EMPRESS

1. Should the Knight of Swords (Mutable Air in the Suit of Air—Gemini) fall near the Empress, there is an indication that his *natural volatility of thought needs some tempering.* The *intellect reigns supreme* with this Knight and his entering the atmosphere of the Empress suggests that he needs to *give some credence to the emotional aspects of the situation.* His *violent opinions and his lofty assertions of the validity of his point of view* call for him *to show more consideration.*
2. Near the Three of Pentacles, the Empress *heightens the artistic appreciation of the work in progress.* Both cards indicate growth, so completion of the project will contribute enormously to the seeker's overall advancement on the path. *Talents, skills, passion, aesthetics, sensitivity, imagination.* The Three of Pentacles, from an astrological standpoint, is Mars in Capricorn: Enthusiastic, ambitious, high energy applied practically to a project.
3. With the Nine of Wands (a battle-weary young man looks suspiciously beyond nine Wands forming a barricade behind him), the Empress suggests that perhaps the seeker *needs to look to the more positive aspects of human nature.* Not that the seeker must let down his or her guard, but here the Empress encourages a bit more acceptance of what Shakespeare called *"the milk of human kindness."* The Moon in Sagittarius (Nine of Wands) suggests alertness and can also be optimistic, in spite of the defensiveness generally attributed to the card. Venus brings tranquillity to the conjunction. The emotions calm. Less suspicious.

IV. THE EMPEROR

1. With Six of Cups Reversed there is an admonition to bring *reasonableness to the thinking in order to eliminate childish emotional outbursts.*

2. The Emperor would also caution *restraint, a rational, analytical outlook and approach* to the Knight of Swords, and *emotional control* to the Queen of Cups Reversed (Water in the Suit of Water Polluted).

3. With the Magician Reversed, the Emperor would insist that *organizational skills be brought to bear upon unfocused, scattered thinking.* He would further encourage the Magician's natural leanings toward *self-reliance and responsible action.*

4. A Reversed Emperor with a Reversed Eight of Pentacles would indicate *incompetence and laziness.*

V. THE HIEROPHANT

1. In conjunction with the King of Swords (Fire in the Suit of Air) we get the suggestion that the King's *intellect,* which is mighty, *might be in the way of the seeker hearing the message of the Inner Voice.*

2. The Ace of Pentacles, Cups and Wands Reversed—*selfishness*—would also block the message of the Hierophant.

3. With the Five of Wands (Strife), the Hierophant would counsel that a *traditional approach* should be employed to solve the problem (i.e., rather than coddling a chronic transgressor, the supervisor fires the troublemaker. Or she gives a poor job evaluation to those causing conflict, etc.).

4. The Hierophant Reversed in the environment of the Page of Wands Reversed says that he has a tendency to hear only the jumble of his own confused thoughts.

VI. THE LOVERS

1. In conjunction with the Two of Swords, a fine sense of *discrimination is called for as the decision is about to be made.*

2. With the Seven of Wands Reversed, the Lovers encourage the seeker to *clearly formulate convictions and stand up for what is right.*

3. Using the Lovers' power of *discernment,* the seeker is counseled to *weigh the alternatives and take the most advantageous opportunity* offered in the Four of Cups (a young man is offered a Cup from a cloud).

4. The Lovers Reversed with the Devil and the Ace of Cups Reversed could indicate a dangerous, raging lust—anything from *Fatal Attraction* to *Last Tango in Paris.*

VII. THE CHARIOT

1. With an *overly emotional*, weepy Page of Cups Reversed, the Charioteer is a model for *self-control*.

2. With the anguish of the Sword-pierced heart of the Three of Swords, the Chariot counsels that perseverance *in the face of difficulties will eventually bring relief.*

3. If the Nine of Cups Reversed ("Well-Being"—a satiated portly man sits at a table surrounded by nine Cups) should appear near the Chariot, the message would center around the idea that the seeker *needs to sublimate his or her instinctual urges to bring back a balance in the personality.*

4. The Chariot Reversed near the Knight of Swords would indicate *violence and excessive force—a destructive lack of restraint.*

VIII. STRENGTH

1. Near the Two of Wands Reversed, the card of Strength would bring a *new hope for the future, directed energy, and an ability to deal with fears courageously.*

2. An awareness of the meanings of VIII. Strength would also help *neutralize conflicting forces* that would affect a situation brought on by a Reversed Justice.

3. With the *body-mind-Spirit harmony* of the Strength card, the *disillusionment* of the Five of Cups is lessened and the seeker can be renewed with *confident expectation* and *clear thinking.*

4. Strength Reversed accentuates *self-gratification*, and in combination with the Five of Pentacles Reversed ("Affliction"), the effect could be one of *cruelty to those less fortunate.*

IX. THE HERMIT

1. The *insight and wisdom* of the Hermit brings a sense of conscience to the *nefarious motives* operating in the Five of Swords.

2. When the Hermit enters the atmosphere of the Ten of Cups and walks beneath its rainbow, magic happens. *Well-being and a delightful tranquillity fill* the personality.

3. The *warm-hearted zeal* of the King of Wands combined with the *power of grace* that the Hermit signifies, will give the entire reading a deep, spiritual aura.

4. In the atmosphere of the Six of Pentacles ("Generosity"), the Hermit is transformed into a great *philanthropist* providing a much needed *service to humankind.*

5. The Hermit Reversed in combination with the Four of Swords could indicate a *petty shirking of responsibility.*

6. With the Four of Cups ("Opportunities Offered"), the Hermit Reversed suggests *rejecting valuable advice.*

7. The Hermit with the Ace of Cups suggests a transcendent opening of the heart *chakra*, bringing in loving, healing Light to the situation.

8. The Hermit discusses the situation with the Archangel Michael in the Fourteenth Portal of Temperance. Enlightened enjoyment in the search for meaning through *experimentation* (XIV. Temperance) and *service* (IX. The Hermit). Gratefulness for the ability to think in adventuresome ways (Temperance and Sagittarius) benefited by the organized thinking of the Hermit, Virgo exalted.

X. THE WHEEL OF FORTUNE

1. In the middle of the conflict of the Five of Wands, the Wheel of Fortune cautions the seeker to *remain calm in the midst of adverse conditions, to stay detached.* There is also a note of caution, in that the conflict of the Five of Wands could draw a nasty turn of the Wheel.

2. The Wheel encourages the seeker to *move with the natural flow of things* rather than *stagnate* in a situation the Eight of Cups Reversed might indicate.

3. When we must experience the negative cycles like the Nine or Ten of Swords portray, the expansive Jupiterian consciousness of the Wheel of Fortune reminds us that *things change, life fluctuates.*

4. The Wheel of Fortune Reversed can point to misfortune and *oppressive circumstances,* and in combination with the Ten of Cups Reversed and the Three of Swords, the seeker needs to take a break and pull up the drawbridge.

XI. JUSTICE

1. When the card of Justice follows the Seven of Swords ("Unstable Action"—An enemy steals five Swords, but leaves behind two that will eventually accuse him), the *perpetrator* of the "crime" is likely to get his just reward: *Severe retribution.*

2. As Justice enters the atmosphere of the Three of Cups Reversed ("Fraternity"), *malicious gossip* reaps *censure by associates.*

3. Justice *cautions a balance of energies* devoted to the material endeavor as it conjuncts with the Four of Pentacles ("Efficient, but Consuming Work").

4. A Page of Swords Reversed that *instigates trouble* and *deliberately stirs up controversy* will find himself the object of scorn as the scales of Justice *balance.*

5. Justice tells us that the seed we plant in the soil of Life will grow into a plant inherent with the qualities of that original seed. That's why the man in the Seven of Pentacles *patiently awaits the harvest:* His original seed ideas had sound ori-

gin, and the fruit of his labors will be rich. The Justice card reminds him that *"What ye sow, so shall ye reap"*—for the good, in this case.

6. Should the Seven of Pentacles be reversed, however, in conjunction with the Justice card, the warning would caution against impetuosity, *a negative quality* that could foster a *premature harvest.* And if the Eight of Wands ("Swiftness") were included, the *heedlessness* could lead to an abortion of the project. *Extreme patience* would be highly recommended.

XII. THE HANGED MAN

1. The Hanged Man brings on *a change of perspective*, a shift in the way the seeker looks at things. He represents a highly desirable frame of mind for interacting with challenging cards such as: Three of Cups, Ten of Wands, Five of Wands, Eight, Nine, and Ten of Swords.

2. With the Hanged Man, *consciousness expands*, so this *opening to the panorama* allows the personality to be *more flexible, less rigid in outlook*, very helpful around cards like the narrowed vision of the Two of Wands Reversed or the Eight of Swords ("Self-inflicted Bondage").

3. *Sacrifice* is also indicated by the Hanged Man, so cards that emphasize *charity and good works* would be heightened by his influence (the Five and Six of Pentacles, for example). In order to soften the effect of certain difficulties encountered in life, the seeker should be encouraged to volunteer his or her time for worthy causes should these cards come up in combination.

4. The Hanged Man Reversed is very self-centered, so in conjunction with the *overweening pride of the King* of Wands Reversed, we get a highly disagreeable example of arrogance.

XIII. DEATH

1. Since Death signifies the *dissolution of outworn emotional response patterns*, in combination with the *guilt feelings* of Nine of Swords, there is the idea that perhaps now the seeker is ready to put an emphasis on *tending to the personal needs of the psyche.*

2. As the card of Death—*transformation of body, mind, and soul*—enters the atmosphere of the Two of Cups, *the capacity to love another expands*, especially to new responses such as *compassion and forgiveness.*

3. With Death near the Ten of Swords ("The End of Delusion"), the consciousness feels freer to experience *movement* and *accept Reality as it is.*

4. The Two of Pentacles ("Balance Amidst Change") near the card of Death signifies a *major life transition*, and a *smooth* one at that.

5. Death Reversed conjuncting the Six of Swords ("Safe Passage") Reversed indicates a *blockage, a stagnation—impasse.*
6. If the Seven of Swords is near, it could mean that a *swindle sinks the project* in midstream.

XIV. TEMPERANCE

1. Since the atmosphere of Temperance is one of *testing, trial and error*, the *hardworking* Knight of Pentacles would *meet these challenges head-on.* He is *patient and persevering* and *will stand up well to dilemmas* that the Portal of Temperance may pose to him.
2. Temperance brings *rhythm and moderation* to any excesses brought on by the personality of the Knight of Wands Reversed, helping him to *modify his egotistical rages.*
3. Temperance helps the Fool Reversed work on his *lack of coordination.*
4. Temperance Reversed is *excessiveness, overreaction*, and a nightmare of *hysteria* in conjunction with the Queen of Cups Reversed.

XV. THE DEVIL

1. The Devil in combination with any of the Four Aces Reversed indicates a *great force for evil; selfishness in the extreme. Decadence, corruption, perversion.*
2. With the Three of Cups ("Fraternity") the seeker must have *peer approval at any cost*; the Devil with the Three of Cups Reversed is *unreasonable attachment to a cult or a gang.*
3. In the Nine of Swords, the Devil is the seeker feeling a *paralyzing guilt*; however, the Devil Reversed with this card *lifts the fears* of the seeker, *lessens the worry.*
4. The Devil encourages the Page of Wands Reversed to live a *shallow existence of lies and facades.*
5. Near the Four of Pentacles (a young prince sits with two Pentacles at his feet, grasping one that blocks his heart *chakra* and a Pentacle crowning his head), the Devil turns the energy of *money-making* into a *ravenous material pursuit*, crushing all who get in the way. Even more extreme if an Ace of Pentacles Reversed is near.

XVI. THE TOWER

1. The Tower in conjunction with the Four of Swords ("Gathering Inner Strength") would indicate that the seeker should seek *rest and reevaluation after trauma.* A time to *appreciate one's efforts* to cope with difficult challenges.

2. With the Eight of Cups Reversed, the Tower could indicate that the seeker is experiencing *fears of being abandoned*.

3. The Tower *shatters an existing structure*, so in combination with the Seven of Pentacles ("Patience"), a project of long duration and devoted energy could be *prematurely terminated*.

4. The Tower brings *awakening* to the Page of Pentacles Reversed: He sees the folly of unremitting *self-indulgence, dissipation, and rebellion for rebellion's sake*.

5. The Tower with the Three of Swords and the Two of Cups Reversed could indicate *divorce*. (In a strange way, the Tower, the Three of Swords, the Two of Cups Reversed, plus the Knight of Swords Reversed illustrates the O. J. Simpson case).

XVII. The Star

1. If the Star should come near the Hanged Man, a clear signal is being sent that the seeker should consider *giving more attention to inner reflection*. Perhaps time set aside for *meditation* every day would be in order.

2. If the Hermit should show up in a reading with the Star, there is a suggestion that the seeker could come in contact with a person, a book, a course or some other *spiritual conduit* that would contribute to his or her *advancement on the path*. The Hermit brings *insight and wisdom* while the psychological forces represented by the Star urge the seeker to move ahead.

3. The Star *draws us inward* to our Center where the powers of love and healing dwell. With the Magician, the powers become even more accessible.

4. If the reading has a concentration of Pentacles—career, business, environment—the Star entering this atmosphere could mean an infusion of creativity and imagination. With the Eight of Pentacles ("Productivity"), the Star indicates that spiritual qualities influence the structure of the project.

5. The Star Reversed is a *loss of confidence*, so should this card be near the Nine of Pentacles, the seeker can be encouraged *to count his or her blessings*.

XVIII. The Moon

1. The Moon is *intuitive and psychic*, so in combination with the High Priestess (*hidden secrets of the Life-power*) and the Archangel Raphael ("God Has Healed") in the Lovers, the Hierophant, the Hermit, the Sun, and the Ace of Wands, one would think of Edgar Cayce.

2. It must be remembered that the Moon also brings *illusion*, so if the High Priestess Reversed were in a reading with the Ace of Cups Reversed—plus the Seven of Cups with the Knight of Cups Reversed, the seeker should consider consulting a psychoanalyst (just kidding). The seeker should consider, however, some

reality-testing. Is my job really as fulfilling as it should be? Am I fooling myself about my lover's affections? Are they real or a manipulative facade?

3. When the seeker is enjoying the euphoria of the Ten of Cups, should the Moon enter the picture, the conjunction could indicate an *illusory happiness*. (In addition to the Moon, cards also in the reading such as the Five or Ten of Wands, *strife and oppression* respectively, increase the shakiness of the well-being of the Ten of Cups).

4. The Moon Reversed is a *more focused energy* dissipating the illusory fogs. With the vision of the Two of Wands, the combination (a Reversed Moon is still highly psychic), the seeker could get a *prophetic insight*; however, a Reversed Moon in combination with the Nine of Cups Reversed, the Seven of Cups, and the Page of Cups Reversed could indicate *drug or alcohol abuse*.

XIX. THE SUN

1. The Sun in a reading is always a dazzling influence. It is *growth, awakening, a reenergized Self moving toward wholeness*. The Sun will *heal the anguish* of the Three of Swords and *lift the burdens* of the Ten of Wands.

2. If a Reversed Eight of Cups leaves the seeker feeling *emotionally restricted*, the Sun will *open his heart* and *give him courage* to make amends or move on.

3. From the rays of a warming Sun, the natural *enthusiasm* of the Page of Wands turns electric.

4. The Six of Cups suggests the *innocence of childhood emotions*. With the Sun, the charm shines outward to affect even the coldest heart.

5. A Sun Reversed can indicate a less happy result. *Fear and negativity* overrun the thoughts and can be very anxiety-producing near challenging Sword cards. The seeker needs to be confident that he or she is not leading a life hidden in the shadows.

XX. JUDGEMENT

1. An intense time, a time for *decision*. Judgement is also a time to make *reparations* for wrongs done. With the Five of Swords, a wrong could go *unpunished, a faulty decision made*.

2. In conjunction with the Six of Wands ("Victory"), heeding the trumpet's call leads to *triumph*. Some hard lessons have been learned, but a *new confidence* awakens.

3. The King of Cups is *emotional power* brought to a situation to get results. Judgement encourages him to *intensify his action*.

4. With the *fear and guilt* of the Nine of Swords, Judgement brings about a *liberation* from this unhealthy state of mind. If the Ace of Wands is also present, then the *will is energized* and a kind of redemption is reached.

5. Judgement Reversed *freezes movement* and the person has *difficulty letting go of an unhealthy situation. Rigidity.* Very unyielding near the King of Wands Reversed, the Eight of Wands Reversed, or Death Reversed.

6. *Conscience is stirred* when Judgement and the Eight of Swords cross.

XXI. THE WORLD

1. The World signifies a dedication to a *higher way* and more r*esponsibilities, many potentials reached;* with the Chariot, *transcendence is experienced*—movement beyond the boundaries of the ordinary self.

2. *A body-mind-Spirit harmony* prevails in the atmosphere of the World, and with the Death card, the seeker awakens to a *new connection with the Divine.* If the Hanged Man is present, then the seeker is likely to smoothly *surrender* to a higher authority.

3. The World is a synthesis of all that has gone before and, therefore, a great level of attainment has been reached. Even more so with cards such as the Hermit or the Magician included in the reading.

4. The World Reversed indicates that success hasn't been reached yet, and with a Reversed Eight of Wands ("Sudden Advancement"), attainment could be further off than expected. If there is a Three of Pentacles Reversed near, then it indicates that expression of artistic talents is *restricted.*

5. The World signifies a certain opening to Universal Consciousness. With the Six of Pentacles, the seeker has become very aware of the plight of the less fortunate. Could become very involved in humanitarian causes.

OTHER FACTORS TO CONSIDER IN A READING

1. More than one Ace: A great deal of Power and decisiveness brought to the original idea, new relationship, or project.

2. More than one Two: Clear communications, clear choices, beneficial opportunities.

3. Two or more Threes: Advancement on the path, spiritual growth, manifestation.

4. Two or more Fours: Tremendous organizational skills brought to the project. A stable foundation.

5. Two or more Fives: Big changes; disruption of the *status quo.* Painful advancement.

6. Two or more Sixes: A very tranquil state of mind; harmony; abundance, warmth.

7. Two or more Sevens: Triumph, recognition for achievements.

8. Two or more Eights: Well-disciplined, powerful will.

9. Two or more Nines: Attainment, reaching goals, success.

10. Two or more Tens: Reaching a point where a new cycle begins; change, rebirth.

11. More than one Page: A very practical state of mind; qualities that make good use of what is at hand.

12. More than one Knight: Explosive events and circumstances, unstable situations, and forceful communications.

13. More than one Queen: Emotionally charged circumstances; strong feelings characterize the reading.

14. More than one King: Fair-minded leadership, honor, mastery; highly successful.

15. If there are several cards of the *Major Arcana* in the reading, then the impact of the meanings takes on greater significance. The message conveyed could have a major influence on the seeker.

16. If the Suit of *Wands* dominate the reading, the issue will be more involved with initiative, ambition, spiritual quest, ideas.

17. *Cups:* Matters of the heart; relationships.

18. *Swords:* Plans, debate, politics, disruption, volatility, difficulties, mental prowess, education.

19. *Pentacles:* Practical matters, career, business, projects, money.

20. A preponderance of Reversed cards: A very negative attitude toward the issue in question; unfulfilled expectations.

GENERAL THEMES IN A READING

1. Advice: V. The Hierophant, IX. The Hermit, Six of Swords, Kings of each Suit.

2. Anguish: XIX. The Sun Reversed, Ten of Wands, Five of Cups, Queen of Cups Reversed, Three, Nine, and Ten of Swords, Five of Pentacles.

3. Arrogance: XII. The Hanged Man Reversed, Six of Wands Reversed, Knight, Queen and King of Wands Reversed, Five of Swords, Knight of Swords Reversed.

4. Artistry: III. The Empress, XIV. Temperance, XVII. The Star, the Court of Cups, Three and Eight of Pentacles.

5. Attainment: VII. The Chariot, IX. The Hermit, XIX. The Sun, XXI. The World, Nine and Ten of Cups, Ace of Swords, Nine and Ten of Pentacles.

6. Boldness: VIII. Strength, XIX. The Sun, Ace, Two, and Seven of Wands, the Court of the Suit of Wands, Ace of Swords, Knight of Swords.

7. Boredom/Aimlessness: Four of Cups Reversed, Seven and Nine of Pentacles Reversed, Queen of Pentacles Reversed.

8. Cruelty: King of Wands Reversed, Five of Swords, Knight, Queen, and King of Swords Reversed, and Six of Pentacles Reversed.

9. Decadence: II. The High Priestess Reversed, XV. The Devil, Seven of Cups, Three, Nine, and Ten of Cups Reversed, Page of Cups Reversed.

10. Decisions: 0. The Fool, VI. The Lovers, XI. Justice, XX. Judgement, Four of Cups, Two of Swords, King and Queen of Swords, Two of Pentacles.

11. Delay: III. The Empress Reversed, X. Wheel of Fortune Reversed, IX. Justice Reversed, XIII. Death Reversed, XX. The World Reversed, Ace of Wands Reversed, Three and Eight of Wands Reversed, Page of Wands Reversed, Two of Swords, Ten of Pentacles Reversed.

12. Enlightenment: IX. The Hermit, XVII. The Star, XIX. The Sun, XXI. The World.

13. Fantasy: II. The High Priestess Reversed, XVIII. The Moon, Seven of Cups, Page, Knight, and Queen of Cups Reversed.

14. Growth: III. The Empress, XIII. Death, XIX. The Sun, Three of Wands, Three of Cups, Ace of Pentacles, Nine of Pentacles.

15. Health: III. The Empress, VIII. Strength, X. The Wheel of Fortune, XVII. The Star, XIX. The Sun, all Four Aces (Spiritual, Emotional, Mental, Physical health), Four of Wands, Nine and Ten of Cups, Ten of Pentacles.

16. Illness: III. The Empress Reversed, VI. The Lovers Reversed, XIX. The Sun Reversed, Ten of Wands, Three, Nine, and Ten of Swords.

17. Immaturity: 0. The Fool Reversed, IV. The Emperor Reversed, Ace of Cups Reversed, Six of Cups Reversed, Page and Knight of Cups Reversed.

18. Journey: 0. The Fool, Eight of Wands, Eight of Cups, Six of Swords, Knight of Swords.

19. Kindness: III. The Empress, VIII. Strength, Ace of Cups, the Court of the Suit of Cups, Six of Pentacles.

20. Laziness: Page of Wands Reversed, Page of Cups Reversed, Four of Swords Reversed, Ace and Eight of Pentacles Reversed, Knight and Queen of Pentacles Reversed.

21. Materialism: Ace of Pentacles Reversed, Four and Six of Pentacles Reversed, King of Pentacles Reversed.

22. Narrow-mindedness: XI. Justice Reversed, Two of Wands Reversed, King of Swords Reversed.

23. Opportunities: 0. The Fool, II. tThe High Priestess, X. The Wheel of Fortune, Two of Wands, Four of Cups.

24. Persistence: Two, Three, and Seven of Wands, Knight of Wands, Seven and Eight of Pentacles, Page and Knight of Pentacles.
25. Quietude: IX. The Hermit, XVII. The Star, Four of Wands, Page of Cups, Four of Swords.
26. Renewal: XIII. Death, XV. The Devil Reversed, XIX. The Sun, XX. Judgement, Ace of Cups, Five of Cups Reversed, Four and Six of Swords, Five of Pentacles Reversed.
27. Selfishness: XII. The Hanged Man Reversed, XV. The Devil, all four Aces Reversed, Knight and King of Wands Reversed, Seven of Swords, Four and Six of Pentacles Reversed.
28. Skill: I. The Magician, IV. The Emperor, VII. The Chariot, XIV. Temperance, Ace of Swords, Ace of Pentacles, Two, Three, and Eight of Pentacles, the Court of the Suit of Pentacles.
29. Truth-seeking: 0. The Fool, VI. The Lovers, IX The Hermit, XI.Justice, XIV. Temperance, XVII. The Star, King and Queen of Swords.
30. Upheaval: VII. The Chariot Reversed, XVI. The Tower, XX. Judgement, Eight of Wands, Ace of Swords Reversed, Three of Swords, Knight of Swords.
31. Wrong choice: 0. The Fool Reversed, VI. The Lovers Reversed, IX. The Hermit Reversed, Four of Cups Reversed, Two of Swords Reversed.

Chapter 30

Reading the Cards

A DYNAMIC INTERPLAY OF ARCHETYPAL SYMBOLISM, SPIRITUAL COUNSELING, warnings regarding challenging trends, personality development, as well as hints about what might transpire at a future time—all can occur within the special environment known as a Tarot reading.

Interpreting the hidden messages in the symbolism of the cards is referred to as *divination,* or an inspired guess. After the seeker has shuffled and cut the seventy-eight Tarot cards (described below), the reader will then "divine" the meanings in light of the present moment.

The reader places the cards in certain patterns that reflect a particular approach or theme, often based on the seeker's query, or "burning issue." In the reading this layout of cards is called a *spread*.

Five spreads or layouts that work best with the text's theme of awareness are as follows:

1. The Yes or No Spread.
2. The Celtic Cross Awareness Spread.
3. The Star of David Spread.
4. The Tree of Life Spread.
5. The Twelve Houses of the Zodiac Spread.

Preparation for Reading the Cards

Before beginning an adventure within the Tarot environment, it helps the consciousness of the reader to be in a spiritually open state of mind, that is, not only *receptive* to the subtle messages that the Inner Self may convey, but also *detached*—a mind free of tension and distraction. Only then can he or she properly and clearly interpret the patterns and combinations of cards without bias or artificial manipulation. It must be remembered that the challenge for a dedicated Tarot reader is to create a spiritual climate that encourages access to Truth, and nothing less.

Many teachers recommend that the cards be wrapped in silk and placed in a wooden box when not in use; further, the reader should not allow anyone else to touch the cards, except in a reading. In this way the reader personalizes the cards and fashions them into a sacred tool used for spiritual inquiry and communication with the Awareness Within.

In addition to the reader's proper inner environment, the outer environment needs to be considered as well. Specifically, the external aura of the room where the Tarot reading is performed should reflect the reader's own inner peace.

If a full room is not feasible for this purpose, choose a place that is set aside just for readings; a nice wooden table or appropriate tablecloth, incense, candles, soft music ,and flowers can add significantly to the Tarot environment.

At the stage that you feel ready to read for another, you should have a reasonable mastery of your emotions and thought processes—as well as a reasonable mastery of the meanings of the cards.

Tarot Awareness, illustrated by the four Suits, encourages us to remember that through our consciousness—when it is clear and uplifted—the soul is then able to shine through us in four ways:

1. The *power to focus* is concentrated in the symbolism of the Ace of Wands;

2. The illustration of the Ace of Cups suggests spiritualized *emotional response*;

3. In the Ace of Swords we see the symbol of spiritualized *thought*;

4. And all three are directed outward into the words, behavior, and circumstances of our Physical Plane *experience* (Ace of Pentacles).

For purposes of a Tarot reading it helps that as we read for another we consciously tap into the natural *enthusiasm* and *confidence* of the Wands' frame of mind—as well as assimilating the natural *tranquillity* and *compassion* of Cups into our emotional reactions. Of course, as a reader we must also be able to wield the Sword with *inspired understanding* and effortlessly express an aura of *authority* in the actual reading (Pentacles).

It is important to be able to observe the interpenetrating movement of the Four Planes of Existence while at the same time appreciating the subtleties that Wands, Cups, Swords, and Pentacles illustrate. It is then that we can see ourselves as the Magician, standing before his or her table of implements, a conduit for the Inner Light.

Meditation for Readings

One good way to begin the preparatory meditation is by slowing down the breath and taking notice of the intake and outtake of air . . .

Slowly inhale and exhale—
drawing in the Light with the in breath,
and letting go of the tension with the out breath . . .
Shut your eyes,
take another deep breath
and feel the sparkling white Light of peace and healing
enter your personal atmosphere;
then as you breathe outwards,
feel the fatigue and tightness of the day dissolve.
Inhaling slowly,
you fill your Inner Awareness with white Light again,
and feel as the great healer Jesus of Nazareth felt
as he spoke of "being in the world, but not of it."
Again, let your mind fill with thoughts of healing and peace,
for yourself and for all whom you come in contact . . .
Take another deep breath and exhale slowly . . .
You can then become more conscious of the responsibility that you take on
to usher another into the Tarot atmosphere . . .
Feel the lovingkindness to all . . .
and the intent to be of service . . .
You take another deep breath,
feeling confident and relaxed,
and on the exhale
you can begin to count backwards
10 . . . 9 . . . 8 . . .
feeling fresh and awake when you open your eyes.

It is vitally important that the reader is clear of intent and professional in presentation. Before the reading you might want to silently bring into consciousness a powerful phrase that focuses the attention. Then as the Magician, you can draw on all your powers of concentration . . . slowly, silently repeating the phrase of intent, the *Tarot Mantram*.

Each reader can invent an original mantram or use one based on what we've learned in the text. For example:

"In the Spirit of Truth and Compassion,
I intend to express
only the greatest Good for myself and others."

Also for clearness of intent, we as readers should be able to move comfortably through all four Planes:

1. Am I peacefully and enthusiastically open to Wand Consciousness, a frame of mind where I consecrate my intent?

2. As I drink of the Cup, are my emotions calm and unobtrusive?

3. Is my Sword sharp and direct so that I may cut through to the core of the issue?

4. And, finally, in the material realm of Pentacles, the actual moment of the reading: Can I express myself clearly and accurately and with compassion?

Prayer before a reading helps tune the consciousness to the finer vibrations, to the Life-power's loving attention. Contemplating spiritual literature (See Bibliography) like the Bible, the Upanishads, the Tao, or other metaphysical writings help prepare the reader for a healing demonstration.

Another excellent preparation for the reading is to compose an original prayer after deep meditation on one's role as a reader. Otherwise, here is a prayer based on the Ageless Wisdom we have been exploring. It repeats the Tarot Mantram as well as contemplates the Four Planes of Existence:

Divine Intent
(A prayer for centering)

O, Lord, use me as a conduit
of what is true
and what is loving.
Fill my mind with the light of Wisdom . . .
I am humbled before Thy vast majesty,
and I feel secure that,
through Thy great beneficence,
Grace shall be granted unto me.
May I only reflect what is Real!

In the Spirit of Truth and Compassion,
I intend to express
only the greatest Good for myself and others.

Let my consciousness be alert
and my voice reverberate with an inspired elegance.
May the words I speak
reflect the beauty of Thy Inner Light.
For now I am transformed,
ignorance fading,
as my consciousness awakens to Thy sublime Fire.
May the words I speak
help those who come to hear.
May they perceive the nuances of the moment—
with all its challenges,
trends
. . . and gifts.
Give me Thy divine blessing
so that I may rest confident
in my demonstration.

In the Spirit of Truth and Compassion,
I intend to express
only the greatest good for myself and others.

For now I don the red robe of the Magician,
a transparent channel
for Thy healing and Thy illumination.
Amen.

1. The Yes or No Spread

We use the Yes or No Spread (Fig. 3) when we want to know about the answer to a question that does not need a great deal of elaboration.

It is important, however, for yourself (and the seeker, if you are reading for someone else) to have contemplated the various angles of the issue so that at least a succinct question can be formed. After a time of inner reflection, ask the seeker the purpose of his or her visit.

Yes or No Spread
Figure 3

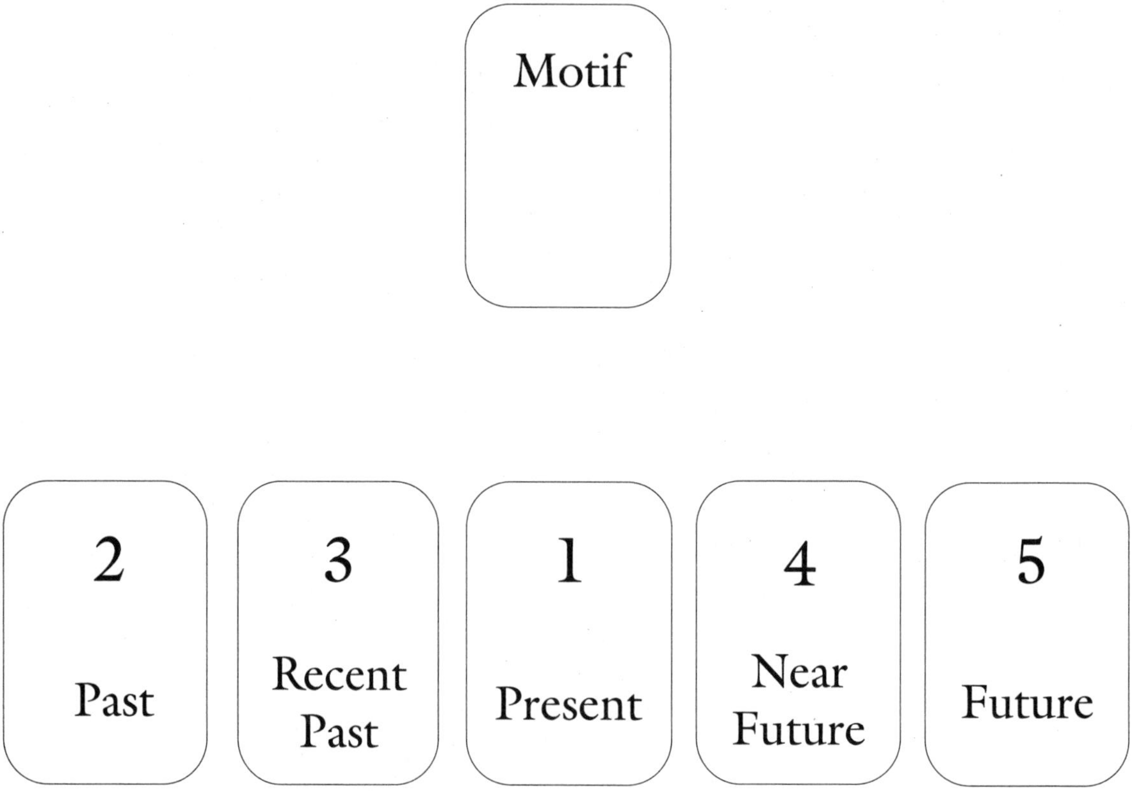

Motif				

2	**3**	**1**	**4**	**5**
Past	Recent Past	Present	Near Future	Future

The Yes or No Spread involves five cards: two representing the Past, one the Present, and two cards for the Future. Formulate a question from the information given and choose a card that generally summarizes the nature of the query. This is called the *motif* card.

For example, if the seeker's issue revolved around a relationship that's gone sour, you might choose the Five of Cups ("Disillusionment") as the motif card. For financial dealings, the Four of Pentacles ("Efficient, but Consuming Work") or the King of Pentacles (Fire in the Suit of Earth) are possibilities. If the question deals with the seeker's creative output, you might consider III. The Empress or perhaps the Three of Pentacles ("Hard Work Recognized"). You can also make use of the "General Themes in a Reading" in chapter 29 as a reference for choosing a motif card.

To continue, have the seeker shuffle the cards.

After he or she feels comfortable with the shuffle, have the seeker cut the deck into three piles with the left hand to the left (as a gesture to the subconscious). Then pick up the piles with your left hand to the *left*, with the first pile dropped on top. If the seeker is sitting across from you (which is the most common position), turn the pile around to face you after you pick up the cards.

Place the five cards face down as follows: (Present) in the center of the table just below the motif card. The second card (Past) goes to the far left, the third card (Recent Past) next to it; the fourth card (Near Future) goes to the right of the center card and the fifth card (Future) to the far right. For the answer to the question, the overall meaning of the cards is interpreted against the number of positive cards viz. negative cards.

The Present, because of the importance of the Now, the Eternal Moment, is worth two points; the two Past cards and the two Future cards get one point each. Turn each card over as you interpret it, with the meaning of Upright or Reversed counting in the direction the card faces the reader, not the seeker (this is true for all Tarot spreads).

Samples based on Actual Readings
for the Yes or No Spread
Reading A

A woman very concerned that good tenants rent her house asked the following question: "Should I rent to the young Polish plumber and his wife and two children?" She had thought they would be fine, except that she did not have their rental history from Poland. The reader got the sense from the woman that she had a favorable reaction to this couple, so he chose as the motif card an image of a happy home life, the Ten of Pentacles.

After shuffling and cutting the cards, the reader chose five cards from the top of the deck and placed them in the order described for the Yes or No Spread (see diagram, Fig. 3).

Card 1, the Present, placed in the center below the motif card, was the Eight of Pentacles ("Productivity"), a positive card indicating *diligence* and *persistent hard work employed in order to get the job done* (2 points +).

Card 2, the Past, placed at the far left, was the Five of Pentacles ("Affliction"), perhaps signifying a period in their lives where the couple may have gone through some *hard times* back in Poland (1 point -).

Card 3, the Recent Past, was XX. Judgement. They *heard the trumpet call* and decided to uproot their lives, difficult though familiar, and emigrated to America (1 point +).

Card 4, the Near Future, was the Page of Pentacles (Earth in the Suit of Earth). This is the young plumber, learning as much as he can about his new country, determined to make a good living for himself and his family (1 point +).

Card 5, the Future, was XIV. Temperance Reversed. Here is an indication that he would rather *avoid too much contact* with the new culture. He prefers to stay close to other emigrants and will come across as somewhat friendly, but distant. (1 point -).

With 4 points positive and only 2 negative, plus an overall hopeful outlook from the reading, the woman felt comfortable in giving the young Polish couple a chance.

Reading B

The seeker asked "Are my priorities in reasonably good order?" The reader chose IV. The Emperor as the motif card—perhaps the finest example of organizational abilities in the deck. After shuffling and cutting in the normal way, five cards were drawn for the Yes or No Spread.

Card 1, the Present: Page of Cups (2 points +). Here the *imagination* is used to find better ways to be organized. Harmony for its own sake. The Page of Cups, Earth in the Suit of Water, rearranges his priorities, schedules, and work space in a *practical and pleasant* way.

Card 2, the Past: 0. The Fool Reversed (1 point -). *Very disorganized, unmoored. Thinking distracted* so that good, creative ideas have difficulty in taking hold.

Card 3, the Recent Past: Three of Wands Reversed (1 point -). *Uncoordinated movement, energy not properly directed toward the project.* A need to visualize the goal and follow through to attainment. Or possibly the Three of Wands Reversed could mean *a superficial interest in too many things,* also leading to loss of energy.

Card 4, the Near Future: Seven of Cups (1 point -). Not a good placement for this card because Seven in the Suit of Water warns the seeker about *delusions.* In this case the seeker could be fooling himself about his progress regarding careful planning and organization.

Card 5, the Future: XIII. Death Reversed (1 point -). Does not bode well for immanent change. The seeker could unconsciously cling to sloppy work habits rather than moving into more detail-oriented thinking. The project could be abandoned due to *inertia or disinterest.*

So the overall reading leads to a negative answer to the question (2 positive for the Present but 4 points negative in the Past and Future). The seeker must work even harder on his organizational skills and be careful not to think he's achieving a level of equilibrium when in reality his working situation is still chaotic. He must test and verify his progress more thoroughly.

2. The Celtic Cross Awareness Spread

The Celtic Cross spread is the most widely used in Tarot readings. Although there is controversy about the positions of some of the cards, several aspects of the Cross do have universal agreement.

The motif card in the Celtic Cross Awareness Spread is often called the Significator. Some teachers say that the Significator should be one of the Court cards that approximate the seeker's outer appearance. For our purposes, however, we will hold to the motif card and use it as a pictorial summarization of the question asked. The Awareness approach to the Celtic Cross is an adaptation of this venerable spread, a dimension added to emphasize psychological integration.

The pattern for the Celtic Cross Awareness Spread is set up as follows (See Fig. 4):

Card 1 (*The Atmosphere Surrounding the Issue*): This card is placed on top of the motif card, and the reader says, "This covers you." This first position describes the matter at hand, present conditions and circumstances. In this placing the question for the seeker becomes, "How well do you understand the situation?"

Card 2 (*The Challenge*): This card is placed across the first card, and the reader says, "This crosses you." The second card represents the obstacles and challenges the seeker must face in order to properly address the issue. Questions in this position for the seeker might be "How do you stand up to opposition?" or "In terms of opposition, can you recognize what will heal you?"

Card 3 (*The Focus*): This card is placed above the motif, first and second card grouping. The reader says, "This crowns you." Here the conscious mind comes into play, and this position reflects what the seeker is aware of regarding the question. Ultimately, at the third position, the question for the seeker becomes, "Can you maintain and direct Awareness to clearly define the issue?" or "Are you comfortable with facing the reality of the situation?"

Celtic Cross Awareness Spread
Figure 4

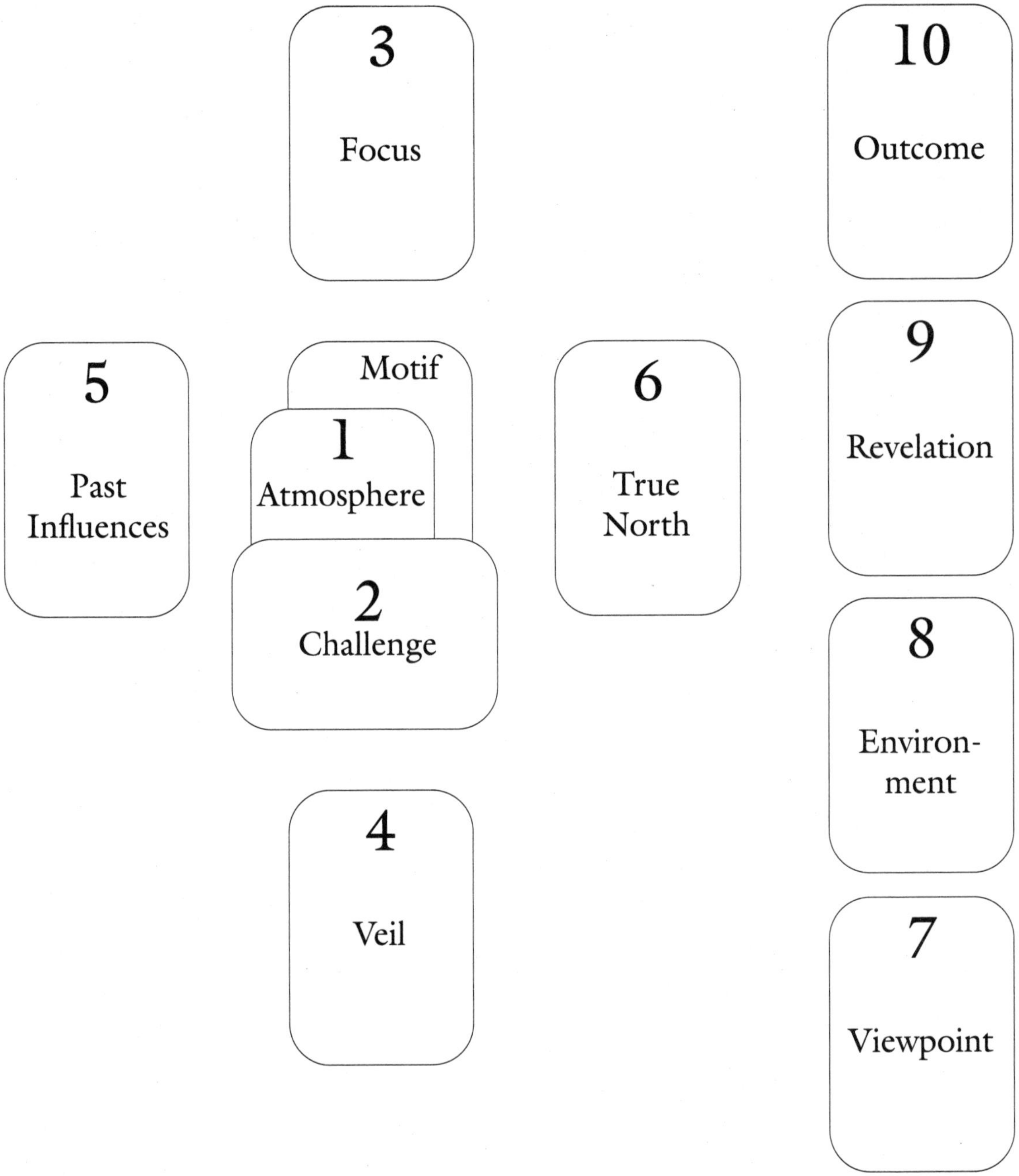

3

Focus

10

Outcome

5

Past
Influences

Motif

1

Atmosphere

2

Challenge

6

True
North

9

Revelation

8

Environ-
ment

4

Veil

7

Viewpoint

Card 4 (*The Veil*): This card is placed below the three-card motif grouping. The reader says, "This is beneath you." It is the realm of the subconscious, the hidden trends of which the seeker may not be aware. The question here is: "Are there any subconscious motivations that you feel you need to recognize or bring to the surface?"

Card 5 (*Past Influences*): This card is placed to the left of the motif card grouping. The reader says, "This is behind you." It is a situation or attitude that is passing from the seeker's life. Card 5 can also be a previous experience connected with the issue that the seeker is analyzing and learning from. If the card is negative in nature, the question at the fifth position is: "Have you learned from previous problematic experiences?" If the card here is positive, then the question for the seeker is: "Have you shown appreciation for past blessings?"

Card 6 (*True North*): This card is placed to the right of the three-card motif grouping. The reader says, "This is before you." The sixth card indicates future trends and/or goals. Here the question for the seeker is in regard to direction: "Can you find your True North and head realistically toward the solution?"

Card 7 (*Viewpoint*): This card forms the bottom of a pillar at the far right of the spread. The reader says, "This is where you stand." It refers to the seeker's attitude toward the situation, with a question like, "How do you really feel about the issue?"

Card 8 (*Environment*): Placed above Card 7 in the far right column, the reader says, "This is how you are seen." It represents how others view the seeker in the atmosphere of the question. If the card is negative, the question is: "How am I influenced by the opinions of others?" If positive, something like "Am I able to make use of good advice?"

Card 9 (*Revelation*): Placed above Card 8, the reader says, "This is the Message." In the ninth position the card represents the strategy the seeker should take regarding the question. What are the hopes (if the card is positive) or the fears (negative) involved? Here the seeker might ask, "Can I keep the faith, can I face my Shadow?"

Card 10 (*Outcome*): Placed at the top of the pillar above Card 9, the reader says of this final card, "This is the result." At the end of the reading, the seeker should consider the following question, "Can I see the core of truth in the situation, thereby building the foundation of the solution to my query?"

Sample Reading

After preparation, the cards are shuffled and cut as before. At first each card is interpreted one at a time, noting relationships with one another as the reading progresses. It is not a good idea to put the whole reading down face up and then interpret; it undermines the reading's suspense.

A female college student asked the following question: "Why can't I study?" The Page of Pentacles (Earth in the Suit of Earth) was chosen as the motif card, an *idealization of the student*—inquisitive, determined, and accomplished. This Page has a reverence for accomplishment on the Physical Plane, beautifully depicted as the youth raises the golden Pentacle in a gesture of awe.

Card 1, *The Atmosphere Surrounding the Issue* (placed on top of the motif card): Eight of Swords ("Self-inflicted Bondage"). Thoughts lingering on confusing, upsetting past memories stir up unhealthy vibrations. The resultant *anxiety* interferes with concentration. The ability to sustain the energy needed for intense study is affected. *Lack of vision, self-defeating thoughts. Inability to concentrate* (Jupiter in Gemini).

Card 2, *The Challenge*: Nine of Cups ("Happiness") Reversed. The seeker should begin addressing the study problem by first discovering where the precious energy is being wasted. Is overindulgence in food, drink, drugs, or sex a problem? What about your attitude toward responsibility? (Jupiter in Pisces can be lazy.)

Card 3, *The Focus*: Ten of Cups ("Joyful Completion") Reversed. The seeker is aware that the poor study habits are damaging the possibility of finishing the many courses left that are required for the degree. Dark gray clouds block out the rainbow of optimism. *Discontent and discouragement* result when the means to a goal are not utilized.

Card 4, *The Veil:* XIV. Temperance. The seeker is not always aware that she can use her powers for *testing and experimentation* to help the situation. The seeker is quite capable of creating new energy with a verve to complete her course of study. All that is required is a shift in attitude: "I am a fine student, and I know exactly how to study properly. I just need some practice. I am tested in school as I am tested in life. I will take on the stance of the Archangel Michael in the Temperance card and find the answer with practice and observation."

Card 5, *Past Influences:* Six of Cups ("Nostalgia") Reversed. Too much *dwelling on negative memories; childish thinking*. The imagination is not put to good use. All this can lead to pessimistic outlook and low self-image. In this case, the seeker has built a picture of herself as a poor student and engages in potentially harmful activities in order to sustain the false image.

Card 6, *True North:* Queen of Swords—Water in the Suit of Air. *Highly intelligent and perceptive* with an individualistic approach. The seeker is encouraged to invent her own way to maintain reliable study habits. The Queen of Swords is the epitome of *reliability;* she will finish what she begins. *Inventive and impartial*. The seeker can keep this Queen in view as she heads North toward the solution remembering the Sword of Discernment which the Queen holds. Then, adopting a Water-in-the-Suit-of-Air consciousness (emotions not in the way of intellect), the seeker will not waste any valuable time in her formal pursuit of knowledge.

Card 7, *Viewpoint:* Six of Swords ("Safe Passage"). The seeker wants to be "delivered." She wants to *remove herself from the troubled shores* of unfocused thought. She is in a receptive frame of mind. She longs to benefit from a comfortable, concentrated thought applied toward academic learning. She wants to arrive at a state of mind that welcomes systematic study.

Card 8, *Environment:* Three of Cups ("Fraternity") Reversed. Partying interferes with study schedule. Having a good time takes precedence over academic achievement. Companions encourage laxity. Possible alcohol and drug abuse interfering with study time.

Card 9, *Revelation:* Two of Pentacles ("Balance Amidst Change"). Here the Message seems to be that study time could be helped with some play time. The seeker need not give up fun in order to succeed in school. But partying should be a reward and done in moderation. Study should be the norm, but *balanced* with play so that the effort it takes to learn does not become oppressive.

Card 10, *Outcome:* XVI. The Tower. Perhaps if the seeker does not adopt a new desire to reach academic excellence (and employing effective study habits), the Tower's lightning bolt could hit in a violent, reality-awakening flash—like a report card full of F's! Or in another sense, the refusal to study properly could lead the seeker into an endless academic drift, an atmosphere that breeds depression and coaxes the lightning flash to strike.

Proximity: The Nine of Cups Reversed in the *Challenge* position and the Three of Cups Reversed in the *Revelation* position reiterates the fact that the seeker must follow the Delphic Oracle's dictum: Moderation in all things. There is indeed a warning here that overindulgence and wasting precious energy bring havoc into the seeker's school experience.

XIV. Temperance as the *Veil* and XVI. The Tower as the *Outcome* suggests that new experimental study habits (done with a Sagittarian enthusiasm and a Mars-like will) will upset the aimless drifting—and lead the attention into action.

This is a huge challenge because the Ten of Cups Reversed as the *Focus* with a Past Influence of the Six of Cups Reversed show a tendency toward stagnation and thoughts wasted in the past. Add to this the Eight of Swords ("Self-Inflicted Bondage") as the general *Atmosphere* of the question, and you have a seeker plagued with thinking processes that need a lot of redirecting.

If she can adopt the inventiveness and intelligence of the Queen of Swords—coupled with her powers of determination and discernment, the seeker should be able to bring about a new approach. Energy can then be directed toward better study habits.

What does the fact that the reading has four Cups in the negative mean to you?

3. The Star of David Spread

This spread (see Fig. 5) can be used as a method of communication with the Higher Self, especially in regard to spiritual healing. First the seeker must form a question clearly and then choose a card which best illustrates the nature of the inquiry (the motif card).

Sample Reading A

A young man found himself stuck in a debilitating aimlessness. He began feeling very unfulfilled and annoyed with himself as the designs for a complicated business ad he was working on sat abandoned and unfinished on his desk. Moreover, he disliked his day job with a big company because it required a lot of mindless detail work, and the atmosphere in his office was poisoned, as none of the other workers liked his or her job either. Cold silence, hard stares, complaining, and nervousness affected the young man's aura so that when he came home, he was high-strung, irritable, and in no mood to work on plans for starting his own desktop publishing business.

He decided to do a Tarot reading for himself using the Star of David Spread. He began his slow breathing meditation (an activity he hadn't done in months) and started to feel more relaxed. Then he contemplated his inner and outer atmosphere and formed this question in his mind: "How can I best make my new business a success?"

After thinking about the question a minute he decided that the theme would be found in the Major Arcana. He then chose XVII. The Star as his motif card and placed it in the center of the table, face up. He picked the Star because *Tzaddi* symbolizes *inspiration,* and he felt that his *natural talent* for design could be restimulated by meditation.

He first began to contemplate the meanings and symbols of the Star for a few minutes, visualizing a fiery white light streaming down from the center of his forehead into the card. Thinking of the question again, he started to shuffle the cards . . .

He then concentrates on the question more deeply while he peers into the eyes of the female figure in the card.

When he feels comfortable about the shuffle, he cuts the cards into three piles to the left with his left hand as a motion to remind him of his subconscious activity. Then, as before, he puts the three piles together to the left, at which point he becomes highly focused.

He will place six cards in a star formation face down around the motif card (XVII. The Star) in the center of the table (see diagram, Fig. 5). At the bottom point of the Star of David he places the first card. This position (1) signifies *past influences* affecting the question.

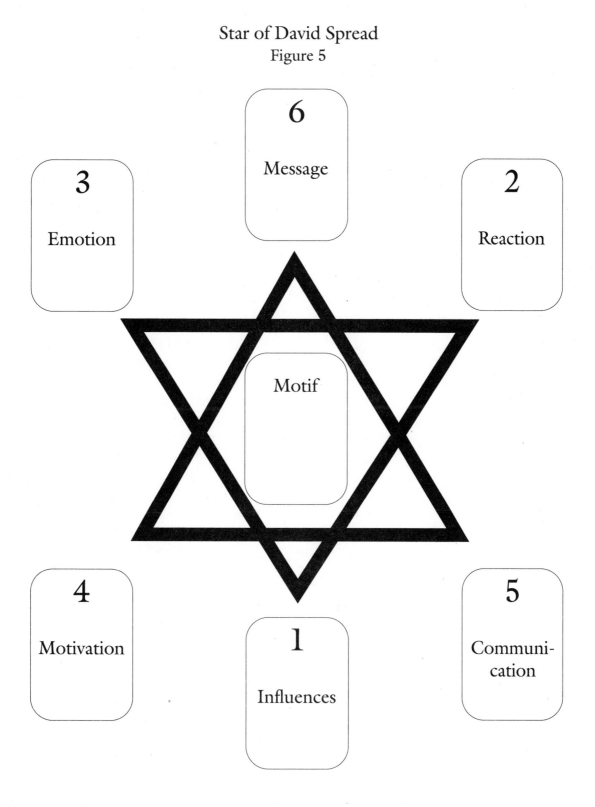

Star of David Spread
Figure 5

Then diagonally to the top right (2)., he places the second card, signifying his *conscious reaction to these past influences.*

He then places the third card across at the top left (3)., forming the downward pointing triangle of the Star of David (representing the descent of inspiration and grace). Position 3 reflects the seeker's *emotional responses.*

The fourth card is placed to the bottom left (4). This position is subconscious and reflects *thoughts that affect you in subtle and profound ways.*

The fifth card is placed across from the fourth (5), bottom right. Here the seeker looks at his power of *communication* and *how he relates to others.*

The sixth and last card is placed at the top point of the Star forming with the 4 and 5 an upward pointing triangle (representing the human heart lifting in prayer). This last card is the *culmination* and represents the healing Message. It is meant to apply to the challenges encountered in the Four Planes (Spiritual, Emotional, Mental, and Physical).

With the motif card (XVII. The Star) in the center, the spread went as follows:

1. *Past Influences:* Two of Wands. Vision, fortitude. The Two of Wands in this case is his energetic attitude (Mars in Aries), his need to see himself successful in the future. It may require him to temper his energy with patience, yet always moving forward and upward like the Ram. This is an important card position for the Two of Wands because it reminds us of holding firm to the belief that *the treasure-laden ship will return* to your safe harbor. Yet you are also reminded to keep an *objective outlook* as you move toward the goal.

2. *Conscious Reaction:* XX. Judgement. He begins to distinguish the *calling of the trumpet*—to stand alone and take the risk. He made a conscious decision to use his talents to organize his business around the services he can perform with his computer, i.e., resumes, letterhead, labels, brochures, etc.

3. *Emotional Response:* Four of Wands. The key to success for him at this point involves his feelings and emotional makeup. Loving and caring in the midst of high energy outlay in starting a new business, the Four of Wands suggests an harmonious atmosphere.

4. *Motivation:* Page of Swords. He wants to create a forum to showcase his talents. The Geminian nature of this Page will stir up the *force of personality through communication* with his Sword, and enter the competition. With a *Libran charm* and *Aquarian originality,* he will *diligently* make his mark in the business community.

5. *Communication:* VIII. Strength. He knows that to spend the countless hours of planning, preparation, study, and actual acceleration of his project will take an enormous amount of *endurance and dedication.* The *inner strength* he must

draw on begins with the Fire of Leo *balanced* with the ability to hear the words of the Hierophant. The business itself is his method of communication.

6. *Message:* Four of Swords. *Meditate. Contemplate. Take time out* to listen to the *intuitive thoughts and revelations* (XVII. The Star) that will come if requested in an attitude of humble receptivity. In solitude *gather inner strength* and proceed confident in your abilities to finish the project, perfected. By looking to the past influence of the Two of Wands, he can see the fruits of the vision. The Judgement card cautions to *consciously rise above* any negativity and complete the project with the purpose of succeeding on the Physical Plane in a state of harmony and lovingkindness.

Drawing on the Page of Sword's mental *agility* as well as Leo's *courage* and *need to be at center stage* (VIII. Strength), he can visualize customers calling and orders being filled all day long.

The Four of Wands and Four of Swords suggest he's on a stable foundation as he tackles the completion of his goal. XX. Judgement and VIII. Strength together encourage him to *draw on his inner powers* in the face of setbacks and changes to come.

Sample Reading B

A woman decided to read for herself because she felt that her Tarot interpretations were off track, and she wasn't reaching a depth of meaning that she felt was appropriate. After deciding to use the Star of David Spread, she formulated the following question: "How can I best untangle myself from the many distractions of my life so that I may clearly hear the Inner Voice?"

After thinking about the question a minute, she decided on V. The Hierophant as her motif card, and placed it in the center of the table, face up. She chose the Hierophant because *Vav* symbolizes the Inner Voice, and she missed the contact she had with her Intuition. She decided that the time had come to reconnect.

She first began to meditate on the meanings and symbols of the Hierophant for a minute or two, visualizing a fiery white light streaming down from the center of her forehead into the card. Thinking of the question again, she started to shuffle the cards . . .

She then concentrated on the question more deeply while she peers into the eyes of the Hierophant. She shuffled and cut as before. The reading went as follows:

1. *Past Influence:* Six of Cups. She had often allowed the light of the soul to flow through her emotions, thereby leaving the channels of communication open for spiritual insight. The Six of Cups reminded her that *beautiful memories of*

past contact can help reconnect her to her Inner Source where the truth of meaning in the cards lies hidden.

2. *Conscious Reaction:* Knight of Wands. Of prime importance in her life is the ability to *express herself confidently.* There is no reason to doubt her abilities as a reader. The *Sagittarian traits of outspokenness and strong opinions* have always contributed to *dynamic* readings. Her sincere and principled character influenced the quality of her Tarot practice.

3. *Emotional Response:* Seven of Cups. She does have a tendency to make *faulty choices* when she lets herself fall prey to *illusion.* She *loses sight of her Ideal,* and dwells more on the commercial aspects of herself as a great Tarot reader. She *fantasizes* herself on talk shows and psychic reading networks, images which interfere with the natural healing of card interpretation.

4. *Hidden Motivation:* Knight of Cups. Air in the Suit of Water, this Knight has an affinity for the mutable Sign of Pisces. She is basically an *intuitive* person with natural *psychic* abilities. She doesn't have to work at it. The revelations will come of their own. She is best when she allows the *idealistic, empathetic, romantic dreamer* to shine forth. There is no need to manipulate or artificially invent (Seven of Cups).

5. *Communication:* Two of Swords. She needs *to block out her biases,* feeling *free to face the ambiguities.* She needs *reasoned judgement* in the choice open to her: In this case, to be the best reader she can be. She needs to put herself in the center between *objectivity* and openness to Intuition (Vav, The Hierophant).

6. *Message:* Justice. This card reinforces the meaning of the previous one, the Two of Swords. She needs to *carefully discern fantasy from reality* in order to reach the *correct conclusion* for the meaning of the particular card in the reading. She must stay focused and to the point, while at the same time, staying open to the Voice of the Hierophant. She will accomplish this if she holds to the confidence and drive of the Sagittarian Knight of Wands, coupled with the intuitive nature of the Knight of Cups. The Six of Cups reminds her to keep an image of herself as the effective reader she has always been, rather than giving in to time-wasting fantasies (Seven of Cups).

4. The Tree of Life Spread

The subject of the Tree of Life Spread (Fig. 6) concerns the direction in which the seeker's life is going. It is based on the central diagram of the Qabala, the Tree of Life, and its ten "way stations." It shows in pictorial form how the Life-power moves through matter.

Tree of Life Spread
Figure 6

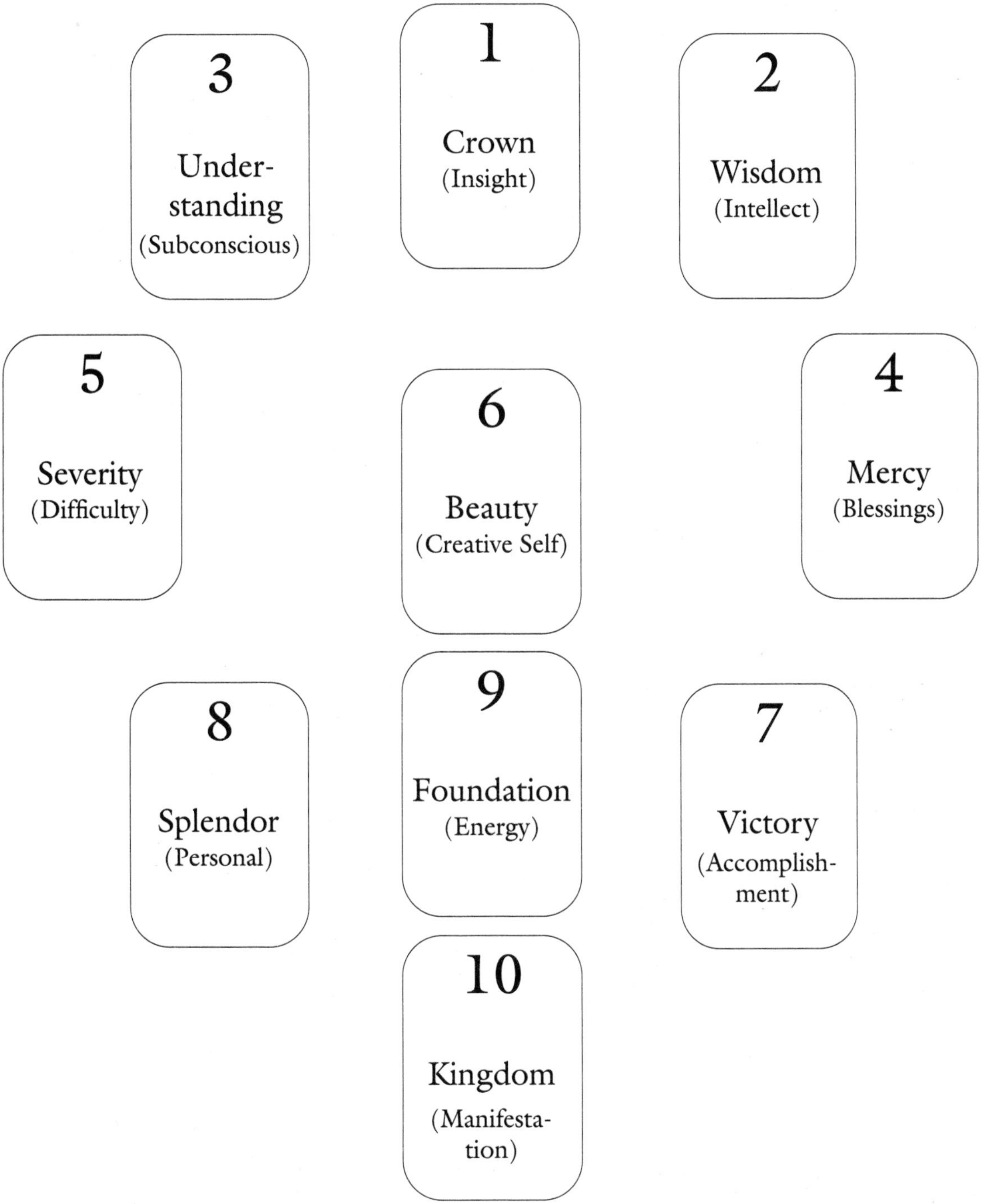

| 3 Under-standing (Subconscious) | 1 Crown (Insight) | 2 Wisdom (Intellect) |

| 5 Severity (Difficulty) | 6 Beauty (Creative Self) | 4 Mercy (Blessings) |

| 8 Splendor (Personal) | 9 Foundation (Energy) | 7 Victory (Accomplish-ment) |

10 Kingdom (Manifesta-tion)

For a Tarot reading we will consider three aspects of experience in the Physical Plane (represented in three columns of the Tree): On the right is the Pillar of Mercy, in the center the Pillar of Mildness, and on the left the Pillar of Challenge. The first card at the apex of the Tree is called the Crown, and it is also at the top of the central Pillar, the Pillar of Mildness. The second card is called Wisdom and is atop the right Pillar, the Pillar of Mercy. The third card (subconscious) is on the left and the top of the Pillar of Challenge.

These first three cards form a triangle and represent the Life-power moving from the Limitless Light into pure Consciousness (Crown), to self-consciousness exalted (Wisdom), to the vastness of subconsciousness (Understanding). In this reading the Crown (Card 1) represents *spiritual insight,* Wisdom (Card 2) is the *thought process* at its most pure, and subconsciousness (Card 3) is *hidden influence.*

The fourth card is at the middle right and is called Mercy, the potential *blessing;* if the card is negative, however, then God's mercy takes the form of a *warning.*

The fifth card, Severity, is at the middle left on the Pillar of Challenge. It represents the *difficulties* we must overcome; if the card is positive, then the card is a *reward* for passing a test.

In the center of the diagram on the Pillar of Mildness is Beauty, the sixth card on the Tree of Life. This position is the same as the heart chakra or Christ Consciousness, and it points to *the love vibration.*

On the lower left on the Pillar of Mercy is the seventh card, Victory, where the *fruits of labor* are discussed.

On the lower left, on the Pillar of Challenge, is Splendor. Here the seeker looks at his or her *outer persona.*

Below Beauty (Card 6) on the central Pillar of Mildness is the ninth card, Foundation. At this way station on the Tree, the seeker explores his or her *energy* level.

Finally, at the bottom of the Tree at the root is the Kingdom, Card 10 and *manifestation* on the Physical Plane.

The question for the Tree of Life would be something like, "Where do I want to go?" or "What do I need to change?" "How is this relationship adding to my life?"

Sample Reading

A young woman wanted to know if her affections were well placed in a rowdy but charming (and attentive) young man. The reader chose a motif card she felt summarized the subject of the reading: The Knight of Swords—Air in the Suit of Air.

After shuffling, the reader took the cut deck and put Card 1 (Crown) down at the top of the Tree. "This card is over you and gives you insight." It was XVI. The Tower. The suggestion is that the Knight of Swords will cause *upheaval* in the life of the seeker, or at least bring on major changes. Are the changes detrimental? It depends on the dynamics of the relationship, hopefully represented in the rest of the cards.

Card 2 (Wisdom): The reader says, "You are wise if you examine the direction of your thoughts on the subject." This second card was the Page of Cups—Earth in the Suit of Water. The seeker has emotional needs that are not being met by the Knight of Swords, at least not right away. It is important that she becomes aware of what she wants from the relationship and makes her needs known.

Card 3 (Understanding): "You may not be aware of this hidden influence." The third card was the Four of Pentacles. Perhaps the Knight of Swords will direct his energy into a money-making career. The seeker must try to answer this question (or at least look at his behavior). Is he capable of focus or is his boisterous energy too scattered?

Card 4 (Mercy): "Does this person bring blessing into your life?" The fourth card was XVII. The Star, a definite *inspiration* in any reading. The seeker feels a great deal of hope for this relationship because she can sense *goodness* and *purity* beneath the Knight's outer *volatility*.

Card 5 (Severity): "What is it that you must face in this relationship?" She then turned up V. The Hierophant Reversed. His *unconventional approach* to life may add to the upheaval of the Tower. Is the seeker willing to "stand by her man" in spite of the fact that she could be ostracized from certain groups because of his temperament?

Card 6 (Beauty): "What is the state of your emotions in the relationship?" The card chosen was Six of Cups. There is a definite *charming* element here. Maybe others don't always see it, but he may have a beneficial effect on her heart chakra.

Card 7 (Victory): XVIII. The Moon. "What needs to be accomplished?" The only way the relationship can work is that she face it without *illusion*. She needs to be aware of potential deception. As long as she looks at her "Knight" with some degree of objectivity, there is at least the possibility for a meeting of the minds.

Card 8 (Splendor): II. The High Priestess. "How does your personality affect the question?" He is very attracted to what he considers her mysterious nature. When her persona reflects her inner beauty, he is drawn to her. Although he may not be aware of it, there is a possibility that they could be soul-mates.

Card 9 (Foundation): Nine of Wands. "How must you direct the energy needed to affect the situation?" He is wary of a deep relationship. The energy that he will put into it needs to be coaxed out of him; he needs reassurance and a degree of encouragement.

Card 10 (Kingdom): Five of Swords Reversed. "What is the likely result?" A problematic card. The relationship will experience opposition. Their devotion to one another must be strong in order to withstand pressure from outside. Challenges are likely to help make the relationship unique.

5. The Twelve Houses of the Zodiac Spread

This spread forms a pattern resembling the astrological birth chart, beginning with Aries and ending with Pisces (See Fig. 7). It is designed to help the seeker get an overview of the Life Mission: Karma, talents, aversions, goals, and potential. From a psychological perspective this spread will look at identity, attitude, and motivation.

As a result, the Twelve Houses of the Zodiac Spread is the most complex and multileveled of all the spreads and is best attempted when the reader has become proficient in the earlier spreads.

First, the position of the card in the spread is taken into account:

1. The House of Aspiration, Aries: Here we look at your attitude toward reaching the goal, what you intend to accomplish, and the level of your enthusiasm. (Fire)

2. The House of Security, Taurus: What is your attitude toward material gain? Are you at peace with your resources? (Earth)

3. The House of Thought, Gemini: How well do you communicate your ideas, your needs, your creative self? Learning and speaking abilities are considered. (Air)

4. The House of Emotion, Cancer: What is the nature of your home environment? What are the areas of your life that need nurturing? Do you have a reasonable understanding of your feelings? (Water)

5. The House of Persona, Leo: What is your outer self like, the personality that you present to the world? How do you express yourself? Do you face life with courage, with flair? (Fire)

6. The House of Detail, Virgo: Is your attention to priority reasonable and productive? Are you well organized? Are you being of service? (Earth)

7. The House of Balance, Libra: Do the activities of your life add to your peace of mind? Is your distribution of energy well proportioned? (Air)

8. The House of Intensity, Scorpio: What is it that you feel strongly about? How do you regenerate your emotions, change how you view your inner atmosphere? (Water)

9. The House of Philosophy, Sagittarius: Does Life hold any particular depth of meaning for you? What are you aiming for? Where do you want to go? What is the nature of your belief system? What do you value? (Fire)

10. The House of Pragmatism, Capricorn: What areas of your life do you need to apply practical methods? Where do you need grounding? (Earth)

11. The House of Originality, Aquarius: The individual searches for identity with a new approach. How do you relate to others in the process? (Air)

12. The House of Intuition, Pisces: Where is listening to the Inner Voice of critical importance? How is your psychic development proceeding? (Water)

Twelve Signs of the Zodiac Spread
Figure 7

11	10	9	7
Aquarius (Originality)	Capricorn (Pragmatism)	Sagittarius (Philosophy)	Scorpio (Intensity)

12			7
Pisces (Intuition)			Libra (Balance)

1			6
Aries (Aspiration)			Virgo (Detail)

2	3	4	5
Taurus (Security)	Gemini (Thought)	Cancer (Emotion)	Leo (Persona)

Secondly, the astrological correspondence of the card drawn is added into the overall picture. For example, if the Knight of Swords (Mutable, volatile Gemini) enters the atmosphere of the House of Persona (card position #5, Leo), the personality's dynamic, talkative qualities are considered. The Knight can be extremely opinionated and wants to tell the whole world how he thinks (Gemini).

Sample Reading

A man asked the following question: "What is the direction my life is taking right now, especially in terms of leadership?"

After shuffling and cutting as usual, the first card is placed to the left (see diagram).

1. The House of Aspiration, Aries: Page of Cups. The *sensitivity and deep feeling* of this Page brings a freshness to the atmosphere and his soothing, responsive nature enhances Aries *aspiring* qualities.

2. The House of Security, Taurus: Three of Pentacles. An excellent match. The Three of Pentacles is *pride in one's work* and a special emphasis put on *quality*. His individual approach and his efforts put out in the endeavor will be *appreciated*. This card reminds him to be sure he brings a *professional approach* to the task. Mars in Capricorn (the Three of Pentacles) is *expressive energy;* Taurus adds to Capricorn's earthy *perseverance*.

3. The House of Communication, Gemini: V. The Hierophant. Activities need to slow down a bit so he can *hear the Inner Voice,* a source of deeply beneficial advice. His powers to get his point across can only improve. The astrological correspondence of the Hierophant is Taurus (where the Moon is exalted), and the indication is a *heightened receptivity to Intuition.* He should be able to *communicate* what he's learned from his own Intuitive Self.

4. The House of Emotion, Cancer: The Two of Cups Reversed. Is he neglecting an *intimate relationship* because of intensified career pursuit? This needs to be taken into account, especially if the Two of Cups (Venus in Cancer) is afflicted. The indication is a lack of commitment because of excessive energy placed on reaching the goal.

5. The House of Persona, Leo: Nine of Pentacles Reversed. A forced *facade* erected. Underneath, troubled things are hidden from view. This is normal, except the Nine of Pentacles Reversed intimates *self-indulgence.* The seeker may be *deceiving himself* about the effect he has on people or may be prey to covert bad habits. There's a danger in giving too much energy to the facade. So much effort is put into acting, the seeker loses thoughts of spontaneity and becomes jaded.

6. The House of Detail, Virgo: Six of Swords. Here we are concerned with how well we organize our immediate environment, and its affect on the outer cir-

cumstances of our life. In the House of Detail we encounter the importance of priority setting so that we don't waste valuable energy. We also learn protocol and propriety.

With the addition of the Six of Swords into the atmosphere of the House of Detail, there is the suggestion that the seeker should take a break, get away from it all for awhile, either literally or figuratively. Take a "Safe Passage" with the Six of Swords to the mountains or a retreat to reassess difficulties. Figure out how you can better organize, but reevaluate your situation a bit distant from the problem. Make use of detailed communication; helpful to public self. Possibly set up meetings to communicate about problems (astrological correspondence of the Six of Pentacles, Mercury in Aquarius).

7. The House of Balance, Libra: Nine of Swords. Out of balance. Energy not well proportioned; too much of it wasted on *worry*. May have a *guilty conscience*. Thoughts of past traumas come to the surface (Mars in Gemini). The Nine of Swords tends to throw Libra's natural equilibrium off. He has a need to put more faith in himself.

8. The House of Intensity, Scorpio: Seven of Wands. *Extremely opinionated*; stimulates the seeker to *express his beliefs vociferously. A passion for principle,* staying at the post no matter what. Unbending. Inner strength of purpose and valor (Mars in Leo).

9. The House of Philosophy, Sagittarius: X. The Wheel of Fortune. Excellent turn of events due to the force of individuality. Beliefs influence destiny. Jupiter, the ruler of Sagittarius and the Wheel, brings movement and growth, expansion of consciousness.

10. The House of Pragmatism, Capricorn: Ace of Cups Reversed. Again, the love vibration needs more attention. Relationships could be adversely affected. *Blockage of the flow of emotions;* love expressed erratically.

11. The House of Originality, Aquarius: King of Pentacles. An excellent connection. As the King of Pentacles enters the House of Originality, his noble qualities are brought into focus, and in some cases, enhanced. The King brings with him a Taurean *ability to focus* energy. He is an *original thinker* with a high sense of ethics. Leadership qualities are highlighted.

12. The House of Intuition, Pisces: Eight of Pentacles. Possible conflicts between the free-flowing atmosphere of the House of Intuition and the rigidly efficient Eight of Pentacles. The Eight, because of the Virgo influence, can focus the Will and should use this determination to quiet the thoughts and listen to the Inner Voice. Or at least have an open mind.

In summary, his life seems to be heading in a more public direction where he can espouse his views and perhaps even dispense some healing. However, his emotional side needs tending. He also needs to be more himself in public. Trying to act like someone he isn't drains the energy.

He may be so hung up on detail he could miss the all-important messages from the Inner Self. It would seem that his leadership qualities would flourish the more he speaks out as long as he's willing to hear the other's point of view and not be overly critical.

The Twelve Houses of the Zodiac Spread takes a lot of interpretation, but for richness of detail, it's very valuable for an understanding of the issue at hand. Taking the proximity of the cards into consideration will add even more details to the overall "story" the cards present.

In Conclusion

WE HAVE SEEN HOW TAROT CAN BE USED AS AN INSTRUMENT TO ILLUMINATE our way through the Examined Life. The bar has been set high at times because the code of moral conduct, attitude, and expression explored in Tarot leads us toward the highest aspiration. Peering into the contents of our consciousness has been disconcerting to be sure, but by looking into the imagery and meanings behind Tarot we are, in a sense, looking into a mirror, a reflection of our own situations and circumstances, of our own mind and heart, and, ultimately, our soul.

It has taken us a great deal of sincere introspection, study, and practice to be able to understand what we see in that mirror, but the rewards of an aware consciousness have brought us a peace and clarity that will eventually lift the Veil to the holy Tabernacle within, if it hasn't already.

In the atmosphere of Tarot you are never asked to accept anything on blind faith, simply because nothing less than your own personal penetration of the subtleties behind the cards will open the secret door. It is hoped that this text has given you some valid guidelines to help you fashion your own keys to that door.

In order to accomplish this understanding we have used the fervor of the Wands atmosphere to fire our aspirations; in Cups we allowed the Water of unconditional love to fill our being; in the airy atmosphere of Swords we have directed the power of our thought processes to solve innumerable problems; and in the earthy world of Pentacles, we grounded our experiences in a common sense approach to reaching our goals. And for some, the ability to read the messages from the cards for yourself and/or another has been heightened.

Ageless Wisdom provides many avenues and many disciplines to reach the Godhead, but few are as varied, and yet inherently cohesive, as the spiritual journey known as Tarot.

Bibliography

Alder, Vera Stanley. *The Finding of the Third Eye*. York Beach, Maine: Samuel Weiser, Inc., 1986.

Arroyo, Stephen. *Astrology, Karma and Transformation*. Sebastopol, Calif.: CRCS Publications, 1978.

Brunton, Paul. *Inspiration and the Overself*, Vol. 14 of the Notebooks. Burdett, N.Y.: Larson Publications, 1988.

————. *The Quest of the Overself*. York Beach, Maine: Samuel Weiser, Inc., 1990.

————. *The Secret Path*. London: Rider and Co., 1934.

Capra, Fritjof. *The Tao of Physics*. New York, N.Y.: Bantam Books, Inc., 1984.

Carter, Charles E. O. *The Principles of Astrology*. Wheaton, Ill.: Theosophical Publishing House, 1925.

Case, Paul Foster. *The Tarot: A Key to the Wisdom of the Ages*. Richmond, Va.: Macoy, 1947.

Crowley, Aleister. *The Book of Thoth*. Berkeley, Calif.: Kashmarin Publications Ltd., 1969.

Dossey, M.D., Larry. *Recovering the Soul*. New York, N.Y.: Bantam Books, Inc., 1989.

Emerson, Ralph Waldo. *The Works of Ralph Waldo Emerson*. Roslyn, N.Y.: Black's Readers Service.

Forrest, Steven. *The Inner Sky*. San Diego, Calif.: ACS Publications, Inc., 1992.

Fortune, Dion. *The Mystical Qabalah*. York Beach, Maine: Samuel Weiser, Inc., 1984.

Foster, Richard J. *Celebration of Discipline*. New York, N.Y.: HarperCollins, 1978.

Fox, Emmet. *The Sermon on the Mount*. New York, N.Y.: Harper and Row, Publishers, Inc., 1979.

Freud, Sigmund. *The Interpretation of Dreams*. New York, N.Y.: Avon Books, 1965.

Goldsmith, Joel S. *Consciousness Unfolding*. New York, N.Y.: Carol Publishing Group, 1990.

———. *The Art of Spiritual Healing*. New York, N.Y.: HarperCollins Publishers, 1992.

Hasbrouck, Muriel Bruce. *Tarot and Astrology, the Pursuit of Destiny*. New York, N.Y.: Destiny Books, 1986.

Hendrick, M.D., Ives. *The Facts and Theories of Psychoanalysis*. New York, N.Y.: Dell Publishing Co., Inc., 1966.

Hickey, Isabel M. *Astrology, A Cosmic Science*. Sebastopol, Calif.: CRCS Publications, 1992.

Holmes, Ernest. *The Science of Mind*. New York, N.Y.: G. P. Putnam and Sons, 1988.

Jayanti, Amber. *Living the Tarot*. St. Paul, Minn.: Llewellyn Publications, 1993.

Khan, Hazrat Inayat. *Mastery*. New Lebanon, N.Y.: Omega Publications, 1993.

———. *The Music of Life*. Santa Fe, N. Mex.: Omega Press, 1983.

Lotterhand, Jason C. *The Thursday Night Tarot*. North Hollywood, Calif.: Newcastle Publishing Co., Inc., 1989.

Moore, Daphna. *The Rabbi's Tarot*. St. Paul, Minn.: Llewellyn Publications, 1989.

Paramananda, Swami. *Book of Daily Thoughts and Prayers*. Madras, India: Sri Ramakrishna Math, 1977.

Patanjali. *How to Know God, The Yoga Aphorisms of Patanjali*. New York, N.Y.: New American Library, 1953.

Pirsig, Robert M. *Zen and the Art of Motorcycle Maintenance*. New York, N.Y.: Bantam Books, 1976.

Regardie, Israel. *The Golden Dawn*. St. Paul, Minn.: Llewellyn Publications, 1990.

Richardson, Robert D. Jr. *Emerson: The Mind on Fire*. Berkeley, Calif.: University of California Press, 1995.

Vivekananda, Swami. *Raja Yoga*. New York, N.Y.: Ramakrishna-Vivekananda Center, 1982.

Yogananda, Paramahansa. *The Autobiography of a Yogi*. Los Angeles, Calif.: Self-Realization Fellowship, 1978.

Zukav, Gary. *The Seat of the Soul*. New York, N.Y.: Fireside/Simon and Schuster, Inc., 1990.

Index

The Buckland Romani Tarot Kit
In the Authentic Gypsy Tradition
Raymond Buckland, art by Lissanne Lake

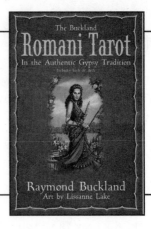

The first Tarot to bring the ways of the Gypsies to life.

This tarot is based on Gypsies (Romanies) as the author knew them, growing up in England before and after the Second World War. They were colorful nomads, with their bright clothes and brilliantly painted wagons, or *vardos*. Following the traditional form of the Tarot—which was originally introduced into Europe by the Gypsies—this deck is unique in its use of Romani scenes to portray the ancient symbolism. Anyone who is familiar with the Tarot will enjoy the refreshing new approach, and anyone new to the cards will equally enjoy this rendition.

- Captures the Gypsy flavor in a deck of traditional Tarot cards
- Discover Raymond Buckland's own method of interpreting the cards
- Learn about the history of the Gypsies, their entry into Europe and Asia, and their introduction of the Tarot cards to the Western world

1-56718-099-X
**Boxed Kit: 78-card deck and 6 x 9, 264-pp. book with illus.,
glossary, appendix, bibliog.** $34.95